TREASURE
HUNT

ALSO BY MICHAEL J. SILVERSTEIN

*Trading Up: Why Consumers Want New Luxury Goods . . .
and How Companies Create Them* (written with Neil Fiske)

TREASURE HUNT

INSIDE THE MIND OF
THE NEW GLOBAL CONSUMER

Michael J. Silverstein
with John Butman

PORTFOLIO

PORTFOLIO
Published by the Penguin Group
Penguin Group (USA) Inc., 375 Hudson Street, New York, New York 10014, U.S.A.
Penguin Group (Canada), 90 Eglinton Avenue East, Suite 700,
Toronto, Ontario, Canada M4P 2Y3
(a division of Pearson Penguin Canada Inc.)
Penguin Books Ltd, 80 Strand, London WC2R 0RL, England
Penguin Ireland, 25 St. Stephen's Green, Dublin 2, Ireland
(a division of Penguin Books Ltd)
Penguin Books Australia Ltd, 250 Camberwell Road, Camberwell,
Victoria 3124, Australia (a division of Pearson Australia Group Pty Ltd)
Penguin Books India Pvt Ltd, 11 Community Centre, Panchsheel Park,
New Delhi – 110 017, India
Penguin Group (NZ), Cnr Airborne and Rosedale Roads, Albany,
Auckland 1310, New Zealand (a division of Pearson New Zealand Ltd)
Penguin Books (South Africa) (Pty) Ltd, 24 Sturdee Avenue,
Rosebank, Johannesburg 2196, South Africa

Penguin Books Ltd, Registered Offices:
80 Strand, London WC2R 0RL, England

First published in 2006 by Portfolio,
a member of Penguin Group (USA) Inc.

10 9 8 7 6 5 4 3 2 1

Publisher's Note
This publication is designed to provide accurate and authoritative information in regard to the subject matter covered. It is sold with the understanding that the publisher is not engaged in rendering legal, accounting or other professional services. If you require legal advice or other expert assistance, you should seek the services of a competent professional.

ISBN 1-59184-123-2

Printed in the United States of America
Set in Janson Text
Designed by Daniel Lagin

*This book is dedicated to my family—
my wife, Gerry; daughter, Heather; and son, Charlie—
who collectively taught me about trading up
and the treasure hunt for bargains and value*

TO THE READER

This book tells the story of how middle-class consumers around the world are reshaping the consumer-goods market by trading down to low-price products and services, trading up to premium ones, and avoiding the boredom and low value that increasingly characterize the middle. These consumers, mostly women, are better educated, have more disposable income, and are buying with more sophistication than ever. They have a sense of purpose and power when they buy and use goods and services. Consumption, for them, is not a tedious necessity or an unavoidable chore. It is a serious effort to use money wisely, it is an important obligation to the people they care for, and it is a treasure hunt—for goods and services that may be cheap or dear, technically sophisticated or whimsical, basic or feature-laden, but are always functionally and emotionally significant.

CONTENTS

How I came to write this book. The story of Lillie and the cockroach. Why listening to consumers is so important and such an underdeveloped skill. The main thesis: the market is bifurcating and the middle is becoming a wasteland.

The story of the Nelsons and their "Daewoo Christmas." A dynamic market meets an unpredictable consumer: confident, savvy, tight with a dime, indulgent, and self-soothing. Why people trade down. Growth at both ends of the market. Trading down: a global trend. How Kraft faces death in the middle. Strategies for winning. Why you shouldn't wait to respond.

2. The New Middle-Class Consumer

The story of the Montforts and their life of trade-offs. Who is in the middle class and how did they get so much power? Lifestage spending. The pivotal role and influence of women. The value calculus. The four emotional spaces. How to listen for actionable insights. The want list. When dreams go on hold.

3. Cheap Is Good

Or, as they say in Germany, geiz ist geil. *The story of Hilda Schmidt and how she stockpiles. Hard discount as a threat. How Aldi grew to become the leading hard discounter in Europe. The rise of the dollar store in the United States. Dollar General is funky, but people love it. How everyday-low-price retailers are fighting back. Not all consumers trade down; some go without. The story of Betsy Vitalio and the three sources of financial vulnerability.*

4. Spanning the Poles

My journey to Korea to meet the LG cadets. How LG started at the low end in home electronics and now spans the poles of high and low ends. The hotel industry transformed by 9/11. The story of Best Value Inn, the fastest-growing hotel company in the industry. Marriott, a late entrant but well-endowed participant in pole spanning. The story of Jim and Anne and why they had to sell their piano.

5. All Treasure, All the Time

Stephanie's scarf addiction. eBay is the world's greatest treasure hunt. Win-win economics. A new language of retailing. The one and only Tchibo: market power from merchandising. The many different types of treasure.

innovation. Viking looks to span the poles. Recutting the data. How The Home Depot aspires to do it for you. How to get started. Serving the middle-class consumer can be a noble enterprise.

INTRODUCTION

One of my early projects as a young partner at The Boston Consulting Group was for a company that made a variety of chemical products for home use, including cleaning agents and bug spray. I invited the head of the bug spray division to join me on a series of in-home interviews to get a better understanding of how the company's products fit into their customers' lives.

One of our first visits was to a sixtyish woman named Lillie, who lived in a mobile home park near Tampa, Florida. She welcomed us in and we perched ourselves on folding chairs while Lillie dropped into a La-Z-Boy recliner. I asked Lillie to tell us a little bit about herself and she launched into the story of her childhood in Mississippi, her first marriage, the birth of her two kids, her hardworking life, her divorce and remarriage.

Just as Lillie was telling us about the sudden death of her second husband, an enormous cockroach emerged from the kitchenette and ambled into the living room. My client and I noticed it at exactly the same moment. We looked at each other, looked at the cockroach, and then looked back at each other, wondering whether we should mention it or pretend we hadn't noticed.

But Lillie spotted the cockroach, too. "Damn!" she growled. She leapt out of the La-Z-Boy, tore open a kitchen cabinet, and pulled out a can of my client's very own brand of bug spray. She closed in for the attack, bent over, aimed the nozzle at the roach, and nailed it. I counted—one-one-thousand, two-one-thousand, three-one-thousand, four-one-thousand, five-one-thousand—as the roach jerked into a deathly paroxysm and the spray formed a toxic puddle around him.

"Take that, you bastard," Lillie said.

My client and I looked at her with raised eyebrows.

"Roaches!" she said with disgust. "Remind me of my first husband." She placed the rim of the can on the carcass and bisected it with a definitive crunch.

What did we learn from our visits? First, that customers use far more spray than necessary. More important, Lillie demonstrated that even a utilitarian product like bug spray can have deeply emotional, even primal, meaning. Our visit with Lillie became a reference point for the bug spray organization as it created news and improvements for its products.

Over the twenty-five years since that visit with Lillie, I have spent a great deal of time listening to consumers, watching them in action, and gaining insights that can be applied to business strategy. I have seen that consumers will always "trade down" and buy the cheapest product in a category if suppliers fail to deliver a stream of innovation and build loyalty based on product superiority. I have come to understand the constant trade-offs that middle-class consumers make in the purchase of goods, how many buying decisions they face in a day, and how much competition there is for their attention. I have come to appreciate how sophisticated consumers are. They have access to a wealth of product information. They do not tolerate poor quality in a product without complaint and a vow that they will "never again" buy it. I know that household budgets are tight and that they are predominantly controlled by women. That's because women, since going to work in large numbers, are responsible for 100 percent of the growth in household income. Women manage the family budget like an industrial purchasing agent who occasionally turns into a hedonist. The home, although still a family haven, has also become a pressure cooker. This smart, educated middle-class population—highly stressed and faced with tremendous choice—increasingly buys at both ends of the price spectrum, while ignoring the middle.

Middle-class consumers have embarked on a relentless, continuous treasure hunt. The treasure hunt is a real and global phenomenon that presents challenges to both retailers and their suppliers, and has delivered death in the middle to the average, middle-market producer—companies like Chevrolet and Kraft.

In *Trading Up*, my co-author Neil Fiske and I explored one aspect of the treasure hunt—how middle-market consumers would distort their spending to buy premium goods that were highly meaningful to them. The book originated, interestingly enough, in a series of conversations we had with young women about their underwear. During the course of that consumer discovery work for Victoria's Secret, Neil and I developed an idea that we called "the ladder of benefits"—an ascending scale of technical, functional, and emotional benefits. A genuine technical difference leads to an advantage in functional performance, which can ultimately result in a positive emotional response, attachment to the product, and brand loyalty. The combination delivers the potential for the company to charge a price premium.

With the ladder of benefits in mind, we worked with the leaders of Victoria's Secret to help create a new line of lingerie called Body by Victoria. It offered technical, functional, and emotional benefits, and Victoria's Secret priced it at a premium to middle-market lingerie. The new line took off and quickly grew into a $500 million business. Its success was evidence that, if you get the ladder of benefits right, consumers will not only pay a premium for your product or service, they will even distort their spending patterns to do so.

At first, we thought this might be an anomaly and applicable only in the fashion industry. But we researched many other categories of consumer goods, including cars, wine, spirits, and home goods, and found that the desire to move up the ladder of benefits was a broad phenomenon. In category after category, up to 20 percent of the market was in goods that sold at a premium of 50 to 200 percent to mid-price offerings. We estimated that "trading up" in 2002 accounted for about $300 billion in annual sales in about twenty-three major categories in the United States. Since then, it has grown to over $500 billion in this country and about the same amount in Europe.

In my work with clients and consumers since 2002, it became increasingly obvious that the trading-up phenomenon, although extremely significant, is actually just one element of the bigger and more important story of the treasure hunt: the bifurcation of the consumer goods market into trading-up and trading-down segments, with death in the middle.

Thus, this book deepens the inquiry and broadens the scope of the work begun in *Trading Up*, with two main purposes. First, it is to help the reader better understand middle-market consumers, who are too often ignored or misinterpreted by businesspeople, the press, and others. Some economists even characterize them as spendthrifts and the culprits behind the U.S. trade deficit. I see middle-class consumers as essentially hardworking and noble people who must deal with an increasing amount of pressure to make choices for their families and themselves. They are generally wise about their spending, although they sometimes carry more debt than they would like to and accumulate more goods than necessary. I hope the stories in this book will bring them more respect and understanding. You'll meet:

Alice and Ben Nelson. The family went on an austerity budget to afford four TVs as a Christmas gift.

Sarah and Rick Montfort. Sarah drives across town to save a few pennies on chicken. Rick blows $500 a month on golf and poker.

Lauren James. Age thirty, she invests heavily in clothing and personal care, and saves money by eating Cheez-Its at the 7-Eleven.

Masako Tanaka. One of millions of young Japanese "office ladies," she lives with her parents and spends liberally on fashion, entertainment, and travel.

Peter Kim. He earns about $80,000 as a waiter, but feels left behind by friends who are starting families and buying big homes.

Hilda Schmidt. With a household spending allowance of €600 per month, she stocks up on goods in case of an emergency or shortfall of cash.

Stephanie Granby. She fell in love with scarves in her early twenties, but couldn't afford to indulge her interest—until she discovered eBay.

The second purpose of the book is to show how companies must take advantage of the treasure hunt phenomenon or be left behind by it. To do so, we have interwoven the consumer stories with accounts of some of the most interesting companies that have affected, or been affected by, the transformation of the consumer goods market, including:

Aldi. The extraordinarily successful hard discount chain, founded in Germany, and now catching on throughout Europe and in the United States.

Bath & Body Works. The unit of Limited Brands that has repositioned itself to meet the changing value calculus of women's beauty.

Best Value Inn. The fastest-growing hotel chain in the United States delivers a quality room at a trading-down price.

Dollar General. One of the many dollar chains that are proliferating throughout the United States with its own funky interpretation of the treasure hunt.

eBay. The world's largest garage sale and the most dramatic manifestation of the consumer-driven market.

LG. The Korean maker of home electronics and appliances that started at the bottom end of the market and now "spans the poles."

McDonald's. McDonald's revitalized its burger and fries and kept the Happy Meal from becoming just "utility fuel."

Tchibo. The innovative German purveyor of coffee and one-of-a-kind goods, with an inventory that changes every month.

By linking the stories of consumers and companies, I hope to deliver a double benefit for the reader: consumer understanding and actionable business ideas—along with a healthy serving of data to support both.

I know from close experience the daunting challenges that businesspeople face in today's dynamic, almost vibrating consumer goods markets. I respect those leaders who find a way to create products, brands, and companies that connect with consumers and energize categories and transform markets, because—in the whirl of meeting investor expectations, complying with Sarbanes-Oxley requirements, and motivating the workforce—it is easy to "forget" the consumer and lose touch with the market.

I also hope the ideas in this book will help entrepreneurs get rich and, in the process, enrich the lives of "average consumers."

TREASURE
HUNT

1.

THE BIFURCATING MARKET

The Nelsons: A Daewoo Christmas

It was coming up to Christmas, and Alice Nelson wanted to make the holiday very special for her family. The Nelsons had not bought a new TV in twelve years. Alice's husband, Ben, was sick of the old television with its twenty-seven-inch screen and mediocre sound. Their three children looked with envy at the big flat screens of their friends and neighbors. Everybody in the family was tired of mediating who would get to watch what and when.

"We needed a new television," Ben says with conviction. "Especially me. I work a seventy-five–hour week. Watching sports on television is one of my few luxuries. Alice and the children wanted a vacation as a Christmas gift. But I knew that if I could convince them to go with the TV as the family gift, we would get years of pleasure from it, rather than just a few days of vacation."

It was an unusual decision for an unusual family. Ben Nelson holds two jobs; one as an engineer, the other as a barber. Alice is a part-time nurse with health issues of her own to attend to. The Nelsons have three children—two girls and a boy—aged eighteen, sixteen, and fourteen. They live in a middle-class suburb. Alice drives a gas-guzzling Durango SUV and Ben tools around in an aging two-seater. He works hard, as much as fourteen hours a day. His engineering work involves selling big-ticket durable accessories to purchasing agents in the railroad industry. His barbering is done in a prestigious men's salon in Chicago, where cuts go for $40 or more. Ben loves his wife and children and hopes the children will achieve success that will far surpass his own. He is a kind man and devotes his life to providing for others. Even so, he really wanted a bigger-screen television far more than he wanted to go on a vacation that he felt would be little more than "a happy memory" within a few months.

So, one weekend in November, Alice and Ben went together to look at new TVs. They started at Best Buy, went on to Sears, and ended up at Circuit City. There, with the help of an unusually attentive salesperson, they studied dozens of sets and carefully compared features and prices. They decided they would have to spend at least $1,500 to get the big-screen television with the quality and features they really wanted. That was more money than they had thought about spending and it would put a strain on their already-strained budget. The Nelsons' total household income—including engineering, barbering, and nursing—is about $100,000 a year.

The Nelsons did not think the television was overpriced. In fact, it seemed like a good value to them, considering its picture and audio quality, as well as its many controls and connection options. Plus, they could imagine the new TV in their lives and the benefits it would bring. Ben looked forward to watching football and baseball with the panoramic clarity of the new set. Alice pictured the whole family together on a weekend night, laughing at their favorite comedies on DVD.

But, as Ben and Alice discussed the purchase, they realized that it would probably make the "who watches what and when" problem even worse. As they talked, they continued to wander through the aisles, looking at different TV sets, which were arranged on the shelves according to size and price. At the very end, they noticed a thirteen-inch color television, a perfectly nice-looking little unit made by Daewoo. Ben checked the price and could not believe what he saw: $57. And, as an engineer, he was satisfied with the technical features and functional performance. The picture quality was good. The sound was fine. You could hook up cable or a DVD player. It came with a neat little remote.

A little nervous, but also quite excited, Alice and Ben debated a new idea. What if they were to buy not just one wide-screen TV, but *four* sets? A thirty-two-inch LG wide-screen flat-panel TFT-LCD TV for $1,999 for the whole family and three thirteen-inch Daewoos, at $57, one for each of the children. The total purchase would come to more than $2,000, but it would bring tremendous pleasure to the family, reduce the number of squabbles, and make for a fabulous Christmas. They decided to go for it. On the way out of the store, Ben crowed, "It's gonna be a Daewoo Christmas!"

Christmas morning came and the children were ecstatic. They could not believe that their parents, who were always looking for ways to save money, had sprung for four television sets. The kids would have been thrilled with one big-screen TV. Now they each had their own. It was nothing short of revolutionary. Ben and Alice loved seeing their son and daughters so happy. That evening, with the big screen set up in the family room, Ben surfed through the channels and the children dashed from bedroom to bedroom, and from set to set, squealing with delight.

A few days after Christmas, Alice called the family together. She said that they had spent a lot of money on the television sets, more than they had planned, but that it was definitely worth it. However, it would mean that they would have less money than usual for a little while. They would have to cut back on spending for things that weren't absolutely necessary. Alice said she would do all she could to save money on food and other household expenses. She expected the children to be frugal and not ask for frivolous things. Ben pledged that he would try to limit his spending on the little gifts he occasionally liked to spring on his family. No more $40 boxes of chocolates for Alice or $85 skirts for the girls or video games for the boy. And that's exactly what they did. For the first quarter of the family's "fiscal year," the Nelson family was like a company on an austerity budget. There was no additional capital spending. No unnecessary purchases. No dining out. Ben kept his splurging instinct in check. Alice cut out her weekly coffee date with her friends. She bought no new clothing. By April, the TV sets were paid for and the Nelsons breathed a little easier.

The Dynamic Market Meets the Unpredictable Consumer

Whatever you think of the benefits of television, or the necessity of one family owning four of anything, the story of the Nelsons and their Daewoo Christmas is a good parable for what's going on in the consumer goods market today.

In the United States and around the world, the consumer markets are bifurcating into two fast-growing pools of spending. At the high end of the market, consumers are trading up, paying a premium for high-quality, emotionally rich, high-margin products and services. At the low end, consumers are relentlessly trading down, spending as little as possible to buy basic, low-cost goods that still deliver acceptable quality, reliability, and, increasingly, elements of fashion and current design. In between the trading-up and trading-down pools lies a vast expanse of mediocre, often low-margin, goods that offer neither distinctive emotional appeal nor better value than cheaper competitors. Whenever they can, consumers steer clear of them. Many businesses that have long prospered by bringing midpriced products to middle-market consumers suddenly find themselves facing "death in the middle." In the television category, for example, Sony is facing death in the middle. Sony has been slow to offer high-end plasma and LCD technologies, clinging instead to conventional

TV tube technology, and watching as lower-cost Korean manufacturers steal market share.

Companies that succeed in this bifurcated market do so by understanding the attitudes, behaviors, and values of the middle-market consumers who are driving the transformation, and constantly adjusting and reinventing their product offering to satisfy the ever-changing "value calculus" of the consumer. This is not easy to do, because today's consumers are highly skilled "shopping experts" who view the purchasing and consumption of goods as an essential activity of modern life—a skill, a pastime, an experience, and a duty. They are very good at separating truth from charade and distinguishing marketing claims from real product benefits. They care about the application of technology, product quality, and features and accommodations to fit their specific needs.

Consuming has become a treasure hunt—a constant search through the world's incredibly vast and ever-changing store of goods and services—with the goal of finding the perfect value every time. There are so many goods available, in so many configurations and at so many price points, that consumers look at the market as a huge bazaar filled with amazing finds and secret delights. It is a place where they can roam freely and always find something of interest, whether it is an unexpected item tucked onto a shelf at a Dollar General, a 30 percent markdown at the Coach factory store, or a one-of-a-kind, limited-time deal at the extraordinary Tchibo store. Sometimes the treasure is not to be found and consumers must settle for something less (or even go without), but when they find exactly the right product at exactly the right price, life is good—even if the product is nothing more than a $2 bar of soap or a $49 motel room with a wi-fi connection.

These consumers spend their money with great individuality, trading up in a few categories, trading down in most, avoiding some altogether, mixing upscale products with downscale ones, and creat-

AVERAGE UPPER-MIDDLE-MARKET INCOME STATEMENT

Item	$100K Pretax Income	
	Monthly	Annual
Income (posttax)[1]	$6,000	$72,000
Car (payments, insurance, gas, maint.)	1,100	13,200
Mortgage/rent	810	9,720
Household utilities and maintenance	640	7,680
Travel and entertainment	380	4,560
Groceries[2]	370	4,410
Eating out[2]	360	4,320
Healthcare/personal health	270	3,240
Home goods (e.g., furnishings, electronics)	240	2,280
Clothing	230	2,760
Charitable contributions	200	2,400
Education	130	1,560
Personal care services	80	960
Life insurance	60	720
Other expenses	200	2,400
Total spending	5,070	60,800
Net savings/(deficit)	930	11,200

(1) Assumes effective tax rate of 28 percent. (2) Includes alcohol.
Source: *Treasure Hunt* interviews, January–February 2005; Consumer expenditure survey 2003.   THE BOSTON CONSULTING GROUP

ing customized lifestyles and standards of living that are uniquely their own.

Every day, middle-class consumers are confronted with choices. They have limited family income and know that their "cash outflow" should not exceed their income. Family members often make requests for more goods than the income providers can afford and they also may "demand" specific brands that put extra strain on the family budget. This causes the decision maker to make trade-offs and to make choices.

Our research shows that the great majority of American consumers trade down relentlessly. (The same is true, as we'll see, around the world.) In our surveys of twelve thousand middle-market shoppers in the United States, 93 percent said there is "at least one category in which I will try to save a little money by spending less." Eighty-four percent said they trade down in five or more product categories. Others are more selective; 62 percent said they focus their spending on just a few categories that matter and ignore the rest. Most interesting, 57 percent of the respondents agreed with the statement, "I never spend money on myself until the needs of my family are met." In that percentage are to be found the diehard penny-pinchers, the sacrificing moms and do-without dads who put their families' needs for food, clothing, school supplies, sporting equipment, and even entertainment ahead of their own wants and needs.

Why People Trade Down

Consumers trade down for four main reasons:

"I'm a smart shopper." Buying and consuming have become skills as fundamental as driving a car or using a computer. As one consumer said to me, "I wake up every day and start a new battle. It's me versus the world. The world is trying to take money out of my wallet. It's my job to make sure it stays in there." These warrior-shoppers take advantage of every weapon and channel at their disposal: sales, coupons, promotions, everyday–low-price retailers, hard discounters, and the Web. Shopping is the work of the everyday trader-down. "I see it as my job to find bargains and get the lowest price," said a consumer in a conversation in a parking lot outside a Dollar General store. "I will shop in three different stores to save fifty cents. I always buy on sale and make our budget work by getting great deals."

"There's no material difference." Another reason that consumers trade down is that they often see no perceivable or material difference between goods at two price points. The quality of goods in many categories has risen so that the difference in price of a few pennies, even a few dollars, does not always translate into genuine technical, functional, or emotional differences. "I don't trade quality for price," one consumer told me. "Instead, I focus on finding the best value. These days you really can find high quality for a low price. You just have to be smart about how and where you shop."

"My Mom taught me." Many trading-down consumers, especially women, were taught frugality at their mother's knee. They believe in being thrifty as a moral value. When they consider a purchase, they ask themselves, "Would Mom approve? Would she have bought this?" In fact, many middle-market consumers will seek their parents' advice and counsel, especially when it comes to a major purchase like a car or kitchen appliance. The great word-of-mouth network, as well as the many online communities of shoppers and buyers, help people to consider and evaluate the features and benefits of every imaginable product, from pet food to food supplements.

"I can go without." Although Americans have gotten a bad rap for being careless spenders and wasteful consumers, particularly in comparison to other cultures around the world, most middle-class consumers do not believe in excessive consumption. They are willing to forgo buying an item in order to save some money. They prioritize their purchases and will only buy certain items when everything else has been paid for. As one shopper said to me, "Making ends meet is always something I'm worried about. We're very careful about where we spend our money. The kids' activities and needs are taken care of first and we just find a way to make the rest of it work."

As a result of these trading-up and trading-down behaviors, middle-market consumers confound the traditional demographic

---

TRADING-DOWN BEHAVIORS ROOTED IN FAMILIAL HISTORY AND COMMON SENSE

"I'm a smart shopper."	"There's no material difference."
■ Buying on sale ■ Shopping with coupons ■ Finding low-price retailers ■ Feeling smart for beating the system	■ Quality perceived to be equal across price points ■ Low-price product is "good enough"
"My Mom taught me."	**"I can go without."**
■ Parents were frugal and thrifty ■ Exhibit spending patterns of parents ■ Always questioning "Would Mom approve of this purchase?"	■ Can forgo an item to save money ■ Unable to justify expense ■ Purchase is last priority and doesn't always happen

Source: *Treasure Hunt* interviews, January–February 2005. Consumer expenditure survey 2003.　　　　　　THE BOSTON CONSULTING GROUP

---

and psychographic stereotypes. These people are unpredictable—completely, delightfully, exasperatingly unpredictable. Our definition of the middle class includes the $150,000-a-year professional who buys $19 jeans at Target, flies AirTran, splurges on shoes at Neiman-Marcus, travels fifty miles to a Coach outlet store to buy a handbag, and pays $100 for her dog to have a "beauty treatment." It also embraces the $50,000-a-year plumber who leases a $27,000 BMW, never dines out, buys clothes at Kohl's, and is a connoisseur of cold-pressed virgin Italian olive oils. Both of them look for the best deals on TVs. Neither one really cares what brand and where they buy canned tomato sauce. More and more, that's the market companies now face.

Growth at Both Ends of the Market

The behaviors of middle-market consumers like the Nelsons and others we interviewed have caused growth at both ends of the market. Of the $3.7 trillion in annual consumer spending in the United States, the trading-up market—which has been growing at the rate of 15 percent over the past three years—accounts for about $535 billion of the total. Trading up has found its way into almost every consumer goods category, including cars, homes, travel, food-at-home and food-away-from-home, and personal care.

The trading-down market, however, is substantially bigger. It is approaching $1 trillion and should amount to $1.5 trillion by the end of the decade. Consumers are eagerly spending less (often much less) on a wide variety of goods in many categories so they can acquire more of what they need and want in a few categories of significance to them.

This is a global phenomenon. The trade-up market is now more than $500 billion outside the United States, principally in Western Europe. In countries like the UK and Japan, the patterns of consumption are very similar to U.S. patterns. The trade-down market is even more developed in most of Western Europe. In Germany, retail specialists like Aldi and Lidl have made the treasure hunt a national pastime.

Trading-down companies have created more than ten times the market value that trading-up companies have created. The top ten trading-up companies have a market capitalization of about $55 billion, an increase of $34 billion over the years 1994–2004. The market cap of the top ten trading-down retailers is nearly nine times as big, about $476 billion, up by $357 billion over the decade. Big recent winners over the past decade include Target, Costco, Lowe's, and Dollar General. We estimate that big-box, low-margin retailers save American consumers over $100 billion per year. No wonder that trading-down retailers have delivered the largest long-term increase in market value of any subsector in the consumer-driven economy.

MASS AND GROWTH HAVE DELIVERED ENORMOUS TRADE-DOWN MARKET VALUE

The Trading-Up Top Ten (retailers)				The Trading-Down Top Ten (retailers)		
Retailer	Market capitalization 2004 ($B)	Change in market capitalization 1994–2004 (real 2004 $B)		Retailer	Market capitalization 2004 ($B)	Change in market capitalization 1994–2004 (real 2004 $B)
1. Coach	10.2	9.7		1. Wal-Mart	233.2	170.8
2. Whole Foods Market Inc.	6.5	4.6		2. Home Depot	88.3	56.2
3. Tiffany & Co.	5.1	4.5		3. Target	41.5	35.7
4. Williams-Sonoma	4.0	3.3		4. Lowe's	43.8	33.8
5. Limited Brands Inc.	10.3	3.2		5. Kohl's Corp.	15.7	13.8
6. Cheesecake Factory	2.2	2.0		6. Costco	17.2	13.1
7. Nordstrom	6.8	1.8		7. Staples	14.0	12.1
8. Neiman-Marcus	4.2	1.7		8. TJX Companies	11.8	10.7
9. Saks	1.9	1.6		9. Family Dollar	8.2	5.3
10. Brinker International	3.4	1.6		10. Dollar General	4.5	6.3
Total	54.6	34.0		Total	476.2	357.8

Source: BCG Value Science.   THE BOSTON CONSULTING GROUP

Almost every category of consumer goods is in the process of forming into pools at both ends of the market. The largest trading-up categories are travel and entertainment, homes and home renovations, cars, food-away-from-home and food-at-home, and personal services. The largest trading-down categories, where consumers buy the least expensive option, are essentially the same ones: homes and home renovations, transportation, dining out, travel, food and beverages, personal items, and apparel and fashion.

What lies between is becoming a wasteland. In category after category, premium entries are growing, bargain brands are stealing share, and the *middle is shrinking*. In cars, for example, the trading-up segment grew by 8 percent from 1994 to 2004. The trading-down segment grew by 4 percent, and the midprice segment shrunk by 12 percent. For General Motors, a company that has always thrived on the middle market and has only a small trading-up business, the shift is cataclysmic.

We see the same result in the market for washing machines over the same ten-year period; the trading-up segment was up 11 percent, trading down grew by 5 percent, and the middle was down 16 percent.

The numbers are similar for televisions—trading up increased by 33 percent, trading down grew by 7 percent, and the middle declined by 40 percent. For hotels, trading down has grown by 13 percent; groceries' middle has shrunk by 24 percent. In women's apparel, the top and bottom have gained 9 percent and the middle has fallen by 18 percent.

As a result, these consumer goods categories have become battlegrounds. Thanks in large part to the economics of contract manufacturing—sourcing, supply chain, and procurement—companies like Wal-Mart, Costco, Home Depot, Lowe's, Dollar General, and Family Dollar have been able to pull the rug out from under the traditional grocery store, department store, and general merchandise retailer, beating the gross margins of those competitors by as much as ten full points. They are leading the revolution as both retailers and producers, forcing suppliers and competitors to cut costs of entire industries to make trading down possible in almost every consumer

TRADING UP $535 BILLION; TRADING DOWN $1 TRILLION

Category	Estimate of 2004 market size ($B)		Ratio of Trading Down to Trading Up
	Trading Down	Trading Up	
Homes and home renovations	220	100	2.2x
Transportation	160	80	2.0x
Dining out	155	80	1.9x
Travel and entertainment	135	130	1.0x
Food and beverage	130	50	2.6x
Personal products and services	90	35	2.6x
Apparel and fashion	60	30	2.0x
Home goods	55	50	1.1x
Total	1,005	535	1.9x

Source: BCG analysis   THE BOSTON CONSULTING GROUP

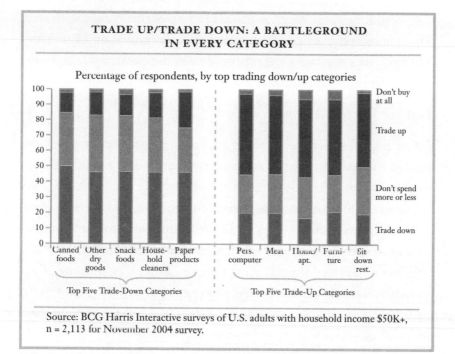

**TRADE UP/TRADE DOWN: A BATTLEGROUND
IN EVERY CATEGORY**

Percentage of respondents, by top trading down/up categories

Don't buy at all

Trade up

Don't spend more or less

Trade down

Canned foods | Other dry goods | Snack foods | House-hold cleaners | Paper products | Pers. computer | Meat | Home/apt. | Furni-ture | Sit down rest.

Top Five Trade-Down Categories

Top Five Trade-Up Categories

Source: BCG Harris Interactive surveys of U.S. adults with household income $50K+, n = 2,113 for November 2004 survey.

goods category. The same supply chain capabilities have enabled trading-up producers to take cost out of their offerings, produce more new products in a shorter period of time, and reduce their need to carry inventory, so they can respond more quickly to changing consumer tastes.

The battle of bifurcation rages across America, although the spending pools tend to have geographic correlations. Trading up in a category usually begins in urban and coastal areas, including New York, Miami, Los Angeles, and San Francisco, and then migrates to other parts of the country.

Trading down tends to start in rural and suburban areas, far from any big cities, and then gradually moves closer to the coasts and urban areas. Wal-Mart's original strategy was to locate in underserved, rural locations, and the company has met resistance as it has worked to establish itself in well-known zones of trading up. Not surprisingly, middle-class consumers who live in states that have low-density populations and are away from the coasts (the Gulf Coast excluded) have the greatest purchasing power of all Americans.

Trading Down—A Global Trend

But trading down is hardly a solely American phenomenon. The same income and spending patterns that drive the trading-up and trading-down behaviors in North America are also causing market restlessness in Europe, China, India, and Japan. Throughout Europe, especially in Germany, the propensity to trade down in selected categories has led to the rise of hard discounting—medium-sized stores that offer little in the way of a shopping experience but a lot in the way of extremely low prices on a wide array of goods, especially groceries. In Japan, the consumer market is distorted by a single demographic

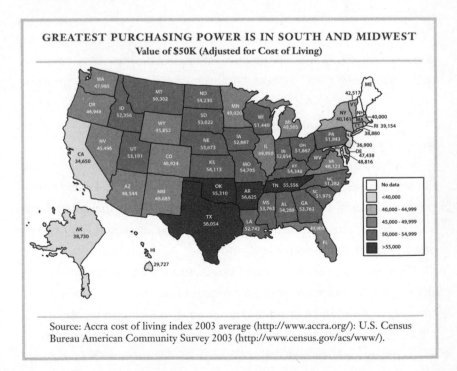

GREATEST PURCHASING POWER IS IN SOUTH AND MIDWEST
Value of $50K (Adjusted for Cost of Living)

Source: Accra cost of living index 2003 average (http://www.accra.org/): U.S. Census Bureau American Community Survey 2003 (http://www.census.gov/acs/www/).

group: young, single, working women with high salaries and few financial obligations. They trade up in fashion and dining out but are ruthless about trading down in many other categories.

There are differences from country to country, but the phenomenon is evident everywhere. You can see it in the streets of Shanghai and Seattle, Mexico City and Montreal, Tokyo and Topeka. Every city has its high street boutiques offering expensive goods with dramatic presentations—and with high operating costs. A few miles away are the discount retailers, such as Wal-Mart, Carrefour, and Costco. Middle-class customers shop at both places on different occasions and with different motivations. They feel a sense of style and sophistication when they buy a Hamptons Signature Stripe Demi handbag at Coach for $200. They smile with secret pleasure as they buy a two-quart bottle of Kirkland Signature Extra-Virgin Toscano vintage olive oil at Costco for just $9.

Worldwide, we expect to see continued growth at the bottom and top of the market and a further decline in the middle. New companies will emerge at both ends; well-known names will be humbled by their inability to escape the middle. Kraft is one of them.

Kraft: Death in the Middle

Kraft—a large and venerable company, with sales of $32 billion in 2004—owns some of the world's most prized brands. Seven of them—Maxwell House, Oscar Mayer, Nabisco, Philadelphia, Post, Jacobs, and Kraft itself—achieved more than a billion dollars in annual sales. Sixty-one other Kraft brands had over $100 million in sales in 2004. But, despite Kraft's size, scope, and wealth of brands, in some businesses it has been so squeezed by competitors from above and below that it has gotten seriously stuck in the middle.

The Kraft brand is most closely associated with cheese, and many of the company's grocery products, including cheese, are used as ingredients in cooking. But, although cheese consumption is on the rise in the United States, many of Kraft's cheese products have been losing share for some time. There are many reasons for this. The main one is that fewer families are cooking at home, mostly because so many women are working and don't have the time to spend planning, shopping for, and preparing meals. So there has been a decline in demand for the ingredients that have traditionally gone into these meals—the very ingredients that Kraft supplies. Another reason for the loss of share is that there are many cheaper brands of cheese and a broader array available now than there were just a few years ago (many of them store labels) and consumers have found that they're just as good as Kraft. You can buy a block of Safeway's store brand Lucerne cheddar cheese, for example, for $2.49. The same size block of Kraft cheddar costs $4.10—about 60 percent more. So, there is plenty of opportunity for consumers to trade down on cheese. And why shouldn't they?

There has also been a boom in specialty cheeses. These are cheeses—like gorgonzola, Camembert, feta, blue cheese, and others—that sell at a premium because they are of superior quality, are flown in from some exotic place, are limited in supply, or have some other technical or functional difference that makes them special. Americans have gone crazy over specialty cheeses. About 66 percent of all supermarkets in the United States had a specialty cheese department in 2005, up from 33 percent in 2000. Dollar sales of specialty cheeses topped $1.5 billion in 2004, an increase of about 13 percent over 2003. Wisconsin's output of specialty cheeses more than doubled in just six years.

Losing Share, Cutting Costs

During the same six-year period, Kraft lost about five share points in the $2 billion market for natural block cheese. The company had to find a way to respond to the decline in share and profits. They did not choose to go into specialty cheeses. Nor did they choose to cut prices on their current products. They chose, instead, to cut costs. Their goal was to increase their margins, so they could hold total profits, even as their market share was falling. They embarked on an effort to cut supply chain costs and marketing expense and to reengineer their main products.

Their cost-cutting efforts can clearly be seen in one of Kraft's most familiar products, Kraft Macaroni & Cheese. Every year, the company has set a cost reduction target of 2 to 3 percent and the managers and scientists who are responsible for Kraft Macaroni & Cheese regularly meet that goal through "value engineering." They are constantly looking for ways to reduce the cost of ingredients, which is the major expense in the macaroni and cheese mix. If you look at the list of ingredients on a box of the current product, you'll see that there is no "real" cheese on the list. That's probably because real cheese is expensive. The product is now made with cheese culture, whey, milk fat, milk protein concentrate, salt, calcium carbonate, sodium tripolyphosphate, and other ingredients. The package says that Kraft Macaroni & Cheese is "the cheesiest," and many consumers still seem to like the taste. But if you were able to compare it to the Kraft Macaroni & Cheese made in 1997, which was made with "real" dried cheddar cheese and buttermilk, you could probably taste the difference.

Kraft Macaroni & Cheese is still the leading brand in its category and a hugely profitable product, but it is also in danger, as is the company, of being caught in the middle and squeezed by competitors at the high and low ends of the market. Kraft Macaroni & Cheese typically costs sixty cents for the 7.25-ounce package. Wal-Mart's store brand, which "is made with real cheddar cheese," costs thirty-three cents. Annie's Creamy Deluxe Shells and Real Aged Wisconsin Cheddar sells for $2.59. Plenty of people still buy Kraft because they love the brand or the particular taste or perhaps because they're not paying attention or just don't like to change brands, in general. But there is no doubt that Kraft is stuck in the middle, and not just with cheese. They have the same problem with their Chips Ahoy! cookies, Kraft salad dressings, and Maxwell House coffee.

Strategies for Winning

What does this pressure on the middle and transformation of the consumer goods market mean for businesses? Opportunity. And danger. There are four principal ways to succeed: trading down, trading up, spanning the poles, and holding the middle.

Trading down. The trading-down market is massive, but, as we've seen, it is extremely knockabout, with ferocious price competition and virtually no consumer loyalty. And you can't succeed at the low end simply by tapping into the global supply chain, taking cost out, and waging a price war with your competitors; consumers still expect value and performance from their low-cost products. More and more, they demand emotional qualities in their low-cost goods and a pleasurable experience while shopping for them.

For trading down, the mantra must be "basic, low-cost, and reliable" (BLCR). The mission is always to find ways to make a product or service cheaper and better. Not only cheaper, not just better—but both at once. As soon as you think your price is low enough and you stop trying to lower it further, a competitor will find a way to scrape a few pennies off the cost and offer the product at a lower retail price. As soon as you think your quality is good enough and stop trying to make it better, a competitor will incorporate a technical improvement or a functional feature that will grab the consumer's attention.

The only way to satisfy the value calculus of the trading-down consumer is to be as cheap as, or cheaper than, any product that is comparable to yours. But "basic" and "low-cost" do not mean that the product is dull or ordinary. They just mean that the product contains only those technical and functional elements that the trading-down consumer cares about. The Mini Cooper, for example, is a basic, low-cost, reliable car but hardly a boring one. At a starting price of $16,750, it can compete with other small models, including the VW Golf, as well as with larger cars that offer more features but—for many drivers—no greater value.

People want quality in everything they buy, and they have many choices in every category. When trading down, consumers still rely on their value calculus—analyzing cost, worth, brand value, design, use, and expected longevity. The trading-down competitor can never stop searching for ways to provide ever lower prices and better quality, because consumers will never stop searching for more value.

Trading down is a global game in which the global low cost producer wins. Success requires the aggressive management of scale, raw materials purchasing, continuous experimentation in design to reduce costs, and a relentless drive to rethink the cost structure to establish advantage.

Trading up. There are still opportunities to succeed in trading up, but you must create distinctive products that offer technical, functional, and emotional differences for which consumers will pay a premium. This is not a one-time event. Competitors that rest on their laurels in trading-up categories will be matched and then trumped by newcomers.

For trading up, the mission is captured in the slogan coined by Ely Callaway of the Callaway Golf Company—"demonstrably superior and pleasingly different" (or DSPD). That is, essentially, a short way of saying that the product must deliver on the ladder of benefits—technical, functional, and emotional—in order to command a premium. After Ely Callaway's death, the company began to drift from that discipline and soon lost share and the momentum to rival Taylor-Made. Taylor-Made escalated the pace of innovation, aggressively discounted the prior season's goods, and became the beneficiary of "hope and pride" for the weekend duffer. Callaway, without its founder at the helm, drifted.

Coach, in contrast to Callaway, has proceeded from strength to strength by constantly delivering on the ladder of differences. The company has grown from $600 million in annual sales in 2000 to $1.7 billion in 2004, with its growth coming from one of the best and most consistent executions of trading-up strategy. Ten years ago, Coach was a stodgy, slow-moving provider of traditional, high-quality, moderately priced leather goods for women, offering a limited selection of products that changed little from season to season. Today, Coach is a lively provider of a wide range of fashion accessories that precisely hits the value sweet spot for women aged thirty to fifty-five with incomes from $40,000 to $200,000. "Coach is all about fashion accessories, and the market for our product is completely elastic," Lew Frankfort, chairman and CEO, told me. "Women buy our product because a new Coach handbag is an instant compliment generator. We do intense market research—thousands of interviews a year—and we understand where our consumers are going." Lew, who is also a principal shareholder of Coach, is proud, successful, and rich. "We have so much growth ahead of us," he said.

However, succeeding in trading up is not as easy as it might look, and there is plenty of congestion at the premium end of the market in many categories. I get a continuous stream of e-mails from entrepreneurs who have developed yet another new and wonderful premium vodka, for example. They have dreams of becoming the next Ketel One or Belvedere and pushing the price point per bottle above $40. My answer to them is this: maybe you should explore a less picked-over category. Vodka has traded up and is highly segmented. There are many other categories where the market is open to a trading-up offering, particularly financial services and healthcare.

Spanning the poles. A very few capable companies have been able to succeed at both ends of the market, "spanning the poles." Toyota is the obvious, and most dramatic, example. The company is a master at cost reduction, with a relentless drive to continuously cut product cost for every component and every make and model. For Toyota, being the global low-cost producer is a minimal standard of performance. The company's executives are expected to achieve as much as a 20 percent global component cost advantage over Ford, General Motors, and its other major competitors. In 2006, Toyota will become the world's largest car manufacturer in units and dollars, surpassing General Motors for the first time. The Toyota and Lexus brands cover virtually all price points from below $10,000 to luxury cars that sell for around $90,000. Each one—at whichever pole, or wherever it falls between them—offers technical innovation, user ergonomics, and a compelling price advantage over comparable vehicles. Toyota gains share through this deliberate, relentless, and seemingly undefeatable execution of a span-the-poles strategy.

LG, the Korean maker of consumer electronics, is a lesser-known proponent of this strategy. The company offers refrigerators that successfully compete at the low end with the Sears store brand and at the high end with new-luxury icon Sub-Zero. But this strategy requires exceptional commitment, skill, persistence, and allocation of resources. For LG, the effort took twenty years and the unflagging dedication of the company chairman Bon-Moo Koo. And, spanning the poles usually means competing in the middle, as well, with all its attendant dangers and difficulties.

Surprisingly, Viking Range Corporation, the Greenwood, Mississippi–based maker of premium stoves and refrigerators for the serious cook, is an unlikely participant in the treasure hunt, as it moves toward a spanning-the-poles strategy.

In *Trading Up*, we profiled Viking as a major player in the premium market. In 1987, founder Fred Carl designed a stainless steel restaurant-quality oven with thirty thousand BTUs in the cooking cavity and sixteen thousand BTUs on the cooktop, and basically invented the superpremium oven for the U.S. consumer. Viking became a legend in the kitchen—a statement of taste, skill, and serious cooking.

The company has brilliantly succeeded in the trading-up market, growing rapidly to over $300 million in sales and with profitability at the top of the appliance industry, and the Viking brand has become iconic in the world of high-end consumer kitchens. Viking has been so profitable that they have been able to self-fund the development of many products in new categories and at a variety of price points—including dishwashers, refrigerators, ice makers, wine storage devices, microwaves, flatware, and knives. As it expands its line toward the lower end of the market (although not as low as the LG line goes), Viking expects to double or even triple its sales volume over the next five years.

"We want more households to be able to afford Viking," Fred Carl told me when I visited the Greenwood facilities and met with his management team. "We need another subline at a lower price to provide this. We don't want to compromise on quality, but there do have to be differences. We think we can do it. We can take Viking features and manufacture them at a lower cost. It's just like BMW and its drive to gradually expand the affordability of its offering."

Holding the middle. The middle of the market is still the biggest piece of the consumer goods pie, with some $2 trillion worth of spending each year in the United States. Companies that aim for the middle can still achieve share and profit growth. The point, however, is that the middle is steadily shrinking, which means that it just gets harder and harder for Kraft, Kroger, General Motors, United Airlines, and other companies that have for years served the middle of the middle class to grow and strengthen their brands.

As the middle contracts, it's likely that a few competitors will remain there and new ones will emerge—companies that can strike a smart balance between low-cost functionality and premium emotion without resorting to bland, me-too conformity and empty marketing messages. It's possible that Kraft will be able to rethink the mid-price food ingredients market that is beginning to seriously care about health issues and also demands speed, convenience, and ease of preparation.

What's particularly intriguing is that successful companies employ a nearly identical set of practices, no matter what strategy they have chosen to pursue in the bifurcating market:

1. *Escape the middle.* If you are in the middle, begin moving up, down, or in both directions. Don't assume your customers will ever come back to the vast desert of mediocrity and don't get stuck there yourself. If you choose to play in the middle, be sure it's not your only playground. Kraft Macaroni & Cheese, for example, is a midprice, midmarket product that is so profitable that the company can't give it up. That's fine, for a while, so long as it puts energy and resources into other products that give it entry into the trading-down or trading-up markets, or that redefine the middle by responding to new consumer tastes and needs.

2. *Drive costs down and quality up.* Never stop searching for ways to provide ever lower prices and better quality, because consumers won't stop searching for more value. There is never a point where all the costs are out or all the quality is in. In this consumer goods market, there can be no resting on the laurels, no moments of catching the breath. Cost reduction efforts that are aimed at one-time reductions are a trap. The world of consumer products has embraced and devoted itself to continuous cost reduction, operational innovation, improved supply chain, and material substitution.

3. *Attack the category like an outsider.* Look at your offering from the perspective of a category outsider. What would it consider your weak spot to be? When your management team quotes industry rules of thumb or describes the "typical consumer," force them to provide more detail and get at the truths beneath the assumptions. If you are in a leadership position, fuel your momentum

by making unpredictable moves and commit completely to the quest for best quality and lowest cost. Change the game. Invent. Don't let "sunk" investments prevent you from invention.

4. *Listen, listen, listen.* Understand all the detail and nuances about consumers' dissatisfactions. Track them down in your products and engineer them out. Invite complaints and systematically track the root causes. Add responsiveness, consumer empathy, and simplicity of presentation to your priority list. Get underneath their skins and understand how you can help provide them with emotional satisfaction, novel solutions to old problems, and a personal connection.

5. *Focus on your best customers.* Follow them up and down the aisles and tailor your offering to meet their needs. As Wal-Mart teaches its associates, "The truth is in the stores." Or, more broadly put, the truth is wherever the consumer engages with or encounters your product or service. Where they are, you should be. The "best customer" or heavy-user consumption pattern can model behaviors you can expand to other groups of consumers. You want to listen to "cravers" who tell their friends about the products they love.

The Trend Will Continue With or Without You

We expect that the bifurcation of consumer goods markets will continue for at least the next decade, with growth at the high and low ends of almost every market segment, and an inexorable shrinking of the middle. We expect that consumer households in the Western world will enjoy a gradual increase in real incomes. Women will inch toward parity income. Education will drive increasing consumer sophistication in purchasing. The bonanza of growth for discount and splurge retailing will not abate.

Health scares and threats, war, terror, and complicated relationships at home and on the job will be the norm for people around the world. Because of this unpredictability and insecurity, consumers will continue to pay a premium for goods that reinforce a sense of place and connection and provide an occasional moment of indulgence. They will also look for value that enables them to save money and protect their futures. This middle-class consuming household will seek to put away a nest egg for retirement. They will relentlessly cut corners and further commoditization will result.

Market challenges are not for the faint of heart. The premium-priced, premium-profitability, really technically advantaged product will grow in power. The low-cost treasure will earn loyalty and referral. The market switch will force the hunt for consumer "truth"—fundamental product improvement and control of the value chain. This means that current category leaders are vulnerable, not only to competitors within their categories, but to emerging startups. So, if you are a leader, you must take the widest possible view of the competitive landscape—that the consumer's discretionary dollars are always up for grabs. (*Discretionary* implies "freedom of choice" or "freedom of decision." For example, a consumer may set out to buy a scarf and come home with a kitchen gadget instead.) If you are not yet a leader, your best plan may be to set your sights on the leader in a category outside your own, who may not see you coming.

Wherever you now sit, no one will thank you, in the long run, for holding back, ignoring the data, or delaying action. No one will laud you for allowing your company to get caught in the middle. They will, however, be delighted to be with you when you have correctly understood the treasure hunt phenomenon and connected your company with the genuine needs of that most powerful market force in the world: the middle-class consumer.

2.

THE NEW MIDDLE-CLASS CONSUMER

The Montforts: A Life of Trade-offs

Sarah Montfort, at first glance, seems to be quite average. She lives with her husband and three daughters in the town of Arlington Heights, Illinois, about twenty-five miles northwest of Chicago, and her demographics are about as close to those of the average resident of this town of some seventy-six thousand people as you can get. The median age is forty. Sarah and her husband, Rick, are thirty-eight. They're both white, as is 90 percent of the population. They own and live in a single-family home, as does about 77 percent of the population. Their annual family income is $85,000, which is almost exactly the median. They have three children.

But there is a lot that the demographics don't reveal about individuals and how they actually live. Sarah Montfort and her family lead a life that is happy and hopeful, but also full of struggle and stress. Much of what Sarah deals with every day is about allotting money and making purchasing decisions that will help her family live a "good life." Unlike people at the top of the income ladder, who rarely have to make substantial trade-offs in their lives, or people at the bottom, who have few options at all, people in the middle constantly face difficult choices. They have to make every dollar stretch. They cannot do all the things they would like to do. They are always comparing themselves to others who they think have more.

The town of Arlington Heights is a desirable suburb known for a good school system with a low teacher–student ratio, and a wonderful network of parks that offers almost every kind of recreational activity, from picnicking to Little League. Sarah's daughters play tennis, soccer, and volleyball. Rick is a golfer. Sarah plays volleyball, too, once a week.

When we drive into Arlington Heights, we see that there are a lot of homes for sale in town. Many of the older homes are being "scraped" and replaced by bigger houses with nicer materials and more amenities. The town is concerned enough about rapidly rising home prices that it is developing new restrictions to try to keep things under control.

We drive by a Just Tires outlet, a Kinko's, and a mom-and-pop convenience store called Buzz-In, Buzz-Out, and then enter Sarah's neighborhood. We come to the park where the kids will soon be warming up for soccer practice and pass the church where the Montforts attend services each week. The building obviously has been recently renovated and expanded.

Sarah's house is on a quiet street lined with two-story homes built about thirty-five years ago. You can almost hear the narrator from *Our Town* talking about the lives of ordinary middle-class families in Arlington Heights. It's not easy to pick hers out because the homes look similar, with only minor variations; they are the kind of homes you'd see in many communities in America. Even so, the house has appreciated significantly since the Montforts bought it five years ago. Their $356,000 investment, which was a stretch for them, is already worth at least $425,000. Having the equity provides a nice cushion, but it is illiquid and Sarah and Rick cannot rely on it too much.

Sarah, dressed in jeans and a white sweater, greets us at the door

THE MONTFORTS' ASSETS		THEIR LIABILITIES	
Savings account	$200	Mortgage	$240,000
Checking account	$600	Home equity loan	$8,000
Investments	$110,000	Credit card	$0
Home value	$425,000	Student loans	$0
Other	$0	Other	$0

with a warm smile and welcomes us in. The girls—twelve-year-old Samantha and eight-year-old twins Carly and Emily—are still at school, so Sarah has time to talk without being distracted. She settles us into the living room. We introduce ourselves and talk a bit about our research. Then we ask Sarah to tell us a little about herself. She does not begin by describing her childhood, education, or her own interests and activities. She says simply, "I'm married to a high school math and science teacher, and we have three daughters."

As we quickly learn, that is how Sarah's life is defined at the moment. As a young woman, she had many dreams. She married a man she loved. They decided to have a family. They agreed that Sarah would be a full-time, stay-at-home mother and homemaker, even though it meant that they would have to rely solely on Rick's earning power. Sarah does not for a minute regret the decision, but she finds herself living a life that is quite different from the one she dreamed of. Even with a solid middle-class income of $85,000, a nice house, a loving family, and a network of friends and neighbors, life is much more of a struggle—financially, practically, physically, and emotionally— than Sarah imagined it would be. She is always busy, with days that begin at 6 A.M. and end at 11 P.M. Although she is exceptionally frugal, she worries about how they will pay for college and wedding expenses. "Growing up, I was idealistic," she said. "I thought life would be a fairy tale. Now I realize that life is a set of trade-offs and you have to make those choices every day."

Rick is always trying to find ways to earn a little more, supplementing his school salary by teaching summer school and coaching golf and diving. Sarah usually substitute teaches a couple of days a week. She is constantly trying to make the most of the money that comes in. "It's a struggle every single day," she says. "With rising gas prices, we have to choose where we're driving and where we're going to ride our bikes. When we go to the store, we have to really think about 'Do we need that snack or do we need food for dinner tonight?' We have to choose and really think about what we're buying and why."

But, now and again, particularly when he's worried about teacher contract negotiations at school, Rick will come home and say to Sarah, "You need to cut back." To which she responds, "Where do you think I'm going to be able to do that?" There is no fat in the Montfort family budget. Rick brings home about $5,200 each month and they spend $4,840 of it. The remaining $360 goes into savings. But they often dip into that, too, and there is only $200 in the account when we talk. Sarah does not feel like an affluent American. She feels squeezed by all the demands on her time and the family money.

It doesn't take long for us to discover one of the main reasons for Sarah's anxiety and the Montforts' pinched lifestyle. Five years ago they made a difficult decision to move out of the house in the town of Algonquin where they had lived for seven years. They loved their house there. It was only ten years old, and had lots of open living space where the family could hang out together. Their neighborhood was clean and safe, and the Montforts had many friends in town. They bought the house in 1996 for $202,000. Rick's salary steadily rose and they came to feel that their finances were under control and they could afford a few extras. Sarah belonged to a health club. She treated herself to a manicure or pedicure now and again, had lunch with friends every week, and regularly had her hair cut at the local salon. Rick indulged his hobby of tinkering with computers and took an occasional golfing trip with buddies.

But, as the twins approached school age, some of the deficiencies of the town began to show. There was a limited park system in Algonquin, and the girls were increasingly interested in sports. Worse, the school system had budget problems. "The school district was trying to put thirty-five students in a single class without a teacher's aide," Sarah said. "One of my daughters was having trouble with reading. That was it. I wasn't going to put her in that situation."

Sarah and Rick decided to move to Arlington Heights. Not only did it have an extensive park district and a better school system, but Sarah and Rick had grown up in the town and both sets of parents still lived there. Sarah also had two elderly aunts in nursing homes in town who needed attending to now and again. She expected a small inheritance from them one day.

Home prices are much higher in Arlington Heights than in Algonquin. Although the Montforts sold the Washington Street house for $262,000, realizing a profit of $60,000, their money bought a lot less house in Arlington Heights. For $356,000, they got a house that was twenty-five years older and, at 2,500 square feet, no bigger than the old house. It has small rooms, low ceilings, no finished basement, and a kitchen that hasn't been updated in years. There's no big open area where the family can hang out together. Sarah hates not being able to see into the cramped family room when she's doing dishes at the kitchen sink. And there is one other feature of the Washington Street house that Sarah misses most of all: the master bedroom with ensuite bathroom, complete with Jacuzzi. "I truly enjoyed relaxing in the whirlpool tub," she said. "It was my little serenity place."

Sarah needs that little bit of serenity more than ever because the move to Arlington Heights put a serious strain on the family finances. They took a $240,000 mortgage on the new house, which increased their monthly payment from $1,750 to $2,000. That's high for a family earning $85,000 a year. The average mortgage payment for a family of similar means is about $880 per month, so the Montforts' budget is distorted by the increased expense. "Moving to Arlington Heights was both trading up and trading down," said Sarah. "We got the better schools and the park system, but we've had to trade down in lots of other ways. I'm happy with the decision, but it's much

Item	Spending	Index vs. Average Household with Same Income
THE MONTFORTS' MONTHLY EXPENSES		
Income (posttax)	$5,200	1.0
Car	480	0.5
Mortgage/rent	2,000	2.3
Household utilities and maintenance	470	0.9
Eating out	50	0.2
Groceries	580	1.9
Travel and entertainment	170	0.6
Healthcare/personal health	30	0.1
Home goods	60	0.3
Clothing	100	0.5
Charitable contributions	170	0.9
Education	150	1.4
Personal care services	20	0.3
Life insurance	160	3.0
Other expenses	400	3.8
Total spending	4,840	1.1
Net savings/(deficit)	360	0.4

harder than I thought it would be to cut things out and say no to so many things I want to do."

The Power of the Middle Class

The Montforts are typical of the American middle-class consumer in many ways, even though their story is uniquely their own. In the United States, we define the middle class as people who live in households that earn between $50,000 and $150,000 per year. There are forty-eight million such households and they control 75 percent of all discretionary spending (spending on nonessential or better-than-necessary items), which means they control the market. Because there has been real growth in household income, middle-market consumers have greater purchasing power and have been able to increase their expenditures on durable goods. They have also benefited from the decline in real prices for both food and clothing.

As a result, they have a greater net worth than the "average" family has ever had in America, and greater net worth than people of similar status have in any other country today. With nearly 86 percent of this income group owning homes, and the percentage still on the rise, it's easy to say that the standard of living of the middle-income American is extremely high.

Middle-class consumers not only control the market, they control themselves and their spending. They may be financially stretched and emotionally stressed, but they are not the wanton, debt-ridden, free-spenders that many observers see. In fact, the net worth of middle-class households is growing more rapidly than their income. Twenty-four out of twenty-five middle-class households take in more money each month than they spend. Debt as a percentage of total assets is stable, and less than 5 percent of middle-market households are in significant financial distress. They rely on credit cards to make special purchases, or to get along at specific periods of stress in their lives—often when they are young or when they suffer a reversal of some kind—but very few American consumers are financing their lives with credit cards.

In addition, contrary to claims by many analysts, there is real savings in the United States. American households possess about $47 trillion of net worth. The savings rate, adjusted for increases in net worth, is basically flat, at about 7 percent of income. The average American household is richer than the average household in Japan, a fact that gets little press coverage. Their wealth may not show up in the savings account at the local bank, but it's there—in the home, the stock market, in cars, and in other assets. For the most part, people are not going into debt to trade up. Nor is debt what's driving people

WHO IS THE MIDDLE-MARKET CONSUMER?

Characteristic	Overall	Under $20K	$20K to $49K	$50K to $149K	Over $150K	Middle Market Indexed to Avg. (US=100)
Number of households (1000s)	97,391	27,100	32,832	44,992	4,002	
Income before taxes	51,128	10,753	33,195	99,739	223,634	195
Male (%)	51.0	38.9	50.7	58.7	59.0	115
Female (%)	49.0	61.1	49.3	41.3	41.0	84
Black or African American (%)	12.0	17.1	11.9	6.7	4.0	56
White, Asian, and all other races (%)	88.0	82.9	88.1	93.3	96.0	106
Average number in consumer unit:						
Persons	2.5	1.8	2.4	3.0	3.1	119
Children under 18	0.6	0.4	0.6	0.8	0.9	133
Persons 65 and over	0.3	0.4	0.3	0.1	0.1	44
Earners per household	1.3	0.7	1.3	1.9	1.9	146
Vehicles per household	2.0	1.1	1.9	2.7	2.8	137
At least one vehicle owned or leased (%)	88.0	70.2	92.5	97.5	96.0	1.11
Homeowner (%)	66.0	44.4	62.8	85.9	94.0	130
With mortgage (%)	41.0	12.7	35.0	67.6	73.0	165
Without mortgage (%)	25.0	31.4	27.5	18.3	21.0	73
Renter (%)	34.0	55.6	37.2	14.1	6.0	42
High school (9–12) (%)	36.0	46.0	43.2	22.0	8.0	61
College (%)	57.0	40.4	50.5	76.8	91.0	135

Notes: Only includes households reporting complete income.
Source: Consumer Expenditure Survey 2003: "Income before taxes: Average expenditures and characteristics" table and "Higher income before taxes: Average expenditures and characteristics" table, http://www.bls.gov/cex/home.htm.

to trade down. They do both because they can and because they want to. Inflation-adjusted assets are growing faster than liabilities. Overall, increases in debt level are modest.

In Europe, the middle class looks different than it does in the United States, particularly in its size. The percentage of households earning the equivalent of $50,000 or more is much lower in the six largest European economies than it is in the United States. In the United States, about 57 percent of all households (about 57 million households) take in $50,000 or more each year. In the United Kingdom, which has the highest percentage of $50,000-plus households

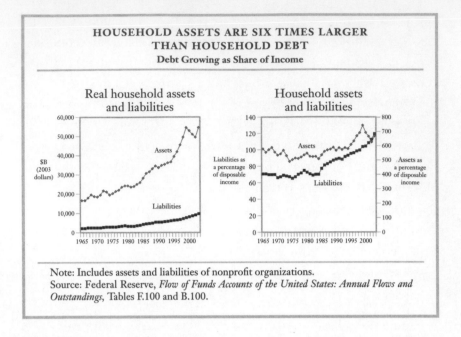

**HOUSEHOLD ASSETS ARE SIX TIMES LARGER
THAN HOUSEHOLD DEBT**
Debt Growing as Share of Income

Real household assets
and liabilities

Household assets
and liabilities

Note: Includes assets and liabilities of nonprofit organizations.
Source: Federal Reserve, *Flow of Funds Accounts of the United States: Annual Flows and Outstandings*, Tables F.100 and B.100.

of the five European economies, the percentage is about 46 percent, or 9.4 million households. Spain has the lowest percentage of the six, at 25 percent, or three million households.

However, incomes have risen strongly throughout Europe, and people are generally wealthier now than they were ten years ago. Over the past fifteen years, disposable income has risen at a compound annual growth rate (CAGR) that ranges from 3.4 percent in Italy to 6.9 percent in the United Kingdom, so there is more money available to spend on goods and services. In the United States, 1.3 million households with income over $250,000 account for 14 percent of discretionary spending; 14 million households with income over $100,000 account for nearly half. These consumers all make trade-offs in their spending. They look across the array of available goods and services when making their decisions about what to buy. They have choice and they know it.

In the United States, the top 20 percent holds about 91 percent of the wealth. Europeans have also seen the value of their homes and other assets grow. Over the past twenty years, home ownership has increased significantly in the five major European economies (France, Germany, Italy, Spain, and the United Kingdom), and accommodation prices have risen sharply, except in Germany. During the same period, household size has been steadily shrinking, with the result that gross domestic product (GDP) per capita has increased. And, as in the United States, although the level of savings has been shrinking and consumer debt has increased, indebtedness—the ratio of debt to assets—has remained quite constant. Our research has shown that trading up is as strong a trend in Europe as it is in the United States—perhaps even stronger. And, primarily because of the large percentage of households earning the equivalent of $50,000 or less, trading down is also a megatrend in Europe.

Lifestage Spending: Beyond Geography and Demographics

The market bifurcation not only transcends demographic and geographic boundaries, it involves people at every stage of life. Businesses must recognize that consumers like Ben and Alice Nelson are driven as much by their circumstances and life decisions as they are by income, profession, or where they live. And, as much as consumers like to see themselves as smart shoppers, expert purchasers, and mall warriors, they freely admit that they are not as confident and carefree as they might like to appear. In fact, the middle-market consumer is under considerable stress much of the time. In our consumer survey, we found that the majority of respondents feel stressed and tired, isolated and fearful, insecure, and underappreciated.

These feelings become important factors in the value calculus. We will see that fears, insecurities, and turmoil factor into purchases in profound ways in each of five lifestages: young singles, couples without kids, youngish parents, high-commitment families, and empty nesters and secure seniors, as well as for people going through hard times.

FEELING STRESSED, ISOLATED, INSECURE, AND UNDERAPPRECIATED

Top two box scores/bottom two box scores**

Stressed and tired		**Insecure**	
I never have enough time.	57%	I'm happy with my body.**	48%
I don't get enough sleep.	51%		
I'm working harder than ever.	46%		

Isolated and fearful		**Underappreciated**	
I don't spend enough time with friends.	55%	I don't feel appreciated for all that I do.	40%
I am anxious about the future.	46%		

Source: BCG Harris Interactive surveys of U.S. adults with household income $50+; n = 2,113 for November 2004 survey.

Young singles. They are dazzled by the world, have few obligations, care little for saving, and see spending as a way to try new things and gain experience. Some are still in school, some are working steadily, some are traveling, and some are jumping from one activity to another. Money is usually tight and income unreliable. Young singles ruthlessly trade down in many categories in order to spend more freely in others. They tend to trade up on well-known brands that their friends admire.

Couples without kids. They spend to enhance their personal identities, to strengthen their relationships with each other and their friends, and to establish their professional credentials. They may start saving to buy a car or get married. They trade down almost as a cause—seeking out the best at the lowest prices—and they often influence the consumption habits of their partners. They have very strong convictions about brands and align their spending with the values they perceive that the brand represents. Many of these young couples enjoy unprecedented cash incomes, usually because both members of the couple are working. They buy convenience goods and indulge themselves by buying a new luxury car, going on adventure vacations, rarely cooking a meal, and becoming expert in consumer electronics and food and wine. Couples that have two incomes and do not have kids have a much wider range of choices than people in any other lifestage. They trade up in a group of categories where they have high interest, including food, travel, cars, and home goods. They trade down in a group of categories where they see no material interest. This is a segment where averages of purchases have little meaning and can even be misleading.

Youngish parents. When children arrive, spending patterns change dramatically. Working mothers, who suddenly have heavy emotional demands on their limited time, are under intense pressure. Spending becomes a family preoccupation—how to spend, where to spend, when to spend. Young parents may trade down in almost everything—except when it comes to the new baby, or when Mom needs a little break or indulgence for herself. These thirty-something parents often vow that their child will not lack material goods—a Bugaboo stroller or a Petit Bateau outfit.

High-commitment families. Families with older children and, often, with aging parents find that managing their spending, and their finances as a whole, takes up a large part of their already busy lives. They are thinking about education, housing, investments, assets, retirement, and inheritances. Children as young as four and five begin to influence the family purchases and brand affiliations. Older children pressure the family to buy brands that they believe will help them succeed socially, academically, or athletically. Parents care less about brands than about finding ways to meet all the family's needs without jeopardizing its future. Spending on small-ticket goods may decrease as spending on big-ticket items becomes necessary: a second or third car, a bigger house, a college education. Trading down becomes a way of life. Mom and Dad, who may have been traders-up in their earlier days, make do with what's already in the closet or settle for the serviceable item that they would have shunned a decade earlier. The patterns the parents choose often become part of the coping schemes of the children.

Empty nesters and secure seniors. Many older couples and singles enjoy good health with minimal financial obligations. They may have very few new material needs—because almost everything has been bought—but many emotional needs. They might be loyal to a handful of brands, but, in general, aren't terribly interested in brand stories. For them, spending often returns to a question of values. They are unwilling to tolerate waste and frivolous spending. They care about quality and performance, but are generally frugal, although price, within limits, is not as important as it used to be. Even so, shopping may become a pastime and an entertainment for them, and the beneficiary of the trip to the mall is usually a child or grandchild. Seniors often trade down on themselves while trading up on goods for younger family members.

Hard times. Experiences can also determine how consumers spend. Patterns change, for instance, when people go through bad times, such as a relationship breakup, loss of a job, illness, death of a loved one, accident, failure, or depression. They often try to compensate for their problems through spending behaviors. Some go on a spending binge, because the act of purchasing makes them feel better. Some become fierce penny-pinchers. Some spend well beyond their means.

At every lifestage, I'm amazed at the skills, behaviors, and attitudes of everyday consumers, both in the United States and abroad. If you spend time listening to consumers about why they buy what they do, you'll find they have a rationale for every purchase. Their buying decisions are not random; they are premeditated and creatively conceived. For major purchases, there is a comprehensive understanding of the technical and functional benefits of the product or service under consideration. Each consumer speaks the language of goods in his or her own way. Single women consume dramatically differently than mothers do, putting themselves first rather than last the way many middle-class mothers do. Single men trade up and trade down in different categories than their friends with steady partners do. In Germany, thriftiness is so prized that it's almost a national character trait, and consumers make it a point of pride to buy everything at the lowest possible price. In Japan, the young, single "office ladies," who earn good salaries but live at home with their parents and pay no expenses, have little need to be thrifty at all. For many other consumers who are scraping along on incomes below $50,000, the language of goods is a pretty sparse one. Trading up may mean buying a low-cost product in a specific category. Trading down may mean buying nothing in that category at all.

For all these consumers, trading down isn't so much about compromising as it is about rejecting the average for a better product at a lower price. It's a shrewd weighing of costs against benefits, and consumers scrutinize their choices as closely as, well, an executive deliberating over a business strategy. Emotional issues play a large role in how they approach trading down and that has resulted in a new math for balancing budgets and a new language for defining *luxury* and *value*. Today's consumers want to feel more comfortable, confident, and expert in the "game" of shopping.

In our interviews, we learned that every consumer has a favorite trick for squeezing the most out of a dollar. The top ten tricks are:

1. Know the market prices to the penny.
2. Buy on sale.

3. Shop with coupons.

4. Find the low-price retailer.

5. Shop at Costco to "guarantee" value.

6. Treasure hunt at Dollar General.

7. Bargain for a lower price.

8. Buy at the end of the season and hold the item for the following year so it will be "new for me."

9. Optimize quantity discount price curves.

10. Go without.

The Pivotal Role of Women

Women, of course, are at the center of household spending and consumption, the driving force behind trading up, trading down, and the shrinking of the middle. Because they have been joining the workforce in increasing numbers, they are responsible for 100 percent of the growth in real household income between 1970 and 2004. They control or influence more than 75 percent of discretionary spending in developed markets worldwide and they are masters of material-goods acquisition. Women's earnings are growing faster than men's earnings, no matter what their level of education. Over 25 percent of married women make more than their spouses do. They earn the majority of bachelor's and master's degrees. Some 85 percent of women over the age of eighteen identify themselves as the principal shoppers in their households. Women buy 50 percent of cars and 51 percent of consumer electronics. Over 40 percent of households with assets of $600,000 or more are headed by women.

Women research their purchases carefully, and they have a sharp instinct for value and a clear sense of their own individual preferences. They can make a brand or a new product concept successful within months of its launch. They can crush a flawed idea in ninety days or less.

Women are the principal influencers of shopping and consumption

- 85 percent of women over eighteen identify themselves as the principal shopper in their household.
- 90 percent of married women identify themselves as the principal shopper.
- 80 percent of consumer goods purchases are made or influenced by women.
- 51 percent of consumer electronics purchases are made by women.
- Women buy 50 percent of all cars and influence 80 percent of their sales.
- 48 percent of stock market investors are women.
- Over 40 percent of households with at least $600,000 in assets are headed by women.

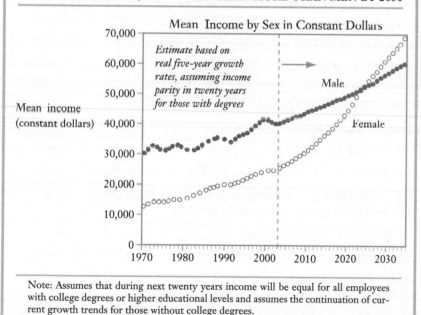

ASSUMING INCOME EQUALITY IS ACHIEVED WITHIN THE NEXT TWENTY YEARS FOR COLLEGE-EDUCATED WOMEN, THEY WILL EARN MORE THAN MEN BY 2030

Mean Income by Sex in Constant Dollars

Estimate based on real five-year growth rates, assuming income parity in twenty years for those with degrees

Male

Female

Mean income (constant dollars)

70,000
60,000
50,000
40,000
30,000
20,000
10,000
0

1970   1980   1990   2000   2010   2020   2030

Note: Assumes that during next twenty years income will be equal for all employees with college degrees or higher educational levels and assumes the continuation of current growth trends for those without college degrees.
Source: Bureau of the Census.

And women will continue to transform the market. Within the next thirty years, the average wage for women in America will exceed the average wage for men. That's because women outnumber men in undergraduate schools, and the percentage of women in graduate schools is steadily increasing and will eventually overtake that of males. The level of education correlates directly with the level of success a person reaches within an organization.

Women's Roles as Consumers

Women, no matter what their level of education, take on many roles as consumers. Although I don't want to deal in stereotypes or archetypes, we have seen three behaviors again and again. In most situations, the female consumer behaves like the industrial purchasing agent, casting an eagle eye on price and value and buying with rigorous care and attention to detail. She knows prices by retailer and by stockkeeping unit (SKU), and her value calculus provides a succinct characterization of each product, such as "a rip-off," "high value," "fun to try," or "a family staple."

Often, especially in families, women behave like martyrs, scrimping and saving and putting themselves last, in order to take care of the other members of the family first. Finally, women will sometimes become consuming hedonists. Especially when the pressure of playing the purchasing agent becomes too great or the martyrdom becomes just too much to bear, women can become very self-indulgent, willing to splurge on comforts and pleasures that benefit themselves. They will pay for a massage, a new luxury face cream, a meal on the town, a beautiful new pair of shoes, or an expensive piece of jewelry. Or they will take the plunge for a big-ticket appliance, fixture, or piece of furniture for the kitchen, bathroom, laundry room, or home entertainment center.

In general, though, middle-class consumers are working hard to live a rich and balanced life and one that is distinctly their own. They develop elaborate coping strategies and smart purchasing tactics to help them buy most of what they want, live their lives almost as they please, and avoid as much financial stress as possible.

Sarah: Looking for Ways to Save

Sarah Montfort may not feel wealthy and she certainly feels stress, but she is not a complainer. Like most consumers we spoke with, she approaches her situation with practicality and selflessness. "I feel that it's my job to look for ways to save money," she said. "Since I don't earn a salary, I look for other ways to help ease the financial burden. I think it's something I learned from watching my mom."

Sarah trades down a lot, spending as little as possible on as many items as possible. "We only buy groceries that are on sale," she said. "For example, I'll buy chicken at Sam's Club for $4.88 for the whole chicken. I sat down and figured out that the chicken on sale at Jewel still costs thirty cents more per pound than the whole chicken at Sam's." The Montforts buy all of their household products in bulk, generally sticking with the low-price store brands or private labels. For clothing, she shops at the discount retailers: TJ Maxx or Marshall's for the girls, Kohl's for Rick, Target for Sarah.

"Right now it's really hard," Sarah laments. "'Do we need that snack or do we need food for the table?' We have to choose and really think about what we're buying and why. We don't buy bottled water. Our tap water is just fine."

With some items, trading down for the Montforts simply means going without. They rarely eat out, although they order in pizza about once a week. They've put off the purchase of a new car, even though the Cadillac they bought from a cousin (a good deal at $12,000 for a nearly new model) gets poor gas mileage. The kitchen remodeling will just have to wait.

I told Sarah that she reminded me of my mother, who was always the last to eat at the dinner table when I was growing up. Sarah laughs when I say it, but I am struck at how much Sarah is carrying on the habits of stay-at-home moms of the generations before her. "I make sure the kids have what they need, then my husband," she said. "Then if there's anything left over, I get something. I just don't spend much on me." Sarah may not be the last one served at the dinner table, but she is definitely the last one on the list when it comes to clothing. She used to buy many more pairs of shoes than she does now. "I can't imagine spending more than $20 on a pair of shoes for myself. Payless is my best friend." She can't remember the last time she bought a new purse.

But there are some purchases that Sarah refuses to scrimp on, especially for things the kids need for school or sports or special occasions. There is no debate about whether to spend $80 on a soccer uniform or $40 on a pair of Adidas soccer cleats. For birthdays, Sarah tries to get the kids at least one thing they really want, even if the cost seems high. When Carly wanted a Gap sweatshirt, Sarah shelled out $40 for it. "I wouldn't ordinarily spend that much on a sweatshirt, because you can buy them for $10. But it was important to her."

Sarah doesn't belong to a health club any more, but she does have a cleaning lady who comes in twice a month, at $60 a visit. "It's a splurge," she said, "but it allows me not to be so exhausted. I can enjoy more time with my family and not always worry about picking up." Now and again, Sarah treats herself to lunch or coffee at Starbucks with friends. "It's my chance to relax and to feel like I'm staying in touch with what's going on," she said. "It's important for keeping a sense of self."

So, Sarah's life is a series of complicated trade-offs. "I gave up so many things when we moved. I'm happy with the decision, but it has been much harder than I thought it would be to cut out these things and say no to so many things I want to do. I miss spontaneity! I so miss it! I just miss being able to do something on a whim."

The Montforts take one family vacation every year, always at spring break. "Vacations provide undivided time for the family to be together," Sarah said. Because the school calendar is set so far in advance, the Montforts can shop for plane tickets early and save money. But vacation spending is hard to control and sometimes they go over their budget. "We took a vacation a few years ago," Sarah said. "It was a family driving trip to the West Coast. We did fifteen states in twenty-three days. It was a big expense. We had saved a lot for the trip in advance, but it wasn't enough. We weren't even close. We went into debt to pay for it. It was worth it though. The memories we have from that trip will last forever. It was really a special time for the family." During the years they lived in Algonquin, the Montforts racked up $10,000 in credit card debt, which took several years to pay off. "Never again," she says.

Some of the splurges are more controversial than the big trip, however. Rick, in particular, is prone to impulse purchases that are not in the budget, especially when it comes to entertaining. He'll spend $100 on new chips for poker nights with the boys or $800 for the annual summer barbecue they throw for friends and neighbors, complete with two roast pigs and a rented inflatable trampoline for the kids.

Even so, Sarah doesn't really regret the barbecue expenditure because it brings the family closer together and helps the Montforts maintain and strengthen their connections with friends and neighbors.

The Value Calculus

Every consumer decides what he or she will spend on any and every item by making a value calculation that involves a host of financial, practical, and emotional factors. The purpose of making the value calculation is not just to find the lowest price (if you're trading down) or highest quality (if you're trading up); it's to determine the right price for the right product at the right time and place.

Consumers' value calculations are much less predictable today than even a decade ago, because they don't seem to line up with the consumer's income or demographics the way they used to. In the past, we would have expected to find lower-income consumers buying primarily low-cost goods at discount stores, middle-income consumers purchasing midprice goods at conventional groceries and department stores, and wealthier consumers shopping in specialty stores and boutiques. Anybody who didn't buy according to the profile was at risk of being negatively stereotyped. The wealthy person who obsessively looked for bargains was a cheapskate or a penny-pincher. The low-income person who now and again splurged on a high-cost item was a high-roller or "living beyond his means." Anyone who cared and talked about goods too much was "flashy" or a "show-off." Those notions now sound quaint and antique. Millionaires scan the aisles at Costco. Teenagers with minimal income frequent Tiffany's. The stereotypes have been exploded.

Middle-market consumers used to be pretty much at the mercy of the producers of goods and relatively uncritical about the relative quality of the things they bought. Today, they are much more knowledgeable about what they're doing. They're aware of their own motives and behaviors. They are well informed about a specific product's features and functions, and how they compare to other products in the category. All that matters to consumers now is value. What is an item worth to me? How much do I want it? How much can I spend for it? Do I need it at all? Does buying this item preclude other, more important, purchases?

Companies that ignore the value calculus are, in essence, trying to escape a force as powerful as gravity. There are six main factors that figure in a consumer's value calculation of any purchase under consideration: price, technical value, functional value, purchase excitement, integration, and emotional value.

Price. How does the price of the item compare to the cheapest alternative that I know of or have heard about? If there is a significant difference, what are the reasons for the gap? If I'm getting a deal, why? If I'm paying more, what benefits am I getting in comparison to the lowest-cost alternative? If the price is not the best price I can get, is it worth it to delay the purchase to another time or make the effort to buy the item at the lower price? Can I really afford this? How will this purchase affect my ability to buy other things I want or need? How will it affect my overall budget? How will it affect my ability to provide for others?

Consumers are extremely knowledgeable about prices. They often know the cost of goods to the penny. This is partly because there is so much choice and information available to consumers. They can compare prices on very similar goods at many different outlets as well as hundreds of price-comparison and shopping sites on the Web. They can also compare them over time.

The consumer seeks the lowest-price, best-quality alternative. Once she has found it, she repurchases it almost without thinking, except for an occasional comparison. Great competitors see the erosive effect of this behavior and continuously invent to prevent commoditization. They find ways to add new value in technical differences such as materials, manufacturing, or packaging. They exploit the

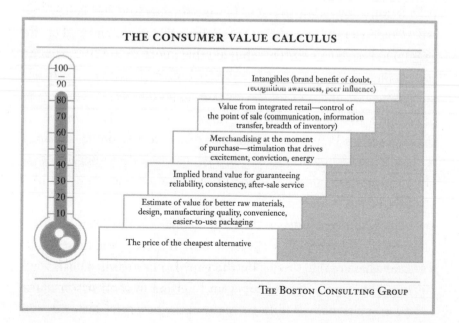

THE CONSUMER VALUE CALCULUS

Intangibles (brand benefit of doubt, recognition awareness, peer influence)

Value from integrated retail—control of the point of sale (communication, information transfer, breadth of inventory)

Merchandising at the moment of purchase—stimulation that drives excitement, conviction, energy

Implied brand value for guaranteeing reliability, consistency, after-sale service

Estimate of value for better raw materials, design, manufacturing quality, convenience, easier-to-use packaging

The price of the cheapest alternative

THE BOSTON CONSULTING GROUP

consumer's fear of buying a lower-cost product by making quality guarantees for their higher-priced products that are genuine and ring true. They provide a series of unique, exciting merchandising and sampling options. They are not content to provide the same old promotion year in and year out. Many leaders seek to further distinguish themselves by setting up their own retail operations, often a small-scale effort that enables them to be closer to the consumer. Sometimes these efforts are intended to rebalance the competition with their direct customers—the retailers. Integrated retail can contribute handsomely to earnings growth, as well as provide brand recognition, regard, and word of mouth.

Despite the big retailers' efforts to create custom product variations that are hard to compare with the same product at their competitors' (thanks to special packaging or different unit counts), consumers are hard to fool. They will figure out the unit cost and strip away all the promotional folderol to get down to the essential price. Sarah Montfort, for example, can rattle off the price of all the grocery items she regularly buys. Every time she shops, in each category, she makes her calculation about what the item is worth to her and her family that week, and what she will pay for it and what she won't. She told us, for example, that she absolutely refuses to pay more than $2.00 a pound for chicken. If the price of the day is higher than that, she'll buy something else and wait for the chicken to go on sale.

Technical value. What are the technical differences in similar products with different selling prices? Are the raw materials the same? Are there any distinctions in design? Is one product better made or assembled than the other? Is the package more appealing, easier to manage, less wasteful, or more useful?

Functional value. Will this product perform as promised? Will it work reliably and last as long as I expect it to? Do I need its performance features? If I have trouble with the product, will I be able to remedy it? And, if so, at what expense and degree of difficulty?

Purchase excitement. Will the process of buying the item be stimulating and engaging, or will it be hard work or even painful? How long will it take? Can I plan the purchase to suit my schedule? Will I be entertained? Have fun? Feel smart and rewarded? Or will I feel harassed and end up feeling as if the purchase stole value from the item itself?

Integration. Companies that have integrated their production and retail operations create consumer context for their products and the brand, often at the point of sale. Integrated retail allows a competitor to control all facets of consumer interaction. Coach successfully sells through multiple channels: conventional wholesaler to retail, their own high-fashion stores in major markets, factory outlets, and on the Web. The combination permits consumer segmentation, authoritative product launches, migration of product from one channel to another, a wonderful set of testing opportunities, and face-to-face communication of Coach benefits in a captive environment.

Apple Computer has taken face-to-face communication one step further, inventing the in-store "Genius Bar." It's a combination of a help desk and service center—staffed by Apple experts who really know their stuff—where consumers can get answers to their questions as well as immediate technical fixes. The full Apple line of products is available in every store, and most items are usually in stock so consumers can walk out the door with their purchases. Integration like this is particularly useful when launching a new product like Apple's iPod Nano. The product can immediately come alive, and be experienced and demonstrated in three hundred stores across the country. Steve Jobs comes on the *Today Show* to demonstrate the new product, and by 10 A.M. the same day, the product is available, visible, and demonstrated in the mall store.

Emotional value. What thoughts, feelings, and attitudes will the item provoke? How will I feel about myself when I buy and use the item? How will others feel about the purchase, both at the time I buy it and once I own it? How important is it that I recognize the item and know about its qualities? Will I give the benefit of the doubt to an item that doesn't quite seem to fit the other factors of the calculus because I know and trust the brand?

When Sarah Montfort went out for lunch and an afternoon of shopping with some friends, she dropped $50 on a Victoria's Secret bra. Her friends urged her to do it, and Sarah's value calculus told her the purchase was reasonable. Fifty dollars wasn't enough to jeopardize the family budget; it would hardly be noticed. It was certainly a lot less than the $100 or more per month her husband spends on golf, poker, and computer gear. It was less than the $90 she'll spend on a pair of athletic shoes for one of the kids. Sarah, the perfect full-time soccer mom, still wants to be sexy and glamorous. She's not a desperate housewife by any stretch, but she still wants her husband to desire her. "Just telling him over the phone what I bought was exciting," she said.

It was the other factors in the calculus that made the bra worth the trade-up expenditure. Most important was the experience of buying. It was a moment of connection with her close friends, a shared experience of splurging, a recapturing of the time when she was single and had control over her own pocketbook. Besides, the bra was comfortable and made her look and feel sexy, feminine, and youthful. When Sarah told us about buying the bra, she shook her head at the memory, as if it seemed a little odd in recollection. However, she didn't regret the purchase at all. It was worth every penny. "I wanted to feel beautiful, sophisticated, even romantic," she said. "It worked!"

It is an intimate and thorough understanding of the value calculus that enables some providers of consumer goods to really connect with their consumers, while others, who can't seem to channel the calculus of their intended audience, continue to offer goods that are somehow "off." They're a little too expensive for the quality or features. Or they're not expensive enough, and short on quality and features for the purpose the consumer has in mind.

The Emotional Spaces

Every purchase, therefore, has meaning and significance, and consumers make a very careful value calculation about each one. Consumers are also driven to buy goods by much deeper emotional factors that affect the value calculus but are not completely contained within it.

In *Trading Up* we identified four important emotional drivers that have become dominant in the past decade, and we've found that they are as valid to trading down as they were—and still are—to trading up.

Taking care of me is about buying things that contribute to personal health, wellness, youthfulness, and taking time for rest and renewal. Examples are a skincare product, fresh foods, a spa retreat, a set of bed linens, or a bottle of wine. This is a particularly important space for women, especially working women with families, because they feel that they are stretched to their physical and emotional limits and have very little time for themselves. In 2003, some sixty-five million American women were part of the workforce, up from eighteen million in 1950. Most important, the percentage of married women with children who are working has climbed dramatically, from 39 percent in 1960 to 77 percent in 2000. For dual-income families, the financial rewards are obvious. The average income in the dual-income household is 70 percent higher than that of the average single-earner household. But, for women, the stresses are just as obvious. Working women still put in more time doing household chores—sixteen hours per week for women on average, in comparison to nine hours for men—and spend more time taking care of children. They are desperate for a few hours per week during which they can relax, regenerate, and regain a sense of self. They find that goods and services can help.

Questing is about buying goods and experiences that enable people to challenge themselves and try new things. Examples include a car, travel, exotic foods, exercise equipment, entertainment, and collectibles. Questing is an exciting emotional space but also a dizzying one. There is tremendous choice available in travel destinations, restaurants, foods, and entertainment options. With the advent of auction sites like eBay, there are endless opportunities for collecting anything and everything. As the world has opened and Americans are better educated and more widely traveled, they are eager to push their limits and constantly move from one thing to the next. Life is short and it's a big world. Goods and services are part of the fun.

Connecting relates to goods that help individuals spend time and engage with other people they care about. Examples include a meal away from home, a time-saving washing machine, a bottle of vodka, a child's toy, or, yes, a new television set. This emotional space has become increasingly meaningful as American life has changed and become more intense, global, and fragmented. For example, people are less likely to pursue their entire career within a single organization than they once did. In fact, Americans will hold nine jobs, on average, between the ages of eighteen and thirty-five. Relationships, too, are less likely to last for long periods of time. In the United States, first marriages have a 52 percent statistical probability of failure and second marriages fail at a rate of 58 percent. It can be a lonely and isolating world. People need ways to connect and affiliate and they find that certain goods can help them do so.

Individual style is the final emotional driver. Many purchases are made simply to enable the purchasers to express their personal style and approach to life. Clothing, personal accessories, foods, home decorations, vacations, personal care items—all these help people define themselves and express their special qualities and distinctive characteristics to others around them.

A Historical Aside

Consumers have long had complex and emotional relationships with the things they buy, own, and consume. In *Trading Up*, we included a brief overview of the thinking about luxury and wealthy consumers since ancient Roman times. But middle-class people—particularly women—and the meaning goods and services have to them have also been the subject of much debate, writing, and analysis over the centuries.

One of the most provocative works of fiction to center on the issues of middle-class life and the role of possessions in it is *Madame Bovary*, written by the French author Gustave Flaubert, published in 1857. Emma Bovary, the main character, is the wife of a "suburban" nineteenth-century doctor. Becoming more and more frustrated with her rather colorless existence, Emma takes lovers in order to find some sense of the romance and excitement she reads about in novels. *Madame Bovary* contains many descriptions of the material aspects of the characters' lives, as well as much detail about their financial dealings. As Emma loses her lovers, and becomes more and more desperate as her life unravels, she increasingly seeks novelty and diversion in the purchase of goods, so much so that eventually she plunges herself and her unwitting husband into such great debt that all their possessions are taken from them. Emma commits suicide by swallowing arsenic. After her death, her husband, longing to find a way to keep her memory alive, adopts her expensive tastes and habits. "He bought patent leather boots and took to wearing white cravats."

In her introduction to the Norton Critical Edition of *Madame Bovary*, published in 2005, the editor, Margaret Cohen, puts her finger on the issue that underlies both *Trading Up* and *Treasure Hunt*. "With their scrutiny of materiality," she writes, "realist novelists capture an allure that Karl Marx identifies as distinct to modern society, in which human relations congeal and become hidden in objects that people make and exchange, leading these objects to exert a fascination beyond the ability to fill a need. Marx called this fascination commodity fetishism, linking it to a moment in the expansion of capitalism when the direct interface of buyers and producers has become abstract and distanced, entirely expressed and experienced through the circulation of commodities." Of course, we don't completely buy the influence of Karl Marx in middle-class purchases, primarily because Marx never contemplated the extremely high disposable income of the middle class in the Western world.

This human interest in goods, not for their own sake, but for their ability to answer emotional needs and to serve as proxies for other experiences and relationships, is probably as old as human history. Cohen writes that Emma Bovary indulges in "spiraling orgies of consumption on credit to console herself for her lost illusions." The middle-class consumers we interviewed did not come close to engaging in "spiraling orgies of consumption," at least not that we observed, but there is no doubt that many of them conflated their hopes and dreams with the goods and services they purchased.

Listening for Actionable Insights

The only way to understand consumers, the value calculus, and these emotional connections they have with goods is to listen for insights that can lead to business action.

Most companies pay far too little attention to their consumers and have too superficial an understanding of who those consumers are as people and how they actually use the company's products and services. What they know, or think they know, is usually based on market research data, focus group findings, polling, and other traditional methods of gathering information about consumers. These methods, while valuable, are incomplete. They don't go deep enough to get at consumer motivations and behaviors. And they are not broad enough to allow companies to see the bigger picture of the entire consumer market and how it is changing.

Given the slightest opportunity, most consumers will explain their consumption habits and how they use products. They'll talk with specificity and understanding about most of the factors that affect the value calculation, from price and features to the experience of buying. They'll reveal who influences their purchasing decisions and why. Instead of gathering "typical" or "average" responses, a much more complete view of consumption will emerge.

However, the element that is the most hidden and the least understood—and therefore is often completely missing from a company's knowledge of its consumers—is emotion. It is almost incredible how emotional most consumer goods purchases are, even ones that you wouldn't expect to be. It may be obvious that certain purchases—such as a new house or an article of clothing for a big occasion or a vacation trip—are emotionally charged. Before our visit with Lillie, however, I would not have put bug spray in that category. In our research for *Trading Up*, we talked with couples who thought of their washing machine and dryer as their "little buddies" and young working women who skip lunches for a week so they can buy lingerie. For this book, we found Sarah, who travels miles out of her way to get a certain brand of chicken at its lowest price, and Arnold, a man who bought a leather couch because he loved it so much, even though it was too big to fit into his apartment.

To get at the emotions that influence the consumer, it is necessary to learn how to listen to them in a different way than you are used to as a marketer or a businessperson. You must listen as a friend, a family member, or a colleague would listen. You have to listen purely for the sake of understanding what the world is like for consumers. Only then can you really hear them empathically.

The best listening can often be done within the context of action. It's important to let the consumer take you where she wants to go and do with her what she wants you to do. I have waxed side tables with consumers in their living rooms, applied lotions to their hands at cosmetic counters, swung golf clubs with them, eaten their favorite soups and stews with them, driven cars with them, and inventoried all the products in their refrigerators. That's when you'll uncover clues that will reveal consumers' emotions and how their behaviors and attitudes might be changing.

The Want List

Every middle-class consumer has a "want list"—a list of things she wants to buy, beyond the very basic necessities that she must buy— and it is constantly being revised. Every day consumers are open to new opportunities to spend their discretionary dollars. But they never have enough money to buy everything on the want list, of course, so they are always making trade-offs and choices, based on a number of emotional and practical factors.

If you can understand the want list of your consumers, you may discover that you are competing not only against other companies in your category, but also against completely different categories where consumers might spend their discretionary dollars. So, if you are a maker of watches, your toughest competition could be a seller of handbags rather than another watch company. If you sell flat-screen TVs, your toughest competitor might be a Caribbean cruise or a high-performance mountain bike.

Consumers arrive at the mall intending to buy one or two specific items, but the entire want list rolls around inside their heads and all the items on it struggle for attention. The consumer is consciously ready to make additional purchases and often has established a spending ceiling in her mind. Which goods will get the nod? There is so much variety available—of different types of categories and of different products within them—that the consumer is dazzled by the options. She does not typically go into the first store she sees that offers one of the goods on the want list. In fact, it can take many "points of interruption" from a particular brand before a consumer will decide to lean in its direction. A retailer, like Bath & Body Works or Coach, can have as many as five points of distribution in a single mall, without cannibalizing its own sales. This heated cross-category competition for discretionary dollars is changing the way companies present themselves to consumers, especially in the three hundred top-ranked malls in the United States.

As you listen to the consumer, look for the interesting mutations, anomalies, and outliers. Pay attention to the consumers who have seen something different in your product, who use it in some new way, who have identified something that is missing in a category, and who may be following a different path that others will follow. They're the ones who see, before others do, that a $65 motel room can be every bit as serviceable as a $130 room in a full-service hotel. Or that buying a scarf online can be more gratifying than a visit to a vintage clothing boutique. Or that a midprice skin cream should do more than just smell good. Or that you don't really need a pair of leather shoes in your wardrobe at all. But these are just the people who are least likely to show up in market research and will be scrubbed clean from scatter diagrams.

Use multiple methods—home visits or standing panels, phone interviews or advisory groups—to listen to consumers. Learn how to interview them so they really open up, rather than give you pat answers and tell you what they think you want to hear. Learn how to listen to their answers, so you can hear between the lines. Ask follow-up questions that will earn their trust so they'll tell you even more. Listen with empathy. Try to understand the context from which they're speaking. Don't judge them. Just listen to what they have to say and try to understand what it means for your product or service. Don't expect to learn everything you need to know in one visit or from one survey or one focus group. In the consumer goods market, the value calculus is always shifting and what was relevant last month is irrelevant now.

Once you start talking with consumers, you'll find that it becomes an invaluable and indispensable part of your creative life. Once you've mastered the skills of listening, you'll find that people will tell you their unfiltered life story. Too often, consumers are treated like lab mice—mere specimens to be examined, prodded, studied, and then discarded. Take interest in what they have to say. Care about them. Most people are eager to tell their stories, and, in every story, there can be a useful insight or a call to action for the listener.

Understanding consumers well enough to create genuine insight about what they want and where they could be headed is difficult, but translating that insight into action is tougher still. It is easier to base a strategic decision on market research data that provides a reasonably sure path to incremental improvement in sales, profits, or share. However, that will rarely, if ever, further any one of the strategies for succeeding in the bifurcated market.

Taking action based on consumer understanding usually requires taking a leap of some kind. You must make an assumption that cannot be "proved" by the data. You must often set off on an uncharted course. But this kind of leap is not the same as acting on a hunch or a gut instinct or a guess or a bet. It is a commitment to an idea that is based on deep consumer understanding and intelligently interpreted in the light of quantitative data. It is the willingness and ability to make a leap that separate the incremental improvers from the breakthrough winners.

Dreams on Hold

Near the end of our visit to the Montforts' home, I asked Sarah to talk about her long-term wishes for herself and her family. "I wish to have our home the way I want it before the kids leave for college," she said. "I really want a new kitchen and beautiful master bathroom. I'd like to get them out of college debt-free. I hope someday I don't have to think about saving daily." Sarah looks wistful. "I hope we can make enough so my husband doesn't have to work in the summer. Then we could travel more. I'd love to take the girls to see other countries."

Tears well up in her eyes. "We had lots of dreams when we were younger. I've had to compromise and put them away. Now I just wish we were a little better off, not so tight all the time."

The demographics say that the Montforts are relatively well off. They live in a decent house in a good neighborhood in a prosperous town. They have a steady income. They are a close family. They have a financial safety net, composed of an investment portfolio of over $100,000, Rick's pension, the generosity of their parents, and the prospect of an inheritance. Apart from an $8,000 balance on their home equity line, which was spent on fixing a leaky cement wall and creating a three-season room, and the $240,000 mortgage, the Montforts have no debt.

But although the Montforts may be successfully living the American dream, there is always a shadow of anxiety and concern. What happens if the teachers' contract is not approved and Rick has to go on strike? What if the house needs a major repair? What if Sarah gets sick? What about college tuition and, eventually, weddings? To a large degree, all of these concerns are expressed in the way middle-income people buy and consume the goods and services that are so central to our lives.

We said goodbye to Sarah, promising to visit again. As we drove out of the neighborhood, we passed the Buzz-In Buzz-Out convenience store again. Sarah had mentioned it during our conversation. It doesn't look like much. It's a one-off store, not part of a chain. It's set far back from the street and the landscaping around it leaves a lot to be desired. Sarah learned about it from other mothers in the neighborhood. It offers a particularly good deal on ham, she says: $2.90 a pound—cheaper than she can get it even at Sam's Club.

A few days after our meeting, Sarah sent an e-mail in response to some follow-up questions we had asked her. "When the twins turned three," she wrote, "there came a time when I felt I had given up everything and there was nothing left of the 'me' there once had been. I decided I had to find something for myself. I chose to go back to my favorite sport, volleyball. Rick has always golfed and played cards. This way we still feel like we've preserved a little of the person inside while giving the rest to the family. Now his hobbies are more expensive and can sometimes cause friction, but I think I let him do it because he gives me that same opportunity. For me, it is crucially important to still feel like a whole person. In the end that leaves very little time for the two of us alone, but there is hope for the future."

Sarah knows that her family's life could be a whole lot worse, but also dreams that it could be a whole lot better. She compares what her family has to what others have, and sometimes feels frustrated that they are falling short. Even so, she is hopeful. She expects that life will get better. She might get another educational degree and go back to work. The kitchen will get redone. The girls will get through college debt-free. Her husband will be able to take off summers. They'll travel. And, eventually, she might even get another Jacuzzi.

3.

CHEAP IS GOOD

Geiz Ist Geil

When I was growing up, cheap meant bad. The cheap product was, by definition, of low quality. It was embarrassing, even shameful, to buy low-cost goods because it meant you couldn't afford any better. If you got your clothes at Kmart, it wasn't something you wanted to talk about. But all that has changed. Today, everybody loves a bargain and they brag about the low prices they get. It's a victory to spend the smallest amount you can, no matter how wealthy you are. It used to be that the janitor would drive a Cadillac to show he had class. Today, the Mercedes driver shops at Target to show she has smarts.

A few years ago the big German consumer electronics retailer Media Markt ran an advertising campaign in Germany with the tagline, "*Geiz ist geil.*" As one of my colleagues explained to me, *geiz* is a word that used to have a slightly pejorative connotation, meaning somebody who is extremely stingy. *Geil* used to be a slightly off-color word, meaning sexually frustrated, but in today's youth slang it means "awesome" or "cool." So Media Markt's theme line was doubly edgy. The company was self-deprecating in using the word *geiz* (not many companies would use the word *stingy* in an ad campaign) and aligned itself with the youth market with the slang word *geil*. It was saying, essentially, that "cheap is good." Consumers around the world, of all incomes, agree.

Hilda at Home

Hilda Schmidt, for example, is a German housewife who has a secret passion for bargains. You wouldn't immediately guess it by looking at her house—a white, three-story home in a suburb about ten miles from Munich—or even by looking at her. She is a sweet woman, nicely dressed, a little overweight—a rather typical forty-year-old fräulein. We went to visit her and, when we first met, she was a little nervous and spoke softly in English. She showed us into the house and led us past her mother-in-law's apartment on the first floor and up the stairs to the two-floor apartment where she lives with her husband, Franck, and their two kids: nine-year-old Johanna and Andreas, eighteen months.

We talked for a while in the kitchen. It was a brisk day and the room felt cool to us; obviously, energy was regarded as a precious commodity and not to be wasted. Andreas was in the bedroom, taking a nap. Johanna was at soccer practice. Franck was on the road, visiting customers. We learned that Hilda Schmidt is a German version of Sarah Montfort. She is a stay-at-home mom whose duty is to run the household, which she does with dedication that sometimes seems to border on compulsion.

"I make a list of what I need to do each day," Hilda told us. "At the end of each day I review the list. It makes me really happy if I can check everything off that list." It is a long list of chores and errands. Make breakfast. Make beds. Clean kitchen. Go shopping. Clean bathrooms and wash floors. Pick up Johanna from school. Drop off Johanna at soccer practice. Cook dinner.

When Franck is not on an extended sales trip, he gets home

around 6 P.M. The family eats dinner together. The little boy goes to bed, Johanna does homework, and Franck watches TV. But Hilda keeps on working, cleaning up after dinner, then washing and ironing until 10 or 11 P.M., when they go to bed.

Hilda shakes her head ruefully when telling us about her work day. "I say to Franck, 'Why am I still working when you get to relax?' I don't understand why his work day only goes until five and my work day goes until ten." I notice a stack of books shoved to the back of a counter and ask Hilda what she's been reading. She sighs and says she doesn't have any time to read. I wonder why she can't take an hour while Andreas is napping to read a book, instead of scrubbing the already spotless floors. "My only job right now is taking care of others," she says. "I do the cleaning, cooking, caring for children. I would really like some time to read a book, or go to the cinema or spend an evening in the city with my husband. We haven't done that in years." Hilda dreams of having a little time to herself or, better yet, a date with her husband. Someday, she hopes to take a trip to a faraway land, perhaps Greece, just with Franck.

THE SCHMIDTS' ASSETS		THEIR LIABILITIES	
Savings account	$26,000	Mortgage	$0
Checking account	$6,500	Home equity	$0
Investments	$13,000	Credit card	$0
Home value	$520,000	Student loans	$0
Other	$0	Other	$0

A major part of Hilda's life is devoted to managing the finances. She struggles to make ends meet each month on the €600 that Franck's annual income of €30,000 (about $37,000) allows for household expenses. She feels it is her duty, even her mission, to shop smartly, which means buying almost everything as cheaply as possible. "I have a strict budget and I have to make it work for all our expenses," Hilda said. "That means I have to get good deals and buy things on sale—that's my job. I will go without things for myself so that the kids and my husband can have them. Sometimes I'll just have bread for lunch, while the kids eat sausage."

Hilda showed us the envelope where she keeps the household allowance money. It was the twenty-fourth of the month, and there were only six euros left to get through to the next paycheck. There were still groceries to buy and Johanna badly needed a new jacket. It was likely that Hilda would have to take a little money out of the savings account, which she doesn't like to do.

HILDA SCHMIDT'S SHOPPING LIST

HAUSHALTSBUCH
Monat:

Datum	ARTIKEL	26.2.	SALDO	€ 600,00	
Sa 26.2.	Getränke		10,99		water beer
	OBI – Wanneneinlage, Kaffeeschale, Tisch,		30,86		household utilities
	Müller		10,–		
	Lebensmittel		24,16	523,99	food
Mo 28.2.	Lebensmittel		13,72	510,27	food
1.3.	"		19,45		food
2.3.	Müller 2x Windeln, Baba usw.		41,76		pampers creams
	Lebensmittel		11,22	437,84	food
4.3.	Lebensmittel		20,–		food
	Apotheke		17,84	400,–	medicine
7.3.	geb. Geschenk Linette-Bücher Julia		15,35	384,65	gifts
8.3.	Lebensmittel		35,92		food
	Stift Julia		2,–	346,73	pen for Julia
8.3.	Müller		7,40		kleenex toilett-paper
	Lebensmittel		14,52	311,81	food
	Ausweis Max		13,–		passport Max
11.3.	Lebensmittel		86,10		food
	IKEA		3,58		snack
	Bazar		2,–	275,13	socks
12.3.	Müller – Cremen usw.		30,03		tooth suncreams
	Lebensmittel		8,80	236,30	food
15.3.	Müller		9,13		cream
	Minimal – Lebensmittel –		5,84		food
	Lebensmittel		4,41	217,92	food
16.3.	Lebensmittel		18,33		food
	Müller		14,80		toilette paper
	Apotheke		23,–	161,19	medicine

Stockpiling

Hilda also had a secret weapon: the storage room in the basement, where she had stockpiled all kinds of goods and household products. She said she had a lot of pasta down there and the family could eat that so she wouldn't have to go to the butcher, as she had planned. As Hilda talked about her strategy for getting through the week, she became very animated and switched from English to German and back to English again, clearly excited. She asked if we would like to see the storage room even though it was a "big mess." We said that we would.

The storage room, far from being a mess, was well organized and tidy. One wall was entirely lined with shelves, neatly stacked with the necessities of everyday life: household cleaners, canned meats, napkins, paper towels, toilet paper, bags of chips, cooking oil, pasta, food wrap, tins of cookies, juice boxes, bottled water, and other basics. The room also contained a large freezer and the washing machine and dryer. This was obviously command central for Hilda, the Schmidt family's chief purchasing agent.

Hilda loves finding bargains. She buys them whenever she sees them and tucks them away in the storage room. She is in the room several times a week, fetching a needed item for the kitchen or adding new purchases to the stock on the shelves. "Getting a good deal makes me very happy," she says. "It helps make my money go further. If I can stay within my budget and buy nice things for my children, I feel like I've done a good job. It's rewarding."

She pulls a bag of chips from the shelf. "I bought these on sale the last time I shopped at Aldi," she says, with a pleased smile. "Half price." The bottled water also comes from Aldi, as do the toilet paper and dishwashing liquid. Hilda opens the freezer and reveals an array of sausages, all of which she bought at Aldi.

Hilda is like many Europeans. They earn less than the average American and have taken the treasure hunt to an art form.

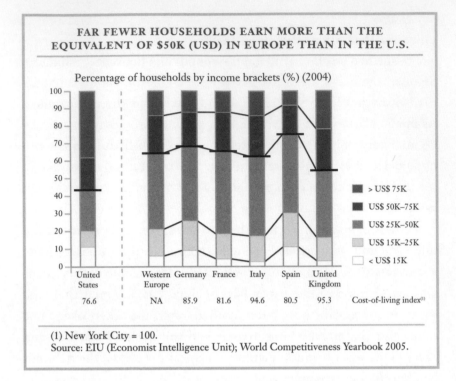

FAR FEWER HOUSEHOLDS EARN MORE THAN THE EQUIVALENT OF $50K (USD) IN EUROPE THAN IN THE U.S.

Percentage of households by income brackets (%) (2004)

> US$ 75K
US$ 50K–75K
US$ 25K–50K
US$ 15K–25K
< US$ 15K

	United States	Western Europe	Germany	France	Italy	Spain	United Kingdom	
Cost-of-living index[1]	76.6	NA	85.9	81.6	94.6	80.5	95.3	

(1) New York City = 100.
Source: EIU (Economist Intelligence Unit); World Competitiveness Yearbook 2005.

Aldi: A History of Low Prices

Hilda, like millions of Germans, has come to rely on Aldi, the $35 billion chain of stores that has become the world's leading "hard discount" retailer for low-cost food and household commodities. At least twice a month, sometimes more often, she treks to her favorite Aldi store in the nearby town of Riemerling, one of five Aldi locations within four kilometers of her house. "I used to think that Aldi was only for poor people," Hilda says. "But I started going there after I had kids. I realized that it's a good place for bargains. And everybody goes there. Not just poor people."

Aldi represents value. Consumers outside an Aldi store in Munich told us:

"Aldi has the best prices. That is why I go there. I can pay a low price but still get good quality."

"I also go to look at the specials. Sometimes you can find a really great deal, but you have to pay attention."

"I spend a lot of time looking through the bins in the middle for that great find."

"Everything is fresh. I know when I come here I'll get great quality at a low price."

"I like shopping at Aldi because I always feel like I'm getting a good deal. They are also well organized and have good quality."

In fact, Aldi appeals to people in all demographic groups in Germany. It is, as Hilda says, not just for poor people any more. About 85 percent of Germans have an Aldi store within a twenty-minute drive of their home. A full 90 percent of Germans shop at Aldi at least once a year, up from 50 percent in 1990. Aldi is a major brand name in Germany and, indeed, throughout Europe, with some seven thousand stores in twelve countries and worldwide revenue in 2003 of $35 billion. It is the biggest hard discounter in Europe with a 31 percent share of the hard discount market in a sixteen-country region.

Aldi is not only a big player; it is, surprisingly, a respected brand name. GfK, a German market research group, says that Aldi is Germany's third most-respected brand, just behind Siemens and BMW and ahead of DaimlerChrysler. The retailer is even on its way to becoming hip. "Twenty years ago you wouldn't walk around with an Aldi bag in Germany because that didn't look cool at all," said one Aldi manager. "Now it's quite the fashion." One of my colleagues, a manager at BCG in Germany, told me that it's common to find Aldi brand sparkling wine being served at upscale dinner parties.

For Germans, Aldi is an iconic retailer, one that deeply connects with their national values of frugality and efficiency. The chain was founded in 1948 as Albrecht Discounts by brothers Karl and Theo Albrecht. They grew up in Essen, in the western part of the country, where their father was a miner and their mother ran a small family grocery. Both men served in the military during World War II and were held in Allied POW camps after the war. When they were released, they returned to Essen and started a retail grocery operation. According to a profile in *BusinessWeek*, "Residents of bombed-out Essen wanted only the products they needed from one day to the next, for the best price. So the brothers restricted their assortment to a few hundred items and carefully monitored quality. 'Our business was managed solely on the basis of the lowest price,' Karl Albrecht said."

Gradually, the strategy of necessity became the strategy of choice and it came to be known as "hard discount."

The Rise of Hard Discount

Hard discounters are quite distinct from everyday–low-price retailers like Wal-Mart in the United States and the hypermarkets like Carrefour in Europe. Hard discounters offer fewer categories of goods, so the shopper may not be able to find any pet food, fresh meat, or hand tools at all. In every category the stores do carry, they stock a very limited selection so the total number of items is small in comparison to supermarkets or hypermarkets. There may be two brands of toilet paper, for example, whereas a supermarket would stock ten. There may be only one size of toothpaste, rather than four. Many of the products are private-label and store-brand. The quality of the store-brand products is generally good, often just as good as the national brand. The stores themselves are relatively small, the shopping environment is functional, and there are few services. Above all, the prices are unbelievably low—as much as 60 percent lower than leading name brands' and as much as 40 percent lower than those of supermarket private-label products.

The hard discount format caught on in the late 1940s and early 1950s, and Aldi added stores fast. In the late 1950s, just ten years after their founding, the company was operating 350 stores. As Aldi grew and prospered, the company and the brothers became famous. In 1971, Theo Albrecht was kidnapped and held by his captors for seventeen days. All of Germany followed the story of the billionaire businessman held hostage and the intense negotiations that went back and forth for more than two weeks. At last, the kidnappers were paid between two and four million dollars (accounts vary) and Theo was freed. The Albrecht family had always been tight-lipped, but after the kidnapping they clammed up entirely and have made few comments in public since then. Theo proved just how *geiz* he was by asking the government for a tax break based on the money the family had paid to the kidnappers. Today, the company is still private and Theo and Karl Albrecht are among the world's wealthiest people. The Forbes 2004 World's Richest People list ranked Karl at number three with a net worth of $23 billion, between Warren Buffett, with a net worth of $42.9 billion, and Prince Alwaleed Bin Talal Alsaud, with $21.5 billion.

The desire of consumers like Hilda Schmidt to get the best deal possible on all of her purchases, and the ability of hard discounters like Aldi to consistently deliver incredibly low prices, have combined to make hard discounting the fastest-growing retail format in Europe. It is growing at 1.6 times the rate of supermarkets. Two hard discounters, Aldi and Lidl, are now among the top ten grocery retailers in Europe. There are some thirty-two thousand hard discount outlets throughout Europe, and they account for more than 10 percent of all sales of fast-moving consumer goods (FMCG). In Germany, hard discounters hold a remarkable 40 percent share of all grocery distribution.

High Discount, High Profits at Aldi

Aldi, the pioneer of hard discounting, has so perfected the format that it can offer consistently lower prices than even everyday discounters like Wal-Mart and still be more profitable than they are. Aldi does this by cutting costs and improving efficiencies in every aspect of its operations.

Aldi relentlessly reviews, tailors, and edits the selection of goods. A typical Aldi store carries between 700 and 1,400 items or stockkeeping units (SKUs) in the major categories. A typical supermarket in Europe carries ten times more, usually 8,000 to 10,000 SKUs. A European hypermarket stocks upwards of 17,000 and a big Wal-Mart in the United States may carry 100,000 or more. "We deliberately keep product range small and under constant review," Karl Albrecht told Dieter Brandes, the author of *Bare Essentials*, a book about Aldi. "We take care that we do not offer similar items alongside each other. We've gone so far as to exclude whole product categories. The reason? Turnover. Our product range is limited to what we can sell fast."

Aldi also prefers to stock items that are easy to handle and don't wilt or crush. That's why almost 50 percent of the products on Aldi's shelves are packaged goods, about 10 percent higher than the percentage at most supermarkets. Aldi stores carry a smaller assortment of fresh, chilled, and frozen products than the typical supermarket because those items are harder and more expensive to handle and display. But Aldi carries proportionately more wines and spirits and household goods, like cleaners and paper products. As much as 90 percent of all the goods in an Aldi are its own store brands, an amazing array of products from cookies to diapers.

Aldi keeps its stores relatively small, usually around 660 square meters (7,100 square feet), to reduce the costs of owning and maintaining real estate and facilities and of having a large number of employees. The typical Aldi store is about half the size of an average 1,200–square-meter supermarket and a tenth the size of some hypermarkets, which can sprawl across 6,000 square meters or more. Aldi stores are often located in working-class neighborhoods, in smaller cities, or at the outskirts of big cities. But, in Germany, particularly, they are also to be found in middle-income and some wealthy communities and near city centers. When Aldi opens a new store, it usually buys the building outright to avoid the costs of financing.

Aldi's rock-bottom prices are matched by its bare-bones shopping experience. The interior of an Aldi store makes Wal-Mart look like Neiman Marcus. No fancy planograms here. No nifty shelf dispensers or off-shelf displays. Most products are stacked in shipping cartons that are cleverly designed with cutouts that can be removed to create displays. All the fresh produce is wrapped in plastic. Some items, like cartons of soft drinks, sit on wooden pallets. To save on staff costs, there is no restocking during the day, so if a carton gets emptied, a customer may have to remove it herself to get to the next layer down. (Usually, customers just leave the discarded box in the aisle or on a nearby shelf.) You have to leave a small deposit—the equivalent of about twenty-five cents—to get a shopping cart. There can sometimes be a wait at checkout—especially at the beginning of the month, when people receive government checks—because there are usually just two or three cash registers open. People often bring their own baskets or bags, because Aldi charges fifty cents for a paper bag and ten cents for a plastic one. You bag your own goods, and you can pay only with cash, debit card, or electronic benefit transfer (EBT)— no coupons, credit cards, or checks are accepted. There is no loyalty program. Customer loyalty, in the Aldi scheme of things, comes about as the result of delivering value every day.

The importance of pricing at Aldi is underscored by the way prices are displayed—printed out on colored 8½x11" sheets and posted above the shelves and on the walls. You get the feeling that the prices could change even while you're shopping, and, in fact, they often do. Indeed, Aldi strongly believes in aggressive pricing action. "If a purchase price drops," Theo Albrecht told Dieter Brandes, "we lower our sales price immediately—even if we have yet to buy at the new prices. We take the position: offensive action is better than defensive action. Maintaining a price when the purchase price has fallen is all very well in theory but is ultimately counterproductive. We want to convince our customers that they cannot buy cheaper anywhere else."

This contention is backed up by the only permanent sign to be found in an Aldi store, the one that says, "DOUBLE QUALITY GUARANTEE: QUALITY, TASTE, AND SATISFACTION ARE ALWAYS DOUBLE GUARANTEED AT ALDI. IF FOR ANY REASON, YOU ARE NOT

100% SATISFIED WITH ANY PRODUCT, WE WILL GLADLY REPLACE IT AND REFUND YOUR MONEY."

Although shopping at Aldi is a visually dull and Spartan experience, it can also be exhilarating, because the prices are so low and the operation is so obviously managed to keep them that way. Every item in the shopping basket costs less than it would elsewhere. Take cookies, for example. Butter cookies from Lu, a leading French brand, cost about €1.92 in a German supermarket. Carrefour, the largest grocery retailer in Europe, sells its store-brand butter cookies for about €1.26. At Lidl, the second-largest hard discounter after Aldi, the same size box of butter cookies—with similar ingredients, including whole wheat flour, 12 percent butter, and sugar—sells for €.69. That's nearly 60 percent lower and, according to highly anecdotal and inexact field tests, the Lidl cookies taste just as good. In a U.S. store, compare a 7.25-ounce box of macaroni and cheese. Dominick's, the grocery store chain, offers its own label product at $.69. Wal-Mart cuts that in half to $.33. But Aldi goes still lower, selling its Cheese Club brand at $.29. A pack of Nanny's diapers costs $5.99 at Aldi in comparison to Wal-Mart's White Cloud brand that goes for $6.97. In a game where Wal-Mart is considered king, Aldi's 14 percent price advantage is remarkable.

Aldi's workers, like Wal-Mart's, are not unionized. Although the number of staff is kept to a bare minimum (there may be just two or three employees in a store during opening hours), employees are well paid—often as much as twice the hourly wage of competitors. As a result, Aldi workers are loyal and there is low turnover.

Aldi Comes to the United States

Hard discount is sweeping through Europe, with Aldi and Lidl leading the pack, but has not become a national obsession in the United States the way it has in Germany. It is still generally seen as the poor man's alternative to everyday–low-price retailers like Wal-Mart,

Kmart, and others. This is partly because Aldi located its early U.S. stores in low-income areas, like southeastern Iowa, where the first Aldi stores were opened in 1976. It may also be that Aldi is filled with generic-sounding store brands that few people have heard of, such as Millville cereals, Sundae Shoppe ice cream, and Sweet Valley sodas. But we also discovered many well-known brands in the stores we visited, including Snickers, Pringles potato chips, Oscar Mayer bacon, Dole bananas, and Sunkist oranges. And in the United States, many of Aldi's own-brand breakfast cereals, like Honey Nut Flakes, are actually supplied by Kellogg's.

The profile of the typical Aldi shopper may be changing. According to Euromonitor, Aldi is targeting the middle-income consumer, with household income of $40,000 to $90,000 per year. Our experience working with Aldi suppliers in Europe supports the assertion that the demographics of the Aldi clientele are changing and, in particular, expanding into the middle (especially the upper-middle) classes. According to our analysis, the critical determinant of Aldi usage is how long the company has been in a market. In ten years, Aldi's share typically grows from nothing to about 2 percent. After twenty years, it usually reaches about 10 percent.

Most of the Aldi shoppers we encountered in store visits in the United States were middle-income earners, although many earned less than $40,000 per year. Whatever their income, all of them readily admitted that the primary reason they shop at Aldi is the low prices. "I go to Aldi first," one shopper told us. "I know I won't find everything I need, but I can try to buy my staples there. It's a lot less cost." But even the bargain hunters pick and choose. "Aldi is for certain things," one shopper told us. "They have great deals, so I get milk and staples like cereal here. I don't like some of their products, but I'm always amazed at how much cheaper things are."

Chuck Voss, an eighty-seven–year-old World War II vet, has become—to his surprise—an Aldi apostle. Chuck lives with his wife,

Mary, in Boardman, Ohio, a town of about forty thousand people not far from Youngstown, which is close to the Pennsylvania border. Chuck and Mary have been married for sixty-three years and have four children—"all college-educated, all dependable," according to Mary. The couple lives on about $50,000 a year, a combination of Social Security and Chuck's pension.

Chuck is a frugal man with simple tastes, but he does have one big indulgence: he likes to buy a new car every two years. For fifty of his past fifty-five years, the car has been American-made—more often than not, a Chevy or Pontiac manufactured in the General Motors plant in Lordstown, Ohio, some twenty miles to the west of Boardman. "Why give the job to the Japanese?" Chuck says. But the quality of Chuck's most recent Chevrolet was so poor that he finally decided to give up on GM. For his next purchase, he traded up and bought a Toyota Avalon for about $28,000, nearly $10,000 more than he was used to spending on a Chevrolet. "It's the best car I've ever had," said Chuck. "Most dependable, best pickup, most thoughtful features."

When it comes to buying food, however, Chuck is all trading down. He is the meal planner, grocery shopper, cook, and clean-up man in the Voss family. This is probably a result of his experience in World War II as an army cook. "I used to make breakfast for a thousand soldiers every morning," he says. "We watched our supplies very closely. Now it's just me and Mary, but I still need to be careful about the money."

Chuck used to shop at the local Giant Eagle supermarket, always looking for bargains and buying specials when they came on sale. Then, about three years ago, Aldi opened a store just a couple of miles away from his house. Chuck did not go in immediately. He had never heard of the Aldi chain before it arrived, but soon after the store opened he started hearing bad things about it from his friends and neighbors. The place was messy, they said, and the selection was limited. Besides, Chuck was satisfied with the Giant Eagle. He knew where everything was on the shelves and he thought the prices were fair.

One day, however, Chuck had no choice but to visit the Aldi

store. He is a big volunteer in Boardman and, for twenty-five years, has been delivering meals on wheels to people who are stuck at home due to age or illness or who are less fortunate and sometimes can't afford to buy groceries, or who just don't have the wherewithal to cook a meal. "I do it because they need me," says Chuck. "The people I serve would not get a hot meal if I didn't deliver it to them."

Usually, Chuck just picks up the prepared meals from the central kitchen and delivers them to whoever needs them. But on one occasion, the Meals On Wheels people asked Chuck to get some emergency supplies at Aldi. He parked in the lot, surprisingly close to the front entrance, and wandered into the store, not knowing what to expect. He was amazed at what he found. "It wasn't nearly as bad as people said," he told me. "And the prices were amazing. The eggs were half the price of the Giant Eagle. The milk was much cheaper. I vowed to go back."

Chuck quickly became an Aldi regular. "I can save 40 percent on everything I buy there. A jar of honey is $2.29 at Aldi and five bucks at the grocery store. I get American cheese that's just the same as Kraft, but less than half the price."

"You should go there yourself," he told me. "Let me make you a cup of tea. You can try the honey. It's delicious. $2.29!"

Chuck is not only a regular at Aldi, he has become an advocate. He scoffs when people look askance at him for shopping there. "No frills is fine with me," he laughs. "Mary never asks me where I bought the food when she eats one of my meals."

But there are still shoppers who just can't get beyond the no-frills shopping experience at Aldi, no matter how low the prices may be. "Aldi just feels poor," one consumer told us. "You have to pay for a shopping cart and buy bags. You even have to bag your own groceries on this long table. I'm not going through that just to save a few pennies."

The Dollar Store

It is this reaction to Aldi that has kept the company's form of hard discount from taking off in the United States the way it has in Europe. But other retailers have found a treasure-hunting format that combines hard discount with a shopping experience that Americans find a little more friendly and familiar—in particular the "dollar stores" like Family Dollar, Dollar General, and Dollar Tree.

People have a funny kind of affection for Dollar General. They shake their heads when they talk about the store, as if they can't quite believe the place and how much they like it. They admit that they come primarily for the low prices, but say there are other reasons for shopping there, too. In particular, there's less hassle at a Dollar General store. Like Aldi, Dollar General stores are located in suburban neighborhoods, shopping malls, and rural locations, rarely in city centers, so they're easy to get to. The stores are smaller than the big-box retailers and so are the parking lots, so the whole shopping experience isn't as trying and doesn't take as much time. We found that the time it took to buy a standard basket of goods, from the moment of entering the parking lot to the moment we had paid for the basket at the checkout, was about twenty minutes at a Dollar General in comparison to fifty-five minutes at a Wal-Mart.

A friendly sort of jumble marks the interior of a Dollar General store. With about four thousand SKUs, there is the pleasure of having more stuff than can be found at an Aldi, but not the daunting variety of goods to be found at a huge discounter. There are more displays, more signs, more activity and color. And, there is the familiarity and reassurance of having many more name brands in evidence. There are both Bounty and Brawny paper towels. Dawn, Ivory, and Palmolive dish soaps. Pantene and Herbal Essences. Colgate, Aquafresh, Pepsodent, Cover Girl, Maybelline, Fruit of the Loom, General Mills, Kellogg's, and good old Kraft.

The top ten items purchased at dollar stores are:

1. Household cleaners
2. Seasonal decorations and supplies
3. Wrapping materials and gift bags
4. Paper products
5. Laundry supplies
6. Housewares
7. Storage containers
8. Batteries
9. Health and beauty supplies
10. Dry groceries

There are three distinct types of retailers that are generally known as dollar stores. The original dollar stores, which sprouted up in the Depression, were just what they said they were. Every item sold for a dollar or less. (In 1930, $1 had about the same buying power as $12 docs today, according to the CPI inflation calculator.) There was a magical sense in these stores that virtually anything could be had for a buck. There are still stores that adhere to the "everything for a dollar" format, such as 99 Cents Only and Dollar Tree. Dollar Tree says that it is the leading operator of "discount variety stores offering merchandise at the $1.00 price point." These stores are, in essence, the modern incarnation of the five-and-dime stores such as Woolworth's and Ben Franklin.

The second category is the overstock, discontinued, surplus, and distressed merchandise retailers like Big Lots, Building #19, and Tuesday Morning. There are many items available for a dollar in these stores, but the quality is wildly inconsistent and the selection varies dramatically from day to day.

Dollar General and its big competitor, Family Dollar, are "extreme-value" stores, the third type of dollar store in the United States. The average price of an item is not actually $1.00; it's $1.50. In general, all the prices are low in comparison to name-brand retailers', but not as low as at hard discounters like Aldi and not always as low as at everyday discounters like Wal-Mart.

Dollar General delivers an interesting illusion to the consumer, one that most consumers are willing to buy into: the prices seem lower than they actually are. This is often because Dollar General stocks smaller package sizes than those on its competitors' shelves. You can buy a package of Pillsbury Fudge Brownie Mix for just $1.00 at Dollar General; the price at Wal-Mart is $1.50. That seems like a good deal, a 33 percent discount, until you look more closely at the boxes. The Dollar General package contains 15 ounces and will fill an 8x8" pan, while the package at Wal-Mart has 19.5 ounces and is intended to make a 13x9" family-size pan of brownies. The mix is still cheaper at Dollar General, but it's only a 14 percent discount, not the 33 percent you might have imagined you were getting.

This is a dialogue I had with some consumers outside a Dollar General store near Chicago:

Me: How often do you shop at Dollar General?

Man #1: Probably once every other week.

Woman #1: About once a week.

Man #2: Practically every day. They have everything that I want when I come here. Sometimes this is the only store I go to.

Me: Why do you shop at Dollar General?

Woman #2: They've got great prices. Everything you see at other stores they have here and it's cheaper than buying it someplace else.

Man #1: I buy Crest toothpaste here for $1. I go to the Jewel across the street, it's going to cost me $3.50!

Man #2: Hello! It's just smart.

Me: Did you make any impulse buys today?

Man #1: I always find new things that are good bargains.

Woman #1: A lot of times I buy more than what I go in planning to buy. I found very pretty pictures here, bathroom sets, bubble bath, skin creams.

Me: How does shopping at Dollar General make you feel?

Man #2: Like Tony the Tiger . . . grrrrrreat!

Smart, middle-income American consumers are discovering that they like the dollar stores because they offer everyday low prices but are often in more convenient locations and of more manageable size than the mass retailers. Although the consumers like the low prices, they also know the tricks of the dollar stores, and will only shop at them for certain items and not for others. They're shopping at them enough, however, that the dollar store segment is growing in the United States at 10 percent annually (CAGR) and the percentage of American households that have ever shopped at a dollar store has risen from 55 percent in 2000 to 66 percent in 2004. Most significant, the higher-income households are the fastest-growing segment of dollar store customers. According to an ACNielsen study, almost half of all households earning $70,000 or more now shop at dollar stores, compared with just 9 percent in 2002. More and more Americans are coming around to the idea that cheap is good.

There is still plenty of room for growth. Dollar General operates more than 8,000 stores, all in the eastern half of the United States and most in rural locations. The company, encouraged by a ten-year growth spurt—zooming from $1.4 billion in sales in 1994 to $7.2 billion in 2004—is expanding to the north and the west and into more urban and suburban spots. And the growth is coming from an increase in sales in the stores as well as from the addition of new locations.

Dollar General: Roots in Rural Retailing

As it has grown, Dollar General has shed its image as a backwater retailer catering to hayseeds and become a much more sophisticated operation and a daunting competitor in the trading-down market. But the company is still as quintessentially American as Aldi is German, with deep roots in rural American retailing. The company was founded in 1939 as a dry goods retailer by J.L. Turner. He was born in 1891. His father died in an accident in 1902, which forced Turner to leave school and go to work to support the family, with the benefit of only three years of education and without the ability to read. In 1908, Turner married and he and his wife, Josiephine, opened a bridal shop. That lasted a year. Then they moved to Kentucky and Turner opened a country store. When it went belly up after four years, Turner abandoned entrepreneurship and went to work as a salesman, first for a wholesale grocery company and then for a dry goods retailer in Nashville, Tennessee.

During the Depression, Turner's entrepreneurial instincts kicked in again. Many general stores in Tennessee and Kentucky were going bankrupt during that time, and Turner began buying them up at fire sale prices and liquidating the assets. He brought his son Cal into the business when the boy was about eleven. Cal would make lists of all the assets of the bankrupt stores for his father, who never did learn to read or write.

In 1939, J.L. and Cal founded J.L. Turner and Sons Wholesale, each investing $5,000. They soon switched from wholesaling to retailing and the business took off. By the early 1950s, they were grossing $2 million a year. And then J.L. had the idea that would really put the company on the map. They would start a new operation where no item would cost more than a dollar. The first Dollar General store opened in June 1955 in Springfield, Kentucky. It was a big success and the Turner family quickly converted all its retail stores to Dollar Generals. By 1957, there were twenty-nine stores and company revenues had jumped to $5 million. Turner died in 1964, but his son Cal carried on as president. The company went public in 1968 and continued to grow. Cal Turner, Jr., succeeded his father as president of Dollar General in 1965 and held that position for thirty-seven years.

Dollar General remained a family business to the core. Cal Turner, Jr., remembered that "Business was all about family. The Turner children would be asked to pray for snow when my dad was overstocked on four-buckle overshoes, because he couldn't sell them otherwise, and he couldn't pay off the banks. Then other times we were asked to pray for the snow to melt, because our customers couldn't get out on the highways to do their Christmas shopping, and Daddy wouldn't be able to pay off the banks. But family, business, and life to a Turner have always been commingled. And it seems natural to take into management the sense of partnership and connection."

Today, there is still a homey feel about most Dollar General stores, but the company is rapidly being transformed into a streamlined, sophisticated retailer that can give much larger competitors like Wal-Mart and Costco fits. Historically, the shelves of Dollar General were stocked with a mishmash of dry goods, cheap knicknacks, obscure brands of cleaning products, lots of shelf-stable foods, and many damaged or overstock goods. Today, the selection of products is much more consistent. There are more brand names, fewer damaged items, and more fresh grocery items. In more and more stores, you'll find electronic registers, product scanners, and credit card swipers. Behind the scenes, Dollar General maintains eight automated centers capable of executing a seventy-two-hour delivery cycle to its stores, down from a ninety-six-hour cycle just a few years ago.

Stealing Share Everywhere

The success of Dollar General, and of the dollar store category in general, is having a major effect on the trillion-dollar trading-down market. Most important, Dollar General achieves higher profits than some traditional stuck-in-the-middle supermarkets like Safeway, even though Safeway can sell many of its products at higher prices. The main reason is that Dollar General keeps its costs down by maintaining the no-frills store environment, pruning the assortment of goods, locating stores in low-cost areas, and investing very little money in advertising and promotion.

On a sample basket of goods, Dollar General is able to earn a higher profit than Safeway even though it charges less—eighty-six cents on average, for an item that would sell for $1 at Safeway. We estimate that Dollar General's cost of goods sold (COGS) is about 13 percent less than Safeway's on the basket, and it spends about 25 percent less on sales, general, and administration costs, including marketing and advertising. But its earnings before interest and taxes (EBIT) are about 6.5 on the dollar, almost two points higher than Safeway's EBIT of 4.9 percent. That substantial earnings difference is remarkable when you think that Dollar General is making it on goods that are priced, on average, about 14 percent lower than Safeway's.

The dollar stores, with Dollar General in the lead, are stealing share from other providers in the trading-down market. People often start their shopping at Dollar General and then, if they can't find what they're looking for, go elsewhere. Shoppers we spoke with told us discount grocers like Cub Foods and Aldi don't always meet or beat the Dollar General price. They said that they shop at conventional grocers, like Jewel and Dominick's, for specific items, like meat, and expect to pay more. They also said that they will go to the big-box discounters like Wal-Mart and Target when they can't find what they need at Dollar General, because they're sure it will be in stock there. But Dollar General shoppers are a loyal group when it comes to competitive dollar stores. "The other dollar stores have good deals," one consumer told us, "but they usually have lower quality and more junk."

And Dollar General is looking to increase its lead and steal more share from the stuck-in-the-middle grocers and big-box retailers.

When Cal Turner, Jr., retired, Dollar General came under the leadership of David Perdue, the first nonfamily top executive since the company was founded in 1939. He says that the company is working to trade up the shopping experience. The stores will be cleaner, there will be more stock on the shelves, and the employees will be friendlier. He also says that Dollar General will get even more efficient by evaluating and improving their work processes. That will free up store managers to spend more time with customers.

Fighting Back

The grocers and big-box retailers are well aware that the dollar stores are stealing away middle-income, trading-down customers, so they're looking for ways to fight back. Wal-Mart has been testing concepts for its own in-store versions of the dollar store. One of them is called the "Hey Buck" section, where food and soft goods sell for an average of ninety-eight cents per item. Wal-Mart is also trying out "Amazing Value" aisles in its supercenters, where all merchandise is priced between $1 and $5. Target has tested a concept called "One Spot" in about 125 stores. It features merchandise such as stationery, toys, home décor, and storage products, with everything priced at $1. Kroger is trying a "dollar aisle" in a few of its markets.

I must confess that I had never shopped at a dollar store before we started doing research for the book. The phenomenon has grown faster and spread wider than I imagined it would. Although it's still not the kind of place that most people are likely to talk about with neighbors or friends, that's sure to change. Cheap is good now, and nobody wants to overpay for anything.

The hard discount and dollar stores will continue to grow and grab share, because trading down is here to stay. More and more, consumers will trade up in categories where they had previously traded down—as Chuck does with his cars. At the same time, consumers will trade down in categories where they had been buying at midprice stores as soon as they find goods of similar quality at lower prices, as Chuck has done with groceries. Chuck, as middle-class and midprice as he might seem, will get out of the middle as soon as he has a choice.

Betsy Vitalio: When Cheap Means Survival

Trading down and trading up involve choices and trade-offs made by middle-class consumers who have the income, flexibility, and emotional wherewithal to make them. The people we spoke with for this book are, for the most part, managing their spending successfully. They can't buy everything they want (who can?), but they're not suffering. A household income of $50,000 to $150,000 does not guarantee a lifestyle of ease and complete freedom, but it does pretty much ensure that the family—barring poor health or a nasty turn of events—can satisfy its needs and indulge at least some of its wants. It does not take much, however, to cause a family to pass through the portal that separates the reasonably comfortable middle class from the constantly struggling group of consumers, especially families, earning $50,000 or less. For them, the availability of trading-down goods ensures access to the basics they need. But hunting for a bargain or taking advantage of a special promotion is a much more fundamental matter of making too few dollars stretch a little farther. These families don't trade up often and, when they do, it looks very different than the trading up of the $100,000 family. A trading-up meal may be a lunch at McDonald's, with a splurge on large fries, instead of a peanut-butter–and–jelly sandwich at home. These families also drop out of many categories altogether. They simply aren't in the market for wide-screen televisions, facial scrubs, or $40 vodka.

Middle-class consumers who are on the margin get in financial trouble, particularly credit card debt, mostly as the result of one of three common (exogenous) problems: loss of a job, divorce, or a health issue. Betsy Vitalio experienced all three.

Far out from the city, past the outlet malls, a left turn puts us into Betsy's subdivision, a calm suburban haven of duplexes adjacent to a strip mall. Betsy greets us at the door with a bright smile, but though it's only Tuesday, the bags under her eyes show the weariness of the week is already upon her. Despite her obvious fatigue, Betsy looks well groomed in a pink sweater and gray dress pants, and very much in control of herself. She is a petite, trim woman who wears no makeup. She invites us in and tells us not to bother taking off our shoes, because the carpet is "junky." (It isn't fancy, but it looks perfectly fine, in good repair, and clean.)

Betsy leads us into a pleasant, nicely kept living room filled with framed photos of her children, and we settle into a couch opposite her. Betsy tells us a little about her two daughters, aged fourteen and thirteen, and her nine-year-old son, and then about her work in special education in the local school district. She had recently taken a new job that she likes better than the previous one. It allows her to spend more time with her kids, but involved a $10,000 cut in pay. Now she makes about $35,000, which includes a child support payment of about $1,000 a month from her ex-husband. They have been divorced for six years.

Betsy's days are packed with her professional work, shopping, meal preparation, housekeeping, and tending to the children. A disproportionate amount of time goes into the kids' athletic pursuits. "I may spend five hours at a stretch in the gym on the weekend, probably ten hours total, and at least twenty hours a week," she says. Although many sacrifices must be made at the Vitalio house, basketball and volleyball do not get short shrift. That's virtually the only trading-up expenditure that is evident in our visit: the Nikes are lined up by the front door. "The kids know they only get one pair every year or year and half," Betsy says. "And they only use them for indoor sports, so they don't get worn down quite as much. Even though Nikes are more expensive than other brands, I buy them because they'll last longer than cheaper ones." Fortunately, Betsy's parents help pay for the kids' activities. Without their contribution Betsy could not handle the $1,300 fee for her daughter's volleyball league.

Betsy lives from paycheck to paycheck. She laughs at the idea of a written budget but says that she has a good handle on the family expenditures. "I know how much can go out every month. I keep track on my checkbook or call the bank and check on the automatic payments." She doesn't use credit cards, except in an emergency such as an unexpected car repair. She has no savings.

In fact, the family lives on a bare-bones budget as Betsy and her kids employ all the tools of the dollar-stretching consumer. Food shopping is a major priority. Betsy scans the newspaper ads for the best deals and will visit three grocery stores to complete the week's shopping and to stock up as well. She makes sure that what she buys for her kids to eat is of good quality, reasonably healthy, and of sufficient quantity to fuel them through the day. She has little loyalty to brands except one, Oreos, which the whole family consumes in quantity (with no apparent effect on their weight—all the Vitalio family members are slim). Occasionally, Betsy will splurge on a tube of Neutrogena face cream for herself. She rarely entertains guests for a meal and seldom eats at a restaurant. When the family vacations, they drive to visit Betsy's brother in Ohio and stay in his house. Even a movie is a rare treat.

Exogenous getting-in-trouble factor number one is divorce. Factor two is a switch to a lower-paying job. The third exogenous factor that can wobble the household finances is a health crisis, and Betsy has had two to deal with. Her son is dyslexic and so requires extra attention and resources to help him read and function at school. A year ago, Betsy became infected after a hysterectomy at the local hospital, came close to dying, and had to spend three weeks away from work. Although most of the medical costs were covered by health insurance, there were lots of incidental and unusual expenses that put more pressure on the already-strained family budget.

Betsy's short-term goal is to save at least a little money so they won't be living paycheck to paycheck. Beyond that, she would like to turn what is now just a place to live into a real home. They moved into the duplex soon after the divorce and Betsy had never intended to stay there five years. The living room needs a new carpet and couches. The backyard needs work. Betsy would also like to go back to school to earn an advanced degree so she could get a higher-paying job. It would be nice to take the kids to California. She needs to start saving for her daughters' college educations—only four years remain before they head out.

How does this lifestyle affect the Vitalio kids? "They're conscious of it," she says. "They tend to be good about shutting off lights and not running water or using electricity needlessly. They know they can't just go to the movies whenever they want, and when they do, it's something they'll often be paying for." The kids understand that cell phones and cars are not guaranteed perks for them, and they'll have to work to help pay for the extras they want.

When we ask Betsy what the good life means for her, right now, she does not mention travel or clothing or dining out. She simply says, "Financial security." Before we leave, we take a picture of Betsy with her children. She throws her arms around them, beaming, as if she had no cares in the world.

The low-cost revolution will continue. The history of retail has always been about entrepreneurs who have a dream to deliver new lower-cost, higher-inventory turn, and consumer excitement. That history is Darwinian and the new player renders the old obsolete.

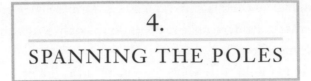

4.

SPANNING THE POLES

LG: Starting at the Bottom and Moving Up

About four years ago, I got a call from a BCG colleague in our office in Seoul, South Korea. "We have a client that would like to meet you," he said. "The name of the company is LG, the $50 billion worldwide manufacturer of electronics goods, chemicals, and industrial products." A few weeks later, I flew to Seoul and landed at the airport late at night. I was met by a car and the driver immediately whisked us off into the dark. After about two hours of driving I got a little nervous. South Korea is a small country, about 400 kilometers north to south. We had been traveling fast and I guessed we had to be very close to the border with North Korea. I saw bright lights and armed guards. "Where are we?" I asked the driver. "Don't speak English," he replied.

The driver stopped the car in front of a large building with only a few lights on, got out, took my bags out of the trunk, and handed them to me. I had arrived, not at the North Korean border crossing, but at the LG Academy, the educational institution where LG trains five thousand new recruits each year and where it holds their management conferences and retreats. I climbed a steep set of winding steps that led to the side entrance of the building. The door was open and I came into a long corridor lined with a bank of vending machines and several signs in Korean. No one seemed to be at home. After several minutes of nervous wandering down hallways, I ran into two young LG recruits, who led me to the reception area. There I was given the key to my room on the third floor. The room was austere. It had a cot, an LG TV, a small desk, and a lamp. The bathroom was fitted with a combination sink-shower and a toilet. I was glad that I had packed a bar of soap and a minibottle of shampoo.

Early the next morning, I rose and, at 5 A.M., arrived at the gym, which was already filled with recruits. I got on the one available treadmill and began my 3.3-mile daily run. I was very slow compared to the LG recruits. At about 5:30, more young LG men arrived and they began a blistering series of calisthenics. I lifted weights and watched as they stretched and pulled. I bought coffee from the vending machine and headed back to my room. I shivered through a short shower in the no-frills bathroom.

I spent the rest of my day with the two hundred top managers of LG as "honored guest lecturer" at their annual management retreat. They had chosen BCG because of our reputation in Korea for expertise in modern management techniques and insight into consumer markets, and especially because of our experience in the American market. During my talk, which was simultaneously translated into Korean, there was not a single question from an audience member. They were far too busy furiously scribbling notes. I told the LG management that there was a large and growing global population looking for best-quality goods and that improvements in technology and design could translate into loyalty and growth. "Imagine if you could someday come into a home and see an array of kitchen, living room, bath appliances—all from LG—sold in fifty million middle-class homes." They roared with applause when I was finished.

In the evening, I had dinner with a select group of about forty senior managers of LG. They brought out Scotch and we grilled beef with garlic on elaborate, smoking, table-top barbecues. We talked and drank for hours and, at the end of the conversation, they said, "We want you to help us conquer the world. We've had success at the foothills. Now we have to climb the mountain." Several of them hugged me and invited me to join them for a round of golf on the company course or to take a swim with them in their Olympic-size pool.

LG had indeed already come a long way when I first met with them, and the company has come even further since then. It has accomplished what very few companies in the world have done: it has transformed itself from a supplier of low-cost, poor-quality goods to a leading producer of home electronics and appliances that serve both trading-down and trading-up consumers.

Transcending a Heritage of Trading Down

LG was founded in 1947, not as LG, but as Lucky Chemical Industrial Corp. Lucky's founder created Goldstar in 1958 to make electric appliances. Goldstar quickly got into radios and refrigerators and introduced its first television in 1966. It then branched out into elevators and escalators, followed by washing machines and air conditioners. As recently as twenty years ago, Goldstar was the world leader in cable-ready, thirteen-inch–screen TV sets, selling at rock-bottom prices. People bought them, just as the Nelson family bought their Daewoos, as a second TV for the basement or study, and kids often used them for playing video games. But the quality of the sets was poor. In 1986, *Consumer Reports* ranked the Goldstar thirteen-inch set as number fifteen out of twenty-one products tested. I remember saying to my wife, "Honey, don't buy Goldstar." But the set sold for just $221, then the lowest price in the category, and Goldstar was a favorite with the trading-down consumer.

In 1995, Bon-Moo Koo, who had been with the company for

twenty years, became chairman. The name was changed to LG (from Lucky Goldstar) and the company embarked on a mission to "climb the mountain" and create what they call "first-class LG."

Today, LG's appliance division is possibly the fastest growing and most profitable in the industry. They offer a $550 top-freezer refrigerator that competes with Frigidaire and Kenmore at the low end, and a $3,100 model that competes with Sub-Zero at the high end. They offer a sixty-inch plasma television at $14,999 and the world's largest production plasma model, at seventy-one inches, that retails for $29,000. LG is the world's third-ranked producer of washing machines and refrigerators and the first-ranked provider of room air conditioners and microwave ovens. It is thriving in a market where so many other electronics providers are seriously stuck in the middle.

LG is not driven by quarterly profit results but instead sees the evolution of its business as taking place in a series of eras. The company is in its growth era now and views capturing market share in key segments as the most important measure of its progress. For LG, spanning the poles is about participating across the whole range of price segments in its markets. It is now intent on the trading-up price points, seeking to deliver the features of the best products available on the market but at a lower price. The threat from competitors like LG is that they are also low-cost, have very long time horizons, and can invest engineering resources to provide cross-category benefits (e.g., a refrigerator with embedded computer capabilities).

The Hotel Industry: Moving in Both Directions

Sometimes the "spanning-the-poles" strategy gets accelerated in response to events, and the insights about the market that follow, rather than by the vision and drive of a company leader, like LG's Bon-Moo Koo. For example, when hotels experienced a precipitous drop in business in 2001, a truth about the industry was revealed—that, despite all the glitter and glamor surrounding high-end hotels and destinations, riches are also to be found at the bottom of the market.

The main factors that determine the financial performance of a hotel are occupancy and operating cost. Room nights, if unsold, can never be sold again. A hotel is a fixed-cost business with high capital investment. When a hotel enjoys high occupancy over a period of time long enough to recoup its investment, it can earn high returns. When utilization drops and occupancy rates stay low, the red ink flows quickly.

That's what happened after September 11, 2001. The $105 billion U.S. hotel industry took a staggering hit. People stopped flying, and both business and leisure travel fell sharply. As occupancy rates dropped, average room rates went down, as well. As a result, a key measure of the financial performance of the industry—revenue per available room (RevPAR)—dropped from $54 in 2000 to $49 in 2002.*

This was a great shock to an industry that had been enjoying growth for several years, experiencing a 5 percent compound annual growth rate from 1994 to 2000. Encouraged by their projections that the industry would continue to expand, many hotel companies were planning or building new properties, in the midst of improving existing ones, and working to attract more customers. But, after 9/11, some hotel companies panicked and abandoned their plans for expansion and improvement. Some unloaded their properties at fire sale prices. Many just held on and put investment plans on the back burner. But others followed a trading-up or trading-down strategy, by adding rooms and building brands that would appeal to specific segments of the market. Some went high. Some went low. A very few found success at both ends of the market.

---

*RevPAR is calculated by dividing gross income by the total number of rooms. RevPAR works well for economy properties where room rental is the only or major revenue stream, but less well for high-end properties that have other significant streams of revenue, such as food and beverage and conference facilities.

A Decade of Transformation

In fact, the hotel industry had been in transformation long before the downturn of 2001, in two important ways. First, the quality of low-end hotels and motels had been improving for years. Long before 2001, the traveler could rent a well-appointed room in a decent property for $65, and there were plenty of national chains to choose from. Second, businesses had been relentlessly putting the screws to the travel budgets of their peripatetic managers and salespeople. The road warriors no longer had the travel allowances they once enjoyed that had enabled them to fly business class, rent a full-size car, stay in a nice hotel, and eat a good meal. They had to make trade-offs. Most business travelers, especially salespeople, had little difficulty deciding what their top spending priority would be: food. The plane ticket came second. The car was third. Lodging was fourth.

As a result of these two factors, the hotel market was, like so many others, bifurcating. There was still enough money being spent by executive business travelers and well-heeled vacationers to feed a slow but steady growth at the very high end. Luxury properties—including Ritz-Carlton, Four Seasons, and Peninsula—which accounted for just over 5 percent of all U.S. hotel rooms in 1994, reached almost 6 percent in 2001. But the luxury and superluxury hotels found themselves in a fight to differentiate themselves from one another and to justify their soaring tariffs by improving their services and transforming a night at a hotel into a beautifully managed guest experience.

The share of rooms in middle-market hotels—such as Sheraton, Hyatt, Hilton, and Marriott—which was more than 62 percent of the industry in 1994, fell steadily year after year to about 51 percent in 2001. The middle-market hotels couldn't seem to offer more features than the trading-down properties, with the exception of room service. Nor could they come close to delivering the emotional experience of staying at a five-star property whose associates remembered your name and where every detail was attended to. The middle-market hotels were becoming like barracks for convention-goers and business travelers who were locked into per diem spending limits and corporate discounts.

Meanwhile, the trading-down properties—Fairfield, TraveLodge, and Super 8—were growing. Low-end room share grew from just over 32 percent in 1994 to just over 43 percent in 2001. They were increasingly able to deliver the essential technical and functional benefits that had once been unavailable at properties with room rates below $100 or so. They improved their bedding, offered cable TV and Internet access, and installed pools and fitness rooms. And, in motel bathrooms across the country, amenity kits replaced that long-time symbol of the roadside hostelry—the tiny, paper-wrapped cake of soap.

In 2003, as the hotel industry started to recover, it became obvious that the extremes of the market were the most resilient and offered the most potential for profit and growth. Average RevPAR for the entire U.S. hotel industry struggled back to $50, with average daily rates of $82 and an average occupancy rate of 61 percent. In the three years after 2001, high-end room share grew by half a percentage point. Middle-market room share dropped three percentage points. Trading-down room share gained three.

Best Value Inn: The Fastest Growth in the Industry

The fastest-growing hotel company in the United States during 2003 and 2004 operated exclusively at the low end of the market. It wasn't one of the familiar brand names, such as Motel 6, Comfort Inn, Red Roof, Econo Lodge, or Best Western. It was America's Best Value Inn (BVI), a chain of more than 500 properties located throughout the United States, Canada, and Mexico. BVI had an amazing compound annual growth rate of 68 percent from 1999 to 2004. With 26,415 rooms at the end of 2004, the company is now the twentieth largest hotel company in the world, although it is still far smaller than most of its trading-down competitors. Days Inn, by comparison, has nearly

2,000 properties and almost 120,000 rooms. Best Western, the largest hotel brand in the world, has about 200,000 rooms in North America, virtually all of which are in the trading-down segment.

Best Value Inns was formed in the early 1990s through a consolidation of a number of independent hotel operators and small chains. In 1999, the company merged with the Independent Motels of America and really took off. To franchisees, the attraction of joining BVI was (and still is) very simple: it charges lower franchise fees than its competitors. Typically, a national franchise will charge its members 3 percent of the property's annual revenue for the right to use the company's name (which has become more and more important to U.S. travelers, who increasingly shy away from mom-and-pop motor courts and one-off hotels). The franchise will pay an additional royalty for a variety of marketing and operational support services, as well as inclusion in the centralized reservations system. BVI charges only 25 to 30 percent of the fees of other national chains. For a property with seventy rooms and a 50 percent occupancy rate, and an average daily rate of $65, a BVI franchisee would pay about $14,000 a year in membership fees. A similar hotel, assessed with the standard fee, would pay about $50,000. That's a significant difference when you consider that a typical trading-down motel property may gross only around $800,000 a year. No wonder BVI had little difficulty getting many members of other hotel chains to defect and could also convince many independently operated motels, that had previously resisted joining a chain, to sign up.

I travel about three hundred thousand miles a year and some years I spend more nights on the road than I do at home. Like most frequent travelers, I am a fanatic about the features I require in a hotel. One of the most important features to me is the fitness center. I'm usually up before dawn working on the computer, after which I need to run, lift, and stretch. I like to be on the treadmill by 5:30 A.M., so a fitness center that opens early or is available twenty-four hours is essential to me. I have a few other requirements in choosing a hotel:

absolute quiet, black-out blinds, a high-speed Internet connection, and early-morning coffee. I don't care about amenity kits, free magazines, a free shoe shine, the contents of the minibar, or how many loyalty points I am awarded per stay. To me, the value of a hotel is almost entirely calculated by how well it enables me to perform my work. When I'm traveling on business, a hotel is a tool, not a destination. However, I still want to have a nice experience while I'm there, so the emotional factors also come into play.

Best Value Inns have become the preferred choice for business and leisure travelers who want a clean room, free cable TV, swimming pool, minifridge, and complimentary morning coffee and can only spend about $65 a night. A stay at a Best Value Inn is a smart use of money, and the company's results prove it. In addition to its strong growth, BVI took third place in the 2004 J.D. Power hotel guest satisfaction survey for its competitive set of economy/budget (trading-down) hotels. And BVI has more than two hundred properties in development that will be opening in the next several years.

Battle of the Beds

As successful as BVI has been, the company's approach to the market has been so straightforward and easy to compete against that it may not be sustainable. The properties themselves are almost indistinguishable from their competitors. They all tend to be nondescript, low-rise buildings surrounded by large parking lots. There is usually a highway nearby. They are generally staffed by local people with minimal training. The rooms are all pretty much the same. For now, the major advantage of being a member of Best Value Inn is the low fee. That has been enough to attract independents and disgruntled members of other national chains, but it may not be enough to keep them. And it may not be enough to build a strong national or international brand that can rival Days Inn or Best Western or even Super 8.

There will likely be a fight to sign up the remaining independent lodging operators who are currently unaffiliated with any chain. There are nearly fifty thousand hotel properties in the United States and about half of them are still independent. Cendant, the world's largest lodging franchiser, may charge higher fees for membership in its group—which includes Days Inn, Super 8, TraveLodge, and several other brands—but they also offer many benefits that BVI does not. Cendant is a huge operator, with 6,400 properties on six continents; this one company franchises over 10 percent of the entire supply of hotel rooms in the United States, far more than second-place Marriott International, which is responsible for 8.5 percent of the domestic supply. Cendant's central reservations system handles bookings for all Cendant properties, at all points in the price spectrum, and booked about fifteen million rooms in 2004. Cendant's loyalty program TripRewards enables customers to win points at all its properties, as well as affiliated car rental companies, and redeem them at any other property.

Cendant also addresses a key issue for small franchises—the need for regular upgrading and maintaining a consistent brand—through a program called Project Restore. It puts the franchise owners on notice to shape up or ship out. "The proposition is really quite straightforward. We are driving to improve property quality and consistency across our brands," said Steven Rudnitsky, chief executive officer of Cendant Hotel Group. "Customer satisfaction is an important component for improving our franchisees' return on investment, and that's only possible when all our brands have consistent products. Our multiyear effort to improve property quality and consistency is called Project Restore and is the underpinning of our efforts to reverse RevPAR decline. It enabled us to grow at a faster pace than our competitors in the economy segment."

Marriott: Masters of Bifurcation

The hotel company that seems to have mastered the difficult trick of succeeding at both poles of the market is Marriott. Long known as a middle-market hotelier, Marriott purchased a 49 percent share of the premium Ritz-Carlton hotels in 1995 and acquired the rest of the company in 1998. They have further built their luxury portfolio with more than thirty signature J.W. Marriott hotels and resorts. They have also aggressively expanded their presence in the trading-down market with their Courtyard by Marriott properties for business travelers and low-price Fairfield Inns for leisure travelers. And, although 47 percent of Marriott's rooms are still in full-service, middle-price hotels—Marriott and Renaissance—Marriott has steadily decreased its midprice room share in order to avoid getting stuck in the middle. The company expects its midrange hotels to account for just 37 percent of room openings from 2006 through 2008.

Although Marriott is now well established as a provider of lodging at every price point, the company's roots are actually in trading down. In 1927, J. Willard and Alice S. Marriott opened a nine-stool root beer stand, which they called A&W, in Washington, D.C. Within a year, they began serving hot Mexican food items along with their hand-drawn root beer and changed the name of their enterprise to The Hot Shoppe. For nearly thirty years, the company prospered and expanded by focusing on restaurants and food services. It did not enter the hotel business until 1957, when it opened the Twin Bridges Motor Hotel in Arlington, Virginia. The founders' son, J.W. ("Bill") Marriott Jr., who had worked with the company throughout his high school and college years and joined full-time in 1956, soon became the hotel's general manager. Bill Marriott was bitten by the hospitality industry and focused on building the company's hotel business. Over the next four decades, with Bill as president and then CEO and chairman, Marriott grew into one of the world's top players in the lodging and food services industry. Today, the company comprises eighteen brands and has revenues of more than $10 billion.

By 2004, Marriott's overall revenue had exceeded what it had been in 2000 and, between 2000 and 2004, Marriott's share price increase exceeded the S&P average by as much as 100 percent, rising

from $30.50 in January 2000 to $62.98 in 2004. During the same period, the S&P 500 declined from 1320.28 to 1211.91. Marriott was
able to achieve revenue growth despite the fact that occupancy continued to decline in most of its properties. Although Courtyard did
experience a revenue decline from 2001 through 2003, it had re-
bounded very strongly by 2004. Neither the low-end Fairfield chain
nor the high-end Ritz chain suffered any decline in revenue, even in
2002, the toughest post-9/11 year for the hotel industry. The revenue
per available room at the Ritz grew more than 11 percent from 2003
to 2004, versus about 8 percent for the Renaissance.

Pushing Higher at the High End

The success of the Ritz-Carlton chain encouraged Marriott to further expand its luxury holdings and even move higher up the ladder
of benefits. In February 2001, Marriott had announced that it would
embark on a joint venture with Bulgari, the Italian jewelry company,
to launch a new hotel luxury brand, Bulgari Hotels and Resorts. The
concept was to create hotels with such an extraordinary level of con-
temporary luxury that they could achieve a "six-star" rating, if there
were such a thing. (Five stars is currently the highest.) Marriott's new
Luxury Group forged ahead, despite the slow market, and opened the
first Bulgari Hotel in Milan in May 2004. Designed by architect Antonio Citterio, the boutique property has fifty-eight rooms and suites,
with an average room rate of about $800. The hotel seeks to redefine
the rungs on the ladder of benefits, with technical differences—such
as complimentary unpacking and meditation corners in the rooms—
that translate into better performance and greater emotional satisfaction for the guest.

Marriott is up against very tough competition in the luxury market, particularly from its archrival Four Seasons, which is roughly the
same size. There are 60 Ritz-Carlton properties in 19 countries, with
nearly 19,000 rooms. Four Seasons has 62 properties in 29 countries
with about 16,000 guestrooms. J.D. Power ranks Four Seasons as

best in its category, just above the Ritz. And then there are the smaller luxury chains, including Mandarin Oriental with twenty properties and the Peninsula with seven hotels, that are beginning to nip at the heels of both of the bigger chains. And, as hearty and resilient as the trading-up market has proved to be, it is still very small in comparison to the middle and trading-down segments.

Expanding at the Low End

The biggest growth in rooms and revenue for Marriott has come from its trading-down brands. From 1994 to 2004, Marriott increased its economy room count by 11 percentage points, adding some one million rooms in its Courtyard, SpringHill, and Fairfield chains. And, as of 2003, Marriott had another thirteen thousand trading-down guestrooms in the development pipeline. Marriott's plan to increase the number of trading-down rooms is not based on current occupancy trends, because occupancy has been flat, or even down, across all segments in the post-9/11 years. Rather, it is based on the conviction that travel will eventually return to the rate of growth it was experiencing before 9/11. From 1994 to 2000, RevPAR for the industry was achieving a compound annual growth rate of nearly 5 percent. From 2001 through 2004, the CAGR was negative 4.4 percent. But the trading-down trend is so strong, and the urge to travel is so much a part of our modern life, that Marriott is confident its bet will pay off.

All hotel owners are looking for ways to differentiate and respond to the bifurcation of the market. The worst place to be is in the middle, where average returns are below the cost of capital. New capacity now coming on the market in the midprice segment is likely to earn a negative internal rate of return (IRR). At the high end, a battle royale is developing. The cost per room will escalate, as hotels try to outdo each other with higher service standards and better amenities. There are sure to be casualties, especially among the small chains that are not sharply focused on either the business or the leisure traveler.

There is no doubt that the best place to be is at the bottom of the market. There may not be glamor there, but there are riches.

Jim and Anne: Up, Down, Rising Again

Jim and Anne Freedman had a transformation and revelation similar to that of the hotel industry, also as a result of taking a hit from 9/11. They found themselves experiencing a leap from one pole (high) to the other (low) and are now finding ways to span the two.

Jim was the owner and general manager of a direct mail processing company that his family had been operating for thirty-seven years. His clients included large companies like MBNA, American Express, JCPenney, and Wal-Mart. In October 2001, after anthrax had been discovered in mailed envelopes, Jim's business hit the skids. Mail volume dropped by 75 percent. Jim cut his staff. He attempted to sell off capacity. But within six months, the business was virtually dead. The bankers called his notes and he was forced to sell the business. He was a victim of exogenous trouble factor two: losing a job.

Although Jim had earned a good living from his business, it was, like the hotel industry, highly vulnerable to a downturn. Like many small business owners, Jim was oriented toward growth. When a customer demanded a new type of mailing insert or a special fold, Jim's inclination was to buy the machine or technology that would do the trick. The problem was that Jim financed his business improvements through debt. He had complete confidence in himself, and believed that he could always make a new sale and gain a new customer to keep the business growing. And, for years, he was right. He is an outgoing, fun, and funny man who makes a super salesperson. He is very knowledgeable about sales and its techniques and has mastered its skills. He has the ability to convince potential customers that his service is worth a premium. He also pays attention to the details of customer relationships, constantly sending out little notes and birthday greetings. But, when the orders stopped coming in, the cash flow came to a halt. Unfortunately, the interest and debt payments did not.

In the last dozen years that he owned his business, Jim had been earning an income in the seven figures and the Freedman family lived a life filled with nice things and expensive comforts. They had three residences. Their primary home was in Hingham, a seaside community south of Boston, and they had vacation houses on Cape Cod and in Florida. They put their three kids through expensive private colleges (Harvard, Wheaton, and Boston College) without taking any loans. They dined out regularly and bought pretty much whatever they liked. However, neither Jim nor Anne had come from money and did not think of themselves as big spenders or high rollers. Home and family had always come first.

Then, when Jim found himself forced to sell his company, the only money coming in was from Anne's job as a kindergarten teacher in the nearby town of Quincy. Her salary, about $42,000 a year, was scarcely enough to keep them going. The Freedmans decided to sell the house where they had lived for thirty-two years and raised their three children. They also parted with many of their precious possessions. The most difficult to say goodbye to was the Steinway piano that Anne and the kids had loved to play. But it was valued at $8,000 and they needed the money. Besides, it wouldn't fit in the new, smaller house they planned to move to. "I cried when it went out the door," Anne told me.

You might expect that Jim would be despondent after such a business reversal and that Anne might feel sad or even bitter about losing their cherished home and possessions. But that is not the case, as we discovered when we visited the couple in their new surroundings. They now live, just the two of them, in a recently constructed community not far from their old town, composed of homes and condos that center around a golf course. (Neither Jim nor Anne plays golf!)

Making the Most of a Downturn

We drove through the entrance gate and past the brand new post office, the two-truck fire department, and the community grocery store. Construction cranes and bulldozers were working on new building sites and there were signs inviting us to visit the model homes. We found Jim and Anne's street, which is lined with detached, single-family homes that have a tidy look and welcoming feel. It was early evening. The porch light was on and Jim and Anne greeted us at the door. They are both in their early sixties. Although there is a little gray in the hair, they are full of energy and vitality. Both are well dressed and smile easily.

The entry is furnished with classic pieces and, when one of my associates comments on how lovely they are, Jim and Anne enthusiastically offer to take us on a tour of the house. It is beautifully and meticulously decorated, but not everything is as expensive as it appears. "Before we sold the business, when we went to a store and saw something we liked, we would buy it on the spot," Anne says. "We didn't really shop around. Now, we think about our purchases more and prioritize." She points out a corner cupboard that she is particularly fond of. They first saw the cupboard in a furniture store, selling for $800, and liked it, but they didn't buy it immediately. A few days later, Anne found the same piece at a discounter for $150 and they snapped it up.

The most striking feature of the house, however, is not the furniture but rather all the photographs of the three Freedman kids and the two grandchildren. The kids are thirty, thirty-three, and thirty-five years old, but Jim and Anne have furnished the bedrooms in such a way that the children and grandchildren can still come home on a moment's notice, and everything will be ready for them. It is clear that family is the heart of this home and that nothing, even the huge financial setback the Freedmans suffered, can disrupt it.

We sit down at the kitchen table for our conversation. Jim and Anne sit very close to one another, elbows touching. "Children are absolutely our top priority," says Jim. "We help them in any way we can, just like they would help us. Our son started a business at the beginning of the year, and we helped him get going. And we've set up college funds for the grandkids." Anne adds that they baby-sit for the grandchildren almost every weekend. "In fact, they've never had a baby-sitter besides us."

"Some of our friends think we're crazy because we put so much money into the kids," Jim says. "Even when the business was being sold, we managed to make Christmas very special. No one could take that away from us."

THE FREEDMANS' ASSETS		THEIR LIABILITIES	
Savings account	$0	Mortgage	$625,000
Checking account	$10,000	Home equity	$125,000
Investments	$100,000	Credit card	$35,000
Home value	$750,000	Student loans	$0
Other	$0	Other	$0

Rather than try to start a new company after his business went under, Jim decided to take a job and soon found a position at a printing company. "I never had a title before," he laughs, "but now I'm VP of mailing." Jim quickly built up the mailing operation and made it very successful. Although he gets a decent salary at the printing company, well over $100,000 a year, that's low in comparison to his previous earnings. But, now that the business is profitable, Jim is preparing to renegotiate his compensation. "I've put two years of my time and energy into the business," he says. "I've created high profits in the past seven months. Now it's time to start talking with my employer about a much more realistic compensation package. It's time to cash in on what I've done." Jim expects that their financial situation will soon improve, although he doubts they will ever get back to the level of prosperity they enjoyed pre-9/11.

After the initial shock of the loss of the business, the Freedmans' life has stabilized and the value calculus has been refined. They trade down much more than they used to and trade up with much more caution and deliberation. When they needed a new computer desk, they looked at Best Buy and Staples rather than Crate & Barrel or an antiques shop where they would have looked before. They chose a particle board desk they could assemble themselves. Their lives are filled with trade-offs, large and small. They're more likely to stop at Dunkin' Donuts now than at Starbucks. Rather than buying jewelry at Tiffany, Anne shops at malls and discount stores. They don't eat out as often as they used to. When they do, it's likely to be for a meal at a local restaurant, rather than at a four-star restaurant in Boston or on the Cape. "We don't go out as frequently as other empty nesters we know, and we don't go over the top the way we used to," says Anne, "but we enjoy a nice meal together."

Joining in the Treasure Hunt

Jim and Anne still appreciate brand-name goods, particularly in clothing and groceries, but they go after the bargain a lot more aggressively than they used to. Jim is wearing a dark blue Polo sweater emblazoned with an American flag, but it was purchased at an outlet, not a mall department store. They generally don't buy private-label goods at the supermarket; instead, they take advantage of sales and stock up on special deals and promotional items.

Anne is a coupon maven. "She loves to search out the best price, rather than just buying the first thing that comes to hand," says Jim. "It's really in her blood." Anne jumps up to retrieve her purse and shows us a stack of coupons she keeps there. "I get my coupons from the newspaper. It takes a few minutes to get them ready for the week, which I do while I'm sitting and watching the Patriots," she says. Jim is not quite so enthusiastic. "The only problem I have is that the coupons still aren't very well organized and people behind us at the checkout have to wait for what seems like twenty minutes while we shuffle through them all," he says. "But, I save so much!" Anne replies.

THE FREEDMANS' MONTHLY EXPENSES

Item	Spending	Index vs. Average
Income (posttax)	$9,950	1.0
Car	810	0.5
Mortgage/rent	4,500	2.7
Household utilities and maintenance	460	0.5
Eating out	250	0.4
Groceries	430	0.7
Travel and entertainment	380	0.8
Healthcare/personal health	200	0.5
Home goods	80	0.2
Clothing	210	0.6
Charitable contributions	420	1.2
Education	0	0.0
Personal care services	130	1.1
Life insurance	210	2.1
Other expenses	120	0.6
Total spending	8,200	1.0
Net savings/(deficit)	1,750	1.1

"I save at least $20 to $30 a week on a $100 order. It really makes me happy when I can get a good product at a good value."

Despite his disenchantment with coupons, Jim is gradually catching on to the excitement of the treasure hunt. "He had never been interested in the big bargain before," says Anne. "But that's changing. We were in CVS and he needed shaving cream. His favorite brand was on special. He came running up to me with five cans in his hand. He said, 'Look, it's only sixty-nine cents!' I was really proud of him."

When the Freedmans were starting out, they didn't have much money, and trading down was a way of life. As they prospered, they left their trading-down ways behind and rarely worried about getting a bargain, or even looking for one. But now they play at both poles with great agility, like so many other consumers around the world.

The experience seems to have given them even greater strength and optimism than they had before disaster struck. Although they miss some of the pleasures of their previous life, they don't feel stuck in the middle or left behind.

"Necessity is the mother of invention and is also a pretty good teacher," Jim remarks. "But our goals have not been diminished."

Anne agrees. "We've talked about going to Hawaii for our fortieth anniversary. It's a goal," she says.

"And it'll happen," replies Jim, squeezing her hand.

"It's a change of attitude. You realize you don't need that much anymore," Anne adds. "We each have our health, and that's the ultimate. We've never been into material goods. Material things you buy and sell, and they don't mean anything. What you're left with is your character."

When we ask them to define the good life, Jim laughs and Anne speaks first. "We are living the good life. Would we like a little more cushion and a little more money for the future? Of course. Would we like our other two kids to be married? Yes. And would we like a few more grandchildren? Definitely."

"For me, the good life would be to work as a teacher, coach little league sports, and live on a farm," Jim says with a laugh. "But that's not realistic right now. It's about getting more time together as a family. And, although I'm a bit of a workaholic, I know Anne would like to spend more time doing volunteer work." He turns to his wife. "Have we fulfilled the dream?" he asks. She nods. "In a limited way," he says, "I guess we have."

"We're proud," she says. "We have a great family. And, knock on wood, we're feeling good at this time in our lives. We're pretty fortunate."

The Freedmans were living at the high end of the market and then were knocked down a few rungs. There, they discovered that they had not lost everything. They still had the most important riches of all—love and connection.

5.
ALL TREASURE, ALL THE TIME

For millions of people, shopping is one of life's genuine pleasures, a form of amusement and recreation. Almost everybody, even the sternest of penny-pinchers, loves to shop when they approach it as an adventure. They love to go "on the prowl," searching for goods they really love and want. It's about beating somebody else to the punch, getting a great deal or a phenomenal bargain, or finding a rare or one-of-a-kind item. Even people with low incomes or who are on a strict budget always have a little bit of extra cash they're willing to spend on a nice piece of loot.

People have engaged in the treasure hunt since commerce began, of course, in the markets and fairs of Europe, the bazaars of the East, and, later, at the peddler's wagons and general stores of America. The ancient allure of the bazaar and the visceral excitement of shopping are the basis for the success of all kinds of retail formats around the world. People are drawn to Trader Joe's, the specialty grocery market, because they're never sure exactly what they're going to find on their visit. Could be a new blueberry ice cream from the Pacific Northwest or an organic pasta from Italy. Carrefour is opening big markets in China to compete with the traditional wet markets, which feature the local produce of the moment and the catch of the day. Destination shopping and cultural venues, like Vila Moda in Dubai and Three on the Bund in Shanghai, feature a constantly changing array of goods, services, and shopping experiences.

The excitement of going on the prowl is also what's behind every yard sale and flea market, including the biggest and most extravagantly profitable embodiment of the concept, eBay. As more than 135 million registered users in thirty-two markets have learned, eBay offers the thrill of discovery every day.

Stephanie, the Scarf Fanatic

Stephanie Granby, for example, has a thing for scarves. She fell in love with them in 1996, the summer of her junior year at Northwestern University, when she was twenty-one and backpacking through Europe. In Paris, something compelled her to attend the once-a-year sale at Hermes, the legendary retailer that is known, perhaps above all else, for its fabulous scarves. Stephanie bought a silk twill scarf, hand-rolled, in a floral pattern. Even at 40 percent off, it cost $120. With that purchase, Stephanie was hooked. She cherished the Hermes scarf and still keeps the orange box it came in tucked away in a drawer. She became enamored of scarves and learned all she could about designers and retailers.

STEPHANIE'S ASSETS		HER LIABILITIES	
Savings account	$19,000	Mortgage	$0
Checking account	$12,000	Home equity	$0
Investments	$65,000	Credit card	$0
Home value	$0	Student loans	$8,500
Other	$0	Other	$0

In her early twenties, Stephanie didn't have the money to buy scarves at full retail prices, which can run to many hundreds, even thousands, of dollars. And even though she is now thirty and makes nearly $100,000 as a business professional, her value calculus does not allow for profligate spending on fanciful fashion items. She grew up in a small town in Iowa, in a household of modest means and a family that valued frugality and hard work. As a teenager, she had after-school and summer jobs to save money for college tuition. She played basketball with as much vigor as she pursued her school studies. After a game, if her team lost, she would shoot free throws late into the night. But Stephanie's lack of money in her early years did not deter her from building a scarf collection. She waited for the sales at the retail stores and searched for good examples in vintage clothing shops and at yard sales.

Then along came eBay. "eBay has changed my life," says Stephanie. "The scarves I wanted to buy were beautiful, but most of them were

STEPHANIE'S MONTHLY EXPENSES		
Item	Spending	Index vs. Average
Income (posttax)	$6,030	1.0
Car	300	0.3
Mortgage/rent	850	0.8
Household utilities and maintenance	25	0.0
Eating out	500	1.3
Groceries	200	0.6
Travel and entertainment	1,000	3.3
Healthcare/personal health	125	0.5
Home goods	1,000	4.2
Clothing	500	2.2
Charitable contributions	25	0.1
Education	125	1.0
Personal care services	100	0.8
Life insurance	0	0.0
Other expenses	200	1.0
Total spending	4,950	1.0
Net savings/(deficit)	1,080	1.1

just too expensive for me. I needed a way to buy them that would provide better value." Since 1999, Stephanie has purchased more than fifteen scarves on the site. "They're masterpieces," she says. "And incredible values. I have bought them for as little as $50 and as much as $400. That sounds like a lot, but not when you consider that the retail price in a store can be as high as $850. I always get a deal on eBay." Stephanie's scarf collection fills the walls of her apartment. When she wants to wear one of them, which she does frequently, she simply plucks it off the wall and replaces it with another one from a drawer.

Every evening when she comes home from work, Stephanie checks eBay to see what's new. If she finds a scarf she likes, she makes a bid. The evening we talked with her, Stephanie put in a bid of $125 on a "beautiful, unique, inspiring" Hermes scarf. Every morning, she gets up at 5:30 A.M. and immediately goes online to see where the bidding stands. eBay has become her major spending outlet.

eBay: The World's Greatest Treasure Hunt

eBay is the world's largest treasure hunt. In just seven years of operation, eBay has created a market value, $42 billion at the end of 2004, that is greater than the entire value of the department store industry in the United States, which has been operating for more than a century. eBay has no debt and a price–earnings ratio of 62 (Wal-Mart's price earnings ratio, by contrast, is 18.6 and Amazon's is 41.1). We estimate that its gross merchandise volume will reach $50 billion in 2006.

What does eBay have that traditional retailers don't? A fantastic business model. It is an online community that brings together approximately 336,000 registered stores worldwide, many of them small or geographically isolated, into one global marketplace. eBay is, according to Michael Dearing, its senior vice president and general merchandise manager, "a wonderful intersection of flexible technology and the entrepreneurial drive of buyers and sellers. For sellers, eBay satisfies the desire to be entrepreneurial and make money. For buyers, eBay enables them to put their hands on the steering wheel of their own consumption. And the Internet makes the intersection possible, bringing together an enormously heterogeneous body of both buyers and sellers. eBay is the single best example of how technology intersects with community."

Because eBay is a community of buyers and sellers who own inventory, eBay carries no inventory of its own. It pays for no goods. It makes no guarantees about accuracy of information, product quality, or delivery. It makes its money as the middle man, taking slivers of the purchase price from the sellers at various stages along the way. As a result, eBay delivers an incredibly high operating margin of 36 percent. That's the highest of all the world's retail companies that generate annual sales of at least $1 billion. Compare it to 19 percent for Yahoo and 5 percent for Wal-Mart.

eBay's business model is made all the more successful because it has behind it the tremendous power of a community made up of people who believe that eBay is performing an important social function. They see the company as an enabler of a people's marketplace, where buyers and sellers can connect with each other in a uniquely direct and transparent way. In fact, eBay was founded as a "thought experiment" by Pierre Omidyar to see if people could trust each other enough to engage in commerce with a minimum of control and intercession from an intermediary. This produces great loyalty on the part of eBay users as well as very high frequency of use. The population of registered eBay users has grown from 2 million in 1998 to 168.1 million by the end of the third quarter of 2005. About half of the users are active, having bid, bought, or listed an item in the past year. In 2003, about 40 million U.S. households (about 37 percent of the 109 million total households) made a purchase on eBay. By the end of 2006, we estimate that the number of registered users will approach that of the entire adult population in the United States.

"There is no other place on earth that offers a greater breadth of categories of goods or more depth within a category," Michael Dearing told me. The 100,000-plus SKUs of a big-box retailer look puny in comparison to the number of items available on eBay—about 60 million listings globally. There are some 18,000 different categories of goods (although some observers count as many as 50,000) and they include just about every kind of item: antiques and art, books, movies, music, coins and stamps, collectibles, computers, dolls and dollhouses, jewelry and watches, photo and electronic equipment, pottery and glass, real estate, sports equipment, and vehicles. When I did a search for scarves, 12,693 scarf-related items came up, 760 in vintage alone.

The inventory on eBay is constantly changing. Whole categories suddenly appear and disappear. Some goods are snapped up within minutes, others remain available for weeks or months. As a result, it is impossible to calculate eBay's inventory turn, but, according to Michael Dearing, eBay's inventory "turns over faster than any other channel on the Web. The duration of listings is only seven days on average. eBay is a high-velocity market. But inventory turn doesn't really matter to eBay, because there are no costs associated with carrying inventory.

"People all over the world come to eBay to look for things they are passionate about," says Dearing. On eBay you can buy a John Deere tractor, a lot on a lake, a Patek Phillippe limited edition watch, Carrie (*Sex and the City*) Bradshaw's Gucci tote, and automobiles that range from a vintage Plymouth to a new BMW M3. In addition to all the relatively normal things available, there are endless numbers of items that are impossible to categorize and end up on the "everything else" page, which includes religious products, personal security items, metaphysical goods, and "weird stuff"—which is subdivided into "slightly unusual," "really weird," and "totally bizarre" (Example: mystery stuffed banana.)

The great majority of the items sold on eBay are relatively inexpensive—excluding autos and real estate, we estimate that the average selling price is about $36—so the population of buyers represents all income levels. Most of eBay's users come from middle-income households who shop there not for commodities or necessities, but for treasure. Marge, a fifty-six–year-old professional, says, "I treat eBay like an online flea market. It's not a place where I'd go for serious shopping, but it's fun. I usually buy things that are hard to find: discontinued china patterns, replacements for glassware that have gotten lost or broken, discontinued cosmetic products. Occasionally I'll buy consumer electronics, software, or costume jewelry if the price is lower than what it's sold for in stores."

Feeling Smart

eBay is a brilliant business model and the most successful expression of an online commercial community, but its success also springs from its incredible appeal to the consumer value calculus. It offers shoppers the opportunity to go on the prowl every day, at whatever hour they desire. They can roam through the categories as if they were wandering the shops of Beverly Hills, the flea markets of London, the bazaars of Morocco.

And, as middle class as they may be, they know they are in the company of eBay fanatics who are far from middle class and hardly anonymous. In fact, eBay has become a celebrity magnet, gushed about by legions of actors and authors, artists and musicians—including novelist Amy Tan (who calls eBay her "secret passion"), *New York Times* crossword puzzle guru Will Shortz, and *Queer Eye* star Carson Cressly, who refers to himself as an eBay addict.

eBay users can shop with the style that suits them best—remaining anonymous or making themselves known. They can bargain and influence the bidding, but they also feel relatively comfortable that the process is well managed and will follow certain rules. They have more control over the equation than they do in any other retail setting, and much more than if they were bargaining on the streets of an unfamiliar city. Many items are offered at a fixed price, but many are sold at auction. Buyers can make a bid, watch the progress, get out whenever they want, and sometimes make a preemptive "buy it now" offer. Although the prices on eBay are not guaranteed to be the lowest in the world, that doesn't matter, because the best price is subjective.

eBay makes buyers feel smart. "Getting the best price is a high payoff for the buyer," Michael Dearing said. "The payoff to winning, to getting the thing you really want at the very best price—the price you think it's worth—is enormous. It's a basic human desire to feel smart, and eBay facilitates that." eBay enables buyers to pay the exact amount for an item that they believe it is worth to them.

However, experienced eBay users say there are "bargains galore" and that "if you have a nose, you can always get more for your money." Our analysis shows that there are considerable discounts to be had in most categories. Best of all, "The best way to save money is to shop eBay," said one user. "For most things, you don't pay sales tax, and the shipping is less than the cost of making a bunch of trips to stores."

eBay is also very easy to use and extremely convenient for the consumer. Almost anyone with rudimentary computer skills can master the site. The hours of operation are the hours the consumer is awake. No driving, parking, walking, or heavy lifting is required. Buyers have access to a great deal of information about the buying process, eBay itself, the seller, and the particular item they're looking at.

Win–Win Economics

Sellers love eBay as much as buyers do, even though they have to pay a premium to sell their goods through the eBay community. Listing, payment, and closing fees are as much as 300 percent or 400 percent higher than they are on other sites, such as Yahoo. But eBay offers sellers many more potential buyers than any other online marketplace—168.1 million registered users.

And, eBay works with sellers as partners. It offers training and education at eBay University. It has defined a number of best practices and created customized selling tools. And, although the fee structure is such that eBay makes a healthy profit, an eBay sale can also be very lucrative for the seller.

Consider, for example, the economics of buying and selling a 2005 Ben Hogan CS3 Neutral golf driver on eBay. The retail price of the club is $299.99. Let's say the eBay selling price is $210, or 30 percent off store retail. For the seller, the wholesale cost of the item sold is $145, which leaves a gross margin of $65. The seller pays an insertion fee which ranges from $0.25 to $3.30 depending on the cost of the item (the average is $.50), and a feature fee for adding an image of the item and displaying text in a bold font. The feature fees average about $.25 each. When the item sells, the seller pays a flat 5.25 percent of the selling price for items up to $25. For items above $1,000, the fee drops to 1.5 percent. For the $210 driver the fee is approximately 3 percent or $6. Sellers who use eBay's proprietary payment system, PayPal, are charged an additional 2.9 percent. That leaves a net profit of approximately $50 for the seller, or about 24 percent. Compare that to the typical $135 profit that a store retailer would realize on the sale, which is more like 45 percent. But, even though the retailer's gross margin is usually slightly lower on eBay than it is at retail, the online marketplace is so much more dynamic than that of an offline store and drives so much more traffic, eBay ends up being more profitable for the retailer in the long run.

724,000 Americans report that eBay is their primary or secondary source of income. There is no question that eBay provides one of the easiest ways to start a new business. You can start up with no inventory, no capital expenditure, no staff, and no offline location.

Many other online marketplaces—such as Yahoo!Auctions and Ubid.com—have tried to compete with eBay, but it has an incredibly strong lead that is very difficult for competitors to overcome. The loyalty of eBay's customers and its big network of buyers and sellers, as well as its ability to track and model consumer purchasing behavior, make it almost untouchable.

eBay has been relentless in its quest to grow, both by establishing sites in new languages, and by increasing its market coverage. It has also been able to expand its community of vendors through the acquisition of PayPal, the world's largest Web payment platform. PayPal solves many of the major problems that can arise in an online marketplace that is made up of so many vendors, many of them small, with so many transactions, many of them also small. Most of these vendors do not want to accept credit cards, because the fee can be as high as 5 to 6 percent of the sale price, and because payment can be slow. PayPal allows individuals and businesses with an e-mail address to send and receive payments online, with lower fees, and faster payments.

A New Language of Retailing

As eBay has grown and refined its processes, a profusion of terms and definitions has emerged, so that doing business on eBay requires speaking a new language of retailing. Here are just a few of the terms you'll need to know to get the most out of buying or selling on eBay:

ACRU: Active confirmed registered user. A CRU who bid, bought, or listed within any given time period.

ASP: Average selling price. The GMV for any given site divided by the number of items sold.

BIN: Buy it now.

CR: Conversion rate. The number of successful listings or transactions divided by the total number of listings.

CRU: Confirmed registered user. A person who registers at eBay and confirms his registration by responding to an e-mail sent out afterward.

EOA: End of auction.

EOT: End of transaction.

FF: Feature fee.

FIT: Fraud Investigation Team.

FLD: Free listing day.

FPP: Fraud protection program.

GDT: Gross domestic trade. The volume of all the purchases that buyers and sellers transact where both the buyer and seller are domiciled in the same country.

GMB: Gross merchandise bought. The dollar volume of all the purchases that eBay buyers make.

GMV: Gross merchandise volume. The dollar volume of all the sales between sellers and buyers. This is comparable to other retailers' online sales (i.e., eBay's GMV is equivalent to Wal-Mart.com's sales).

LA: Live auction.

MBG: Money-back guarantee.

MIB: Mint in box (describing an item).

NARU: Not a registered user.

NIB: New in box (describing an item).

NWOT: New without tags (describing an item).

NWT: New with tags (describing an item).

ODR: Online dispute resolution.

P2P: Person to person.

ROW: Rest of world. All countries where eBay does not currently have a local-language Web site or a minisite.

SYI: Sell your item.

TnS: Trust and safety.

TPV: Total payment volume. The total of all the money transmitted between PayPal users.

UPI: Unpaid item.

VeRO: Verified rights owner (program for copyright/trademark owners).

An Addiction, Too

There is a downside to eBay. For some people, it can become an obsession. Heavy users will log on every day and track six or more items.

Fanatical users are constantly on eBay, at home and at work and at play. Some 12 percent of acknowledged heavy users say they are "addicted."

"eBay sucks you in," said one user. "I've bought tons of items that I don't need, just because they were selling at a great price. This would make sense if I resold them for profit, but I never do!" Another admitted that, "eBay can be quite addictive. Those of us who are real avid buyers who spend a lot of time shopping and buying on eBay realize that at some point we've got to start selling things to be able to support our habit."

Auctions, in particular, fuel the addiction. "Bidding tends to get really frenetic at the end of the auction. That kind of excitement is infectious," explained Jim Griffith, dean of education at eBay. "The best part of eBay is the thrill of an auction," said a frequent buyer. "I love to jump in just at the last second and score something at a great value. It's called 'sniping' an auction." Another user told us, "There have been times I've had to go cold turkey because I had so many auctions I won, it was hard to keep track of all my purchases!"

For such users, eBay is rarely a money-saving activity. "Sometimes I save using eBay," said one self-confessed eBay addict, "but as much as I spend on the site, I really don't think I'm saving anything. I don't have a problem spending more for unique items, and because they are unique, there's no way to know their actual retail value."

Addiction can lead to problems both for buyers and sellers. As eBay has grown, it has attracted its share of shady sellers and fraudulent offers and there has been an increase in disputes between buyers and sellers. Of the more than eight thousand people who work for eBay, some one thousand of them work full-time to root out fraud and resolve disputes.

"Unlimited Growth" Ahead

Despite these frailties in the system, eBay has enjoyed remarkable success to date. eBay transactions now account for 24 percent of all e-commerce revenues. Its international business has grown 79 percent from 2001 to 2004, and is likely to surpass the U.S.-based business by 2006. And eBay is looking to increase share of wallet among its heavy users, providing purchase options—such as Half.com, which offers a fixed price, online Web site to buy and sell high-quality, previously owned goods at discounted prices—that go way beyond auctions.

eBay may come across as a community based on trust, but the company's leadership is intensely competitive and obsessively tracks the metrics of the business, including market share and customer satisfaction and loyalty. "We have a real blessing in the amount of data we collect," said Michael Dearing. "We monitor consumer satisfaction across about fifteen different dimensions, including pricing, customer support, features, and many others. Right now, buyer satisfaction with sellers and seller satisfaction with buyers are at about 90 percent. That's much higher than you'll find with retail stores."

eBay sees more growth and success in the future. "eBay has a significant runway ahead," said Dearing. "Over the last five years, we've focused on broadening the geographic footprint and category structure. To continue our growth we're focusing on high-volume buyers and specializing the experience. Sometimes consumers come to eBay with a specific item in mind. Sometimes they just like to bounce along the site. We're trying to make a visit to eBay more of an experience. We want to draw in more users and get them more engaged once they're on the site. We're also seeing amazing growth in specific categories, such as books, music, computer hardware and software, passenger vehicles, and, most surprising to us, apparel."

Stephanie certainly sees no end to her involvement with eBay. "eBay is my secret answer," she said at the end of one of our conversations. Before we left, she checked back online to see what was happening with the Hermes scarf she had bid on. "I could buy it outright for $175 right now," she said. "Or I could wait for the auction." After a half second of mental debate, she let out a yelp, and declared, "I can't wait. It's gonna be mine now." She hit the purchase key and a smile spread across her face.

The Terrestrial Version

Be it for scarves or cars, golf clubs or books, everybody is on the prowl for something, and eBay is just one place to look for whatever it is. The hard discount stores, including Aldi and the dollar stores, and even some of the big-box retailers, also have aspects of treasure hunting to them.

Kmart, for example, is famous for its selling gimmick, the Blue Light Special. It was created in the 1960s as a way for store managers to draw shoppers' attention to slow-moving merchandise that was to be sold at a special discount for a limited time. A flashing blue light that looked like the bulbous light fixture on a police car would be erected near the merchandise. The click of the loudspeaker would be heard, followed by an announcement that always began "Attention Kmart shoppers . . ." and would then describe the merchandise. Shoppers would dash to the display beneath the flashing light to snap up the item while supplies lasted and the discount price still held. The Blue Light Special got tired in the mid-1990s, had a brief renaissance in the late '90s in a bluelight.com Web site, and returned in the form of special in-store promotions in 2005, but the blue light itself was gone.

Wal-Mart is well known for its treasure chest, AKA the DVD bin, a container some three feet deep filled with hundreds of movies of all descriptions, looking as if they had been thrown in willy-nilly by a sales associate. It is not unusual to see three or four people sorting through the DVDs for hours at a time, exclaiming when they make a find, stacking up their treasures, burying their heads deep in the bin, digging for more. The price is usually well below the standard retail price, around $5.99 for one movie and $11 for two.

At Dollar General, there are always special buys and limited-quantity goods available, and they are often displayed in unexpected locations or tucked away among other items, to increase the surprise of discovering them. On one visit to a Dollar General outlet we found a one-of-a-kind 6x9' area rug rolled up behind a bunch of brooms in the cleaning supplies section, decorative bird houses on a shelf beneath towels and sheets, and a children's stool next to a space heater. Treasure is in the eye of the beholder.

Aldi saw the power of the treasure hunt when, in 1998, the store made a special buy of a large quantity of personal computers, the Real 3.0-Ghz Intel Pentium 4 Processor Titanium MD 8080XL. People stood in line for hours for a chance to buy one of the computers for around €750, some 25 percent below the typical retail price of €1,000. Aldi sold two hundred thousand of the computers in one day, an amount equal to approximately 4 percent of total computer sales in Germany for the entire year. *Computer-Bild*, the largest Europe-based computer magazine, called the event the "most popular computer release of 1998." Its success prompted Aldi to expand its offering of computers and personal electronics goods. In the fourth quarter of 2004, Aldi sold more than three hundred thousand units, raising the sales of all computers in Germany by 15 percent over the previous quarter. Aldi is now considered to be the second largest seller of PCs in Germany.

The One and Only Tchibo

None of these stores can hold a candle to Tchibo, probably Europe's best-loved and most unique treasure hunt retailer. Tchibo was founded in 1949 as a mail order purveyor of high-quality coffee and evolved into a most unusual kind of specialty retailer. Tchibo is still centered around coffee—selling ground coffee, coffee beans, and coffee-making accessories in its coffee bars and retail shops, as well as by mail. But Tchibo also offers a variety of other nonfood items, mostly home-related. The unique distinction of Tchibo is that the nonfood items are offered—not in departments or categories—but in themes, and the themes change week by week. Every Wednesday, about fifteen items are introduced around the new theme—such as Italian cuisine, beautiful garden, easier workout, enjoy nature, surprise your partner—with a mix of offerings from jewelry to travel arrangements. All of the items are branded with Tchibo's own label, TCM, and are available for a limited time only. None of the products is available at any other retailer, or at least not in exactly the same form. "A new experience every week" is the Tchibo promise.

Consumers know they can always get the coffee they need at Tchibo, but they are never quite sure what other delightful surprises will be awaiting them on a visit to the store or when browsing online. Possibly a stainless steel waffle iron, a backpack, a decorative toilet seat, or a set of hand-painted wine glasses? Because the merchandise is unpredictable and the quantities are limited, Tchibo is a paradise for impulse purchases. People buy things at the shops they had no intention of buying that day and may not have even thought about buying at all. There is something almost completely irresistible about snapping up an item that looks good, is well made, is highly affordable, fits the value calculus, and brings an element of surprise into one's life. Who knew that I would so badly want a Nordic Nights reversible bedspread with soft fleece filling at £24.99?

Tchibo is very different from the European hard discounters like Aldi and Lidl and the funky U.S. dollar stores. Its "thematic worlds," as the company calls them, are developed to respond to current trends, and all the items are deliberately sourced and tested. The theme may be seasonal, such as "back to school" or "here comes Easter," but it may also be linked to needs or wants, such as "time to clean the house" or "horseback riding." This is quite different from the opportunistic sourcing behaviors of other discounters, who make special buys simply because the goods are available from a supplier or who sell closeout or distressed merchandise.

Tchibo cares about quality and guarantees all its merchandise. Customers can return any item that doesn't suit them, no questions

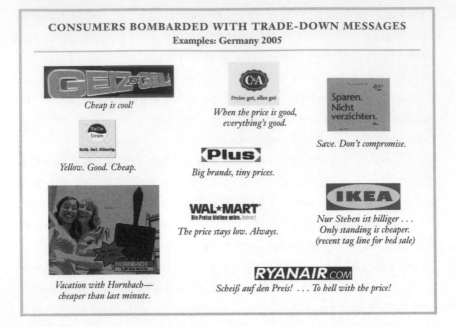

CONSUMERS BOMBARDED WITH TRADE-DOWN MESSAGES
Examples: Germany 2005

Cheap is cool!

*When the price is good,
everything's good.*

Save. Don't compromise.

Yellow. Good. Cheap.

Big brands, tiny prices.

The price stays low. Always.

*Nur Stehen ist billiger . . .
Only standing is cheaper.
(recent tag line for bed sale)*

*Vacation with Hornbach—
cheaper than last minute.*

Scheiß auf den Preis! . . . To hell with the price!

asked. As a result, the Tchibo name and its store brand, TCM, are well known, respected, and trusted. As one German shopper told us, "The Tchibo brand has a good reputation. You can openly say that you shop there. I might even buy a present for somebody there." That would not always be the case with Aldi or Lidl or Dollar General.

Ilse Kessler, thirty-three, is a hardworking stay-at-home mother of two children, aged eight and five. Her husband, Conrad, is a plumber. Ilse quit her job as an office assistant when the couple's first child was born. The family now manages on Conrad's modest income of €1,900 a month. Ilse has to shop smartly and find bargains, yet says she feels good about it. "I love scouting for information and comparing prices, I will get up early and get to a store at 7:30 A.M. to make sure that I get the item I want."

Beginning with the Bean

Tchibo was founded in 1949 by two businessmen, Max Herz and Carl Tchilling-Hiryan. (The name Tchibo is a combination of Tchilling's name and *bohne*, the German word for bean.) At that time, in postwar Germany, coffee was a rarity that consumers longed for after many years of going without. Direct mail of coffee was an innovation. Herz believed he could deliver the highest-quality fresh coffee. He was right; Tchibo found that there was great demand for its high-quality beans. Tchilling-Hiryan was responsible for the coffee, charged with finding the best beans from the growers, and overseeing the roasting and blending. Herz was the distribution man. At that time, there simply was no distribution network suitable for retailing coffee, so Herz hit upon the then-novel idea of delivery by mail.

The company ventured beyond mail order in 1955, opening the first Tchibo shop in the city of Hamburg. It was in the shops that the idea of selling nonfood items was born. To build loyalty with customers, Tchibo began offering small promotional items along with the coffee. The first was a recipe book, which proved to be a big hit, and other promotions followed. Rather than pack up the coffee in standard paper bags, for example, the shop assistants would dispense it in reusable items such as a kitchen towel or a bright-orange metal container.

Customers liked the practice, and Tchibo's containers and promotional items became a regular sight in kitchens around the country. But Tchibo's competitors were not so pleased, and the bundling of food and nonfood products eventually ran afoul of retailing regulations. Tchibo was forced to make a separate business of its nonfood items and it quickly found a niche. The rise of Tchibo went largely unnoticed by the then-dominant specialty retailers, because its offerings cut across many product categories. Discounters were primarily focused on food and would not compete with Tchibo on nonfood goods. Some gas station chains tried to compete—often promoting the advantage of their longer opening hours—but they didn't really master the processes and did not succeed.

Today, Tchibo has expanded throughout Europe, with more than sixty thousand outlets, and operations in twelve countries in Central and Eastern Europe as well as the United Kingdom. The company reaches customers through four formats: online and mail order, Tchibo retail stores, specialty coffee bars, and Tchibo shop-in-shops in bakeries and food retail chains. The company has grown steadily, with a compound annual growth rate of 10 percent since 1989. It is the number one seller of coffee in Germany as well as in Hungary, the Czech Republic, Austria, and Poland—and the number one seller of many items, including bras and socks, in Germany.

"If I can buy good quality at a low price," says Ilse Kessler, "I may be able to afford some little extras." Ilse works hard to make the family's money go further. She shops at the hard discount stores for many essential household goods. "I buy things like toilet paper, kitchen roll, and detergents in doubles or in larger sizes if it is cheaper," she says.

Ilse visits Tchibo to buy nonfood essentials, such as clothes, linens, toys for the children, pet supplies, and little things for home decoration, like candles. "The quality is fine, the price is low—although not the lowest in the marketplace—and the service is very good," she says.

Occasionally she'll splurge on a "hidden treasure" for the home or for the kids. "I have become even more focused on treasure hunting now that we have a second child," says Ilse. "But I'm willing to wait until the right thing comes along."

The Attraction of Coffee and New Merchandise

The Tchibo concept is a clever combination of deliberation and spontaneity, practicality and sensuality. Many people plan a visit to Tchibo because they genuinely need to buy coffee in whatever form, or because they want to meet a friend to share a cup. While they're there, they can't help but take a look at what's new. The theme of the week is highlighted in the window, and every new item is displayed there. According to my colleagues in Germany, "everybody" looks in the Tchibo window when they pass and "everybody" buys something there now and again.

Once at the shop or coffee bar, customers find themselves in a very pleasant atmosphere that is conducive to treasure hunting. Above all, every Tchibo customer identifies the comforting aroma of coffee as the signature of the brand. When we asked shoppers what one thing should never be changed about Tchibo, they said, "the smell of coffee." But there's more to the experience than aroma. "It feels nice inside the shop," one consumer told me. "It is neat and clean, and the staff looks good in their uniforms." While contemplating the coffee purchase, it's impossible not to look around at the new items. The shelves are chock full of a variety of goods. They are not extravagantly displayed; most of the items are packaged in clear plastic bags.

Perhaps it's the psychophysiological effect at work. With the rich aroma of coffee in the air and with the helpful attendance of the staffers (and possibly with the encouragement of your co-shopper), it suddenly makes sense to buy a new steam iron to replace the aging one at home, or pick up a pack of dog chews, or get an egg boiler as a gift for a friend. Often the shop gets crowded, but that only increases the effect—goods always seem more attractive when other people want them and it becomes a race to get to the best merchandise before it sells out, which it often does at Tchibo.

"I started shopping at Tchibo with my mother when I was a kid, and we always bought nice things for the home or sometimes a toy for me," says Ilse. "Now I visit there about once a week. The display in the window and the posters in the store give me ideas for decoration at home. The shop always smells of freshly roasted coffee. There is lots to look at and you can touch and feel the items. The salespeople are friendly and leave you to look on your own."

Sometimes Ilse gets to the shop and finds that the item she had planned to buy has sold out. "If it is something that I absolutely want," she says, "I will ask the staff to call another Tchibo shop close by and check if they have my item. If so, I will drive there and get it."

Ilse may shop Tchibo more deliberately than most; many shoppers find that they pop into the store regularly just to see what's new, and pick up several things that were not on their list.

Their value calculus may go a little haywire. Customers buy things on impulse that they wouldn't necessarily buy otherwise. You might think that this would lead to a great deal of buyer's remorse or that there would be an inordinate number of returns at Tchibo, given the easy-return policy. That's not the case, however, because the quality of the merchandise is high, the brand is respected, and the typical cost of an item is fairly low. Even the most spontaneous purchase of the most unneeded product will not get the family in financial trouble.

Not the Perfect Housewife

The most typical Tchibo shopper is a married woman, with kids, with a household income of €32,000. Gerda Bauer, fifty-five, has been shopping at Tchibo "forever," as she puts it. Both Gerda and her husband, Dirk, work in the travel industry and, with a combined annual income of more than €50,000, they are a little better off than many Tchibo shoppers, including the Kesslers. Gerda considers herself a bit of a rebel and scoffs at what she sees as the German need for everything to be too tidy and too perfect. "Look at my older sister or at my neighbor. They want to be the *die perfekte Hausfrau* [the perfect housewife]. My sister cleans the windows every week. It's an obsession. If she did not want to make it so perfect all the time, she would be a lot more relaxed!"

Gerda likes to be a little freer and more open with her life and her time. Twice a month, she visits Tchibo to buy coffee and have a look around. "I usually buy lots of things that I don't really need, but which I find beautiful and well priced, especially textiles like clothes and linens, baby items for friends, electronics, and accessories for decorating my house, such as cushions and candles."

Tchibo's success at attracting and keeping customers like Gerda, who are open to the idea of the treasure hunt and are not particularly price sensitive, comes from the company's ability to develop and deliver a stream of products that are not exactly new or innovative, but that are fresh and timely. The products are well designed and attractive, they perform well, and they're always linked to emotional occasions and needs. It's rare that you will find a breakthrough product at Tchibo, but you will find new interpretations, combinations, colorations, and packaging. For example, the fabric wardrobe looks pretty much like any other fabric wardrobe, except the Tchibo version is in blue-striped, "breathable" fleece. The garden shears are similar to other brand-name shears, except the handles are a little different and the price is about 15 percent lower. The six-pack of hand-painted, self-adhesive, decorative sea creatures for the tub and shower may be available elsewhere, but maybe not. Many items are unavailable anywhere else. For example, Tchibo sells a little holder for the artificial sugar tablets that many Germans use to sweeten their coffee and tea. The holders are to be found in offices and homes throughout the country; about 70 percent of them were purchased at Tchibo.

Although Gerda does not aspire to be "perfect," she does value organization and prides herself on being a capable shopper. She manages the family finances and carefully plans her shopping trips. She trades down only for commodities and such "low risk items" as cleaning supplies and small appliances, where the price difference is significant. "We don't really have to trade down," Gerda says. "With two incomes right now, we feel fairly secure materially." However, she still gains satisfaction when she finds a good bargain.

Gerda says that she also savors the occasional "guilty pleasure." She loves a good glass of wine from her upscale wine shop in the evening, enjoys fresh pasta from the Italian delicatessen nearby, and, every Friday, visits her favorite butcher and grocer at the open-air market.

Tchibo is filled with such guilty pleasures. Gerda visits Tchibo regularly to buy her supply of coffee, for which she pays a premium price. "I always buy my coffee from Tchibo," she says. "It is absolutely the best mild coffee and has a wonderful aroma, both in the store and when I brew it at home." In addition to the coffee, Gerda will search the shelves for "new and beautiful things" and, on most visits, she will make a purchase of some kind. "I buy underwear and baby items there. I would even buy a tennis racket—the quality is always good!" Gretchen also favors Tchibo for small electronics. "My favorite Tchibo item is my small radio in the living room. I bought it three years ago for about €90. I just loved the design, which is why I didn't buy a different model from Media Markt, where I usually buy electronics."

Although Gerda enjoys her guilty pleasures, she is constantly finding ways to offset them. In addition to bargain hunting, she saves money by driving an aging Golf that she says is good for at least twenty more years on the road. "But I won't drive all over town to save a few cents on commodities," she says. "I am not that kind of penny saver."

Different Types of Treasure

Tchibo and eBay appeal to the treasure hunter in very different ways. Tchibo is remarkable in that it is able to consistently anticipate and create themes that strike a chord with consumers, and is able to create an atmosphere that puts the shopper in a treasure-hunting state of mind. It is a unique combination of trading-up, trading-down, and treasure hunting—with the premium coffee set amidst a wide variety of affordable and differentiated goods and service offerings. Tchibo has created a model that goes beyond the current Starbucks practice of blending coffee and music. The company has built its success with sophisticated innovation management, supply chain, pricing, sales and marketing processes—all working together to constantly reinforce and enhance a trusted brand. Competitors find it very difficult to successfully imitate the Tchibo model.

eBay is a far more outlandish concept than Tchibo, built on the assumption that everybody in the world is a buyer and seller of something and that almost everybody is willing to purchase goods over the Internet, mostly sight unseen. Is there a limit to the growth potential of eBay? Not only does it have plenty of room to grow geographically, there appears to be no end to the amount of stuff that is available to be sold and that people are willing to buy. For every category, and every item, there is a Stephanie.

6.

WHEN THE CALCULUS SHIFTS

Lauren: A Personal Mystique

There is usually a single dominant factor in each person's value calculus, a factor that is always more important than price and that drives each and every purchase. For Sarah Montfort, the dominant factor is family—the health, safety, and well-being of her three kids, her husband, and herself, in that order. Lauren James, a thirty-two-year-old single woman who lives by herself, has a completely different dominating factor: fear of the future. She worries that she will be unable to find a mate and will never form a lasting and stable relationship. She is afraid that she will grow old alone, lose her ability to earn money, and end up on the streets, carrying shopping bags stuffed with dirty clothes and bits of food and sleeping under a bridge.

You would not guess this about Lauren when you first meet her. She is a charming, attractive, confident-appearing young woman who seems like a quintessential trading-up consumer. She lives in an upscale section of Chicago, in an apartment that used to be a storefront, which she has converted into a unique and distinctive living space. The front door is painted scarlet and Lauren opens it, offers a warm smile, and enthusiastically invites us in. She wears her blonde hair in long, artfully-cut layers. Petite and slim, she's stylishly dressed in expensive jeans, brown high heels, and a tastefully low-cut brown sweater. She wears fashionable, colorful rings on several fingers of both hands. There is a row of shoes and high-heeled boots along one wall—a sure sign of a trading-up fashionista.

We settle onto the couch and Lauren fetches us drinks—individual bottles of Fiji water. "Why Fiji?" I ask her. "It's good for you," she says, as she passes the bottles around. "It's supposed to help with weight loss. The nutrients are easier to absorb because of the way it's bottled or the way the water flows." She chuckles at herself. "Or something like that." As she curls up in an overstuffed chair, Roscoe, her little Maltese dog, jumps up and nestles in her lap. She seems very open and relaxed and, although it's late on a Friday afternoon, she doesn't seem particularly worn out from her work week, and is perfectly willing to talk frankly about her financial situation.

LAUREN JAMES'S ASSETS		HER LIABILITIES	
Savings account	$1,000	Mortgage	$0
Checking account	$650	Home equity	$0
Investments	$30,000	Credit card	$800
Home value	$0	Student loan balance	$22,000
Other	$3,000	Other	$0

We learn that as a marketing manager for an ad agency, Lauren earns a base salary of $80,000, which usually climbs to $92,000 with her yearly bonus. She rents the apartment for $1,000 a month, gets a free car, and has $30,000 salted away in retirement accounts. She had student loans of $40,000, which helped her through graduate school, but their interest rate is so low that her monthly payment is only $98.55. Her monthly after-tax take-home is $4,900 and she tries to save about $500 of that each month. She calls it "something for sammy." She has contributed the maximum allowable amount to both her Roth IRA and 401(K) plan. "I have the bag lady fear," she says, un-expectedly. "I picture me and Roscoe out on the street corner."

Taking Care of Herself

When we talk about Lauren's monthly expenditures it quickly be-comes obvious that she directs her spending disproportionately toward personal care and clothing items. She tells us that she limits her spending on clothes to $200 a month, but when we go over the actual receipts from the past few months, it's clear that she almost always exceeds that amount and often spends three or four times that much on apparel and accessories, especially handbags. Unlike Sarah Montfort, who thinks of a $50 bra as a splurge, Lauren regularly spends $600 to $1,000 per month on clothing and accessories.

In fact, Lauren's whole budget is distorted toward goods and services designed to make her look good and feel attractive. When we point that out to her, she laughs and readily admits the importance of investing in herself. "I believe that your outer appearance is reflective of how you feel inside," she said. "If you spend the time to take care of yourself, then even on your worst days you've got something to smile about. Especially at this point in my life, it feels good to have that."

When I ask what her most important "outer appearance" expen-diture is, she says, without hesitation, "My hair. I'm getting high-lights on Saturday. That'll cost about $250. A trim is $80. I also get a shampoo and a conditioning scalp treatment." In all, Lauren invests about $600 a month on nonapparel personal care items, including a specially formulated skin cream that costs $60 a jar, daily yoga classes, and a pedicure every other week. That total is ten times more than the "average" consumer of similar income would pay. Sarah Mont-fort, with a household income a few hundred dollars higher than Lauren's, spends just $20 a month on personal care services.

It's not unusual for young, single women to spend a dispropor-

LAUREN'S MONTHLY EXPENSES

Item	Spending	Index vs. Average
Income (posttax)	$4,900	1.0
Car	40	0.0
Mortgage/rent	1,000	1.2
Household utilities and maintenance	270	0.5
Eating out	440	1.4
Groceries	100	0.3
Travel and entertainment	370	1.5
Healthcare/personal health	0	0.0
Home goods	80	0.4
Clothing	640	3.4
Charitable contributions	50	0.2
Education	190	1.8
Personal care services	600	10.2
Life insurance	0	0.0
Other expenses	620	6.4
Total spending	4,400	1.1
Net savings/(deficit)	500	0.6

tionate amount of their income on clothing, accessories, and personal appearance. But Lauren's spending seemed high to me; something was missing from my understanding of her value calculus. Plenty of young women get married past thirty and have satisfying family lives. Plenty of women do not get married and lead fulfilling professional lives that bring them enough money to retire in comfort. Where did the bag lady fear come from? I ask her to tell me a little bit about her background.

An Unstable History

The oldest of four children, Lauren was born and raised in St. Louis. Her father was a teacher and the family was "lower-middle-class" according to Lauren, until he left teaching and started his own business. "My mom was a bit of a social climber and my dad was always more involved with my brothers," Lauren said. "I don't think he knows what to do with girls." Her father sold his business in Lauren's senior year of high school and the family's fortunes improved. They moved to a five-bedroom house on two acres of land. But Lauren still needed loans to pay for her graduate school tuition.

As an undergraduate at the University of Mississippi, Lauren was highly social and dated several boys, at least three of whom she refers to as "serious" boyfriends. After graduating with a major in English, she moved back to St. Louis and went to work for an automobile manufacturer, earning about $30,000 a year. There, she reconnected with an old classmate, on whom she had had a crush in sixth grade. "I guess I'd been carrying a fantasy of him for fifteen years," Lauren said. They dated for three years and then he asked her to marry him. "We were engaged for six months but then broke it off," she said. "We weren't in love with each other. He became very boring. He had no pulse. It got claustrophobic." After the breakup, Lauren stopped dating for six months and then had an affair with a married man. "I liked the relationship because he encouraged me to be something and do things," said Lauren. The affair lasted a year until Lauren broke it off. "I told him it wasn't going so well. There were no crazy fireworks."

Then she met Rick, a tall, good-looking guy with sandy blond hair and blue eyes. "I loved Rick more than anyone else," Lauren told us. "He is the smartest man I've ever met. Smart guys are the sexiest thing in the world. They are intriguing and make the journey interesting." Rick was from St. Louis, but was attending law school in Chicago. After a year and a half of long-distance dating, Rick sent Lauren a letter, begging her to move to Chicago and live with him. "I want to be the prince in the fairytale life that you deserve," he wrote. "I won't be truly happy until we're under the same roof. I know that you're scared about coming to Chicago, but I know everything will be wonderful."

Five months after Lauren moved in with Rick, they broke up. "Living together was not good," she said. "It wasn't the same. He was determined to get me here, and once I was here I felt like my stuff was in the way." After the breakup, Lauren dated many other men, some of whom she found interesting, but none of the relationships turned into anything serious or lasting. And, yet, when I asked her about her vision of the future, she said, "I want to have a companion but it doesn't have to be the traditional house, husband, and kids." She does not relish the idea of being alone when she is forty or fifty or sixty years old.

Lauren is insecure and in search of the "perfect" relationship, but she finds it much easier to find men than to keep them, because her criteria for the perfect mate eliminate most of the real men she dates. As a result, she worries that her thirties will be difficult. She looks in the mirror and sees hints of wrinkles to come. A serious change of family fortunes, lack of a father's love, a social-climbing mother, and several failed relationships—isn't that enough instability to make Lauren fear for the future?

Self-Control

Lauren freely admits that she spends much more on goods and services designed to improve her appearance than other people do, but she does not think of herself as a trader-up or as at all profligate in her spending. She thinks of purchasing these items as one of her jobs and tries to carefully weigh every purchase and spend only on those things that her value calculus says are worth it. For example, she makes a list of the clothing items she wants to buy, carefully prioritizes them, and makes a note in her day planner of the sample sales and designers' previews where she may be able to buy what she wants at a discount. This takes time and effort, and she often builds a weekend around store events and special sales. "I'm such a nerd," she says, as she shows us her handwritten budget and a well-organized file folder of receipts.

Lauren is a reader. In addition to the four books she is currently "working," she reads every issue of *Lucky* magazine. "*Lucky* is my bible," she says. "I use the 'yes' and 'maybe' stickers for all the things I want to buy. It's fun. It teaches me things."

Nearly a million people read *Lucky*, Condé Nast's hugely profitable magazine about shopping, fashion, beauty, and lifestyle. Unlike *Cosmopolitan*, *Lucky* runs no articles about relationships or about the ten ways to please a man. It's a picture book, with virtually no editorial content, in which a Web address or customer-service phone number is provided for every item the reader sees. Products featured in *Lucky* often enjoy instant commercial success. Lauren says, "*Lucky* is visually stunning, fun, an escape."

Lauren may be a rocketer in personal care spending, but she's not out of control. Rocketers distort spending in one category over another. They spend much more than you would expect in one area and scrimp and save in several others. You see the phenomenon in our income tables for the individuals in the book with indexed spending compared to "average" households. Lauren is always balancing the fear of becoming a bag lady (by spending too much and having no savings) with the desire to invest in herself (by spending enough so that she feels good and perceives herself attractive to others). Sometimes the two desires come in conflict and she has to make trade-offs. For example, she fell in love with a "very Bollywood, very Bohemian" necklace at Neiman Marcus but decided she could not afford it at $200. She scouted around and found a similar necklace selling for $28 at Marshall Field's and bought it immediately. When money gets tight, she will spread out the highlighting appointments, going at ten- or twelve-week intervals, rather than her normal eight-week cycle.

Lauren also trades down or goes without in categories that she doesn't care about or are not directly related to her self-investment. This is evident in the decoration of her apartment. The shabby-chic décor looks more like what you'd expect to find in the apartment of an early-twenty-something. Almost everything was purchased on sale, was found on the street, or is handmade. Lauren made the cushions for the window reading nook, created the window treatments, and sewed the curtains. She reupholstered the chair she's sitting in and is planning to reupholster the couch as well. She found the TV table in an alley and refinished it. She bought six dining room chairs at Pottery Barn for a total of $250, and the sleigh bed was a floor sample at Ethan Allen.

But the most obvious demonstration of Lauren's cost-cutting strategy is found in her refrigerator. Like Hilda Schmidt with her store room, Lauren is reluctant to let us look in her fridge. When at last she relents, we can't help but laugh at what's inside: four cans of Diet Coke, three bottles of Budweiser, a bottle of mustard, a jar of mayonnaise, a bottle of A1 sauce, and one more Fiji mini. Unlike Hilda, who has stored up enough food to get her family through a month if necessary, Lauren wouldn't last a day on her supply. "I have an aversion to grocery shopping," she said. "There's something very mundane and boring about the shopping cart and buying a month's worth of food. I find no joy in it. I don't like the experience. And I don't like spending the money on it. I'd rather have that money to use somewhere else if I want to, and then scrimp on food." Lauren tries to limit herself to $10 daily for lunch on her own and will often make a meal out of a bag of Cheez-Its or a cup of soup at the 7-Eleven with lots of free crackers.

For all her trading down in food for the fridge, Lauren's fear of being alone and abandoned is a factor in another area of spending distortion: eating and drinking with friends and prospective lovers. She is a trader-up who loves to drink premium Belvedere vodka and will spend $50 to $60 for a dinner, complete with appetizer, entrée, dessert, and a few drinks. "I'd rather spend $100 going out to eat with friends—sharing with people and catching up with them—than I would on the grocery cart. I'd rather have one great meal than eight good ones."

To Lauren, shopping and spending to make herself and her life with friends as rich and distinctive as possible is an art form. That's why she doesn't like grocery shopping and you'll never find her at a deep discounter like Aldi or Dollar General. "They take away from the art in shopping," she said. "They remove the thrill and joy." She never shops in bulk. She loves smaller retailers and limited-edition goods—like a colorful handbag made out of juice boxes—that enable her to show her funky and creative side.

At the end of one of our interviews, I noticed an inscription on the cushy pillow on Lauren's chair: "Too much of a good thing is simply wonderful." It looked to me as if she had stitched the words herself.

The Office Lady: Young and Single in Tokyo

Even though Lauren's value calculus seems very distinct to her, it is only a slightly more mature and complex (and darker) version of the calculus that is typical of the young, single "office ladies" in Japan. These are women, generally under thirty years old, who work in various kinds of offices in Japan's major cities, earn good salaries, and live at home with their parents. They typically pay no rent or utilities and are only responsible for their personal expenses, such as clothing, eating away from home, travel, and entertainment.

But the office ladies we spoke to do have their worries, and the dominating factor in their value calculus is the stress of finding a husband. They are not haunted by gloomy views of the future, as Lauren is, but do feel the tremendous pressure of identifying, attracting, and securing a suitable young man. They are not so worried about putting money aside, because it is the Japanese custom that their future husbands, wherever they may currently be, are attending to the saving of money. In our conversations with Japanese office ladies, the subject of retirement accounts does not come up. As a result, office ladies are amazing traders-up, and will distort their incomes with great ferocity toward high-fashion items such as handbags, sunglasses, watches, and other personal adornments and accessories. But they will also go without. They simply do not participate in many categories—including autos, home goods, and electronics. And, like Lauren, they will trade down in many categories, particularly food at home.

Masako Tanaka is an office lady, twenty-six years old, who lives with her parents outside Tokyo. She graduated from Tokyo University, where she studied English literature, when she was twenty-three. She works for an asset management firm, providing administrative support to two managers. She earns the equivalent of about $54,000 a year, and takes home about $4,500 a month.

MASAKO TANAKA'S ASSETS		HER LIABILITIES	
Savings account	$8,000	Mortgage	$0
Checking account	$1,500	Home equity	$0
Investments	$0	Credit card	$0
Home value	$0	Student loans	$0
Other	$0	Other	$0

Masako does not really follow a budget or attempt to keep track of her spending. "I try not to go over $1,000 a month," she says. "That includes eating out, going out with friends, buying groceries, and paying for the cell phone. I just withdraw $1,000 in cash from my account at the beginning of each month. Then I always know where I stand by looking at the cash in my wallet." But the $1,000 rarely lasts the entire month and she usually ends up spending $1,300 to $1,500 each month in cash. Masako has no debt and has savings of about $9,500, most of it in a savings account.

If, toward the end of the month, she runs low on cash, Masako is more likely to go without than to trade down. "I just won't call my friends to go out. But, if they call me, I'll still go out, even though it costs $50 to $100 every time. That's quite a bit of money, but I'm very social and going out is important to me." Going out with friends is

MASAKO'S MONTHLY EXPENSES		
Item	Spending	Index vs. Average
Income (posttax)	$3,290	1.0
Car	230	0.4
Mortgage/rent	0	0
Household utilities and maintenance	0	0
Eating out	400	1.9
Groceries	370	1.8
Travel and entertainment	360	2.2
Healthcare/personal health	130	0.9
Home goods	80	0.6
Clothing	670	5.3
Charitable contributions	0	0
Education	40	0.6
Personal care services	140	3.6
Life insurance	50	1.5
Other expenses	40	0.6
Total spending	2,510	0.9
Net savings/(deficit)	780	1.5

important enough to her calculus that she will skip lunch for herself or save money on DVD rentals.

In addition to her cash expenditures, Masako uses her credit card to pay for large-ticket items, particularly clothing and jewelry, and she spends at least $1,000 per month on such goods. She tracks her credit card purchases online and, when she gets close to $1,000, she stops buying.

For Masako, the physical and emotional experience of shopping is as important a factor in the value calculus as the product itself. "Shopping is one of the ways I have to release my stress. I like shopping. It's very stimulating." She is very brand conscious and values high-fashion brands like Gucci, Prada, and Chanel. She spends five times the amount that the average Japanese consumer spends on clothing, but she does not consider her buying habits to be extravagant. "The four seasons are separate and you need different clothes for each one. I don't want to look too fashionable, but I always want to look neat and decent."

Now and again, however, Masako will splurge, especially when her stress level is high. She loves gold jewelry and, three or four times a year, will spend $100 or more on a pair of earrings, a nice ring, or a necklace. Her most memorable purchase was an antique watch that cost $1,000. "I bought it because I needed a watch and this one felt special to me. It makes me feel great when I wear it."

When we ask Masako if she has ever made a purchase she regrets, she thinks for a moment and says, "No. I really haven't bought anything I regret. I'm usually very careful with my purchases."

Whatever is left over after cash expenses and clothing purchases goes into Masako's short-term savings account. She will often dip into it, however, especially for travel. "I love traveling overseas and take at least one or two trips per year," she says. For Masako, travel is a form of questing, a way to try new things and push her limits. "It's very stimulating and not something you can experience in Japan," she says. "Just by walking you see different things." Travel is also a form of connection, because she usually travels with friends. She has visited the United States, Mexico, Taiwan, Indonesia, Thailand, France, and London. "I feel like I can do these trips because I live at home and don't have other expenses."

Masako, like many Japanese travelers, also thinks of travel as a way to buy goods that are not available at home or that sell for much less than they would in Tokyo's department stores. In Korea, for example, she bought two pairs of shoes for $35 a pair that would have cost at least $100 a pair in Japan. "I felt fantastic for finding such a great deal! This is another reason I like to travel overseas—you can find amazing bargains."

But Masako admits that, even when she is out with friends or traveling overseas, she is always thinking about marriage. "I'm only twenty-six years old," she says. "But on the other hand I'm already twenty-six years old." In Tokyo, women are generally married by the time they're twenty-six and Masako has watched with concern as many of her friends have gotten married and had children. "I wish I had a boyfriend," she says. "What if I can't find a partner I can marry? This worries me."

Recently, Masako has been trying to save a little more money for the future. "I hope to get married by the time I'm thirty. For me, the good life would be to have two kids. One kid would be lonely, and it's economically difficult to bring up three kids in Tokyo. I just want a family where everyone is healthy and happy." The money she puts aside would go to the apartment Masako might share with her future husband. "Usually the man pays for the apartment. But I don't think it's fair for him to pay for all of it, which is why I'm saving a little." She also dreams of having a house in France one day. "Although I know that's impossible."

Masako and Lauren may seem to fit a single stereotype—the young, single woman who is focused on her personal appearance, preoccupied with relationships, and highly social. But, although they may have similar concerns, it would be a mistake to characterize them simply as "female singles, 18–34." Masako's value calculus is driven primarily by hope, Lauren's primarily by fear. These are value factors that cannot be easily quantified or plugged into a spreadsheet. The maker or retailer of consumer goods must learn to understand them both intellectually and intuitively.

A New Value Calculus at Bath & Body Works

That ability is precisely what is driving the success of Neil Fiske, chief executive officer of Bath & Body Works (BBW).* For more than a decade, Bath & Body Works has been selling, with great suc-

---

*Neil is a former partner at BCG and was my co-author in writing the book that preceded this one, *Trading Up: The New American Luxury.*

cess, midprice body and personal care products for women who want bright colors and intense fragrances. The BBW "look" was cheerful and wholesome, if a little superficial and unsubtle. It was a "farmstand from the heartland," as the company described it, brimming over with fruit- and flower-scented soaps, creams, lotions, scrubs, oils, butters, and gels, not to mention scented candles and other home accessories.

Founded in 1990, Bath & Body Works (part of The Limited Group) had been positioned as a masstige brand, offering its own-brand products at a premium to drug store brands but below the price of the big designer names. Leslie Wexner, founder of The Limited, invented BBW based on a hunch that women wanted to shop for moderately priced health and beauty products—a step above the drug store, a step below the department store. For millions of women, BBW products fit neatly into their personal value calculus, delivering a combination of wholesomeness, effectiveness, and personal indulgence, at a price that was high enough to be exciting but not so high as to be unaffordable, even on a middle-class income.

Wexner invented "Kate," the fictional proprietor of BBW. According to the invented story, Kate was raised on a farm in Ohio, and started making candles and fragrance products based on the crops grown on her family farm. She expanded the business, but continued to pay rigorous attention to detail and provided her customers with good value and honest products. Wexner believes that all successes in retail start with a story—an inventor who lives the brand lifestyle, oversees every detail of production and design, and moves the brand to reflect his or her taste and aspirations. He believes this character defines the brand and makes it possible to capture the emotional energy of every associate. "Good retailing starts with good storytelling," he says. "Everyone in the enterprise has their role and their scripted parts."

Bath & Body Works became one of the most successful specialty retail concepts in the world, growing from fifteen stores in 1990 to more than 1,300 in 2000. And, from 1993 to 2000, the company achieved an astounding compound annual growth rate (CAGR) of 51 percent, soaring to nearly $2 billion in annual revenue. BBW had a huge customer base and the consumers represented a remarkably broad set of demographics. Girls of ten loved BBW, as did women of seventy. Household incomes were as low as $35,000 and as high as $250,000. About thirty-five million women visit a BBW store every year.

By the year 2000, however, the company's growth began to slow. In the previous few years the market had changed. Competing retailers such as Sephora, Aveda, and Origins expanded into malls throughout the country—including BBW's heartland—offering new technical benefits to the consumer, particularly all-natural and organic compounds, a wider range of sophisticated shades and colorings, more complex fragrances based on exotic herbs and spices as well as florals and fruits, and more innovative and distinctive packaging. Their stores were cool, well organized, and carefully lit, with well–thought-through traffic flow and signature music always playing. They looked like a cross between a department store fragrance department, a European boutique, and a science lab. They offered a wide selection of their own-brand products. Some of them, such as Sephora, stocked other brands, as well. Just as important, these retailers surrounded their products with a different story of beauty. It wove together elements of science, design, fitness, relaxation, psychology, celebrity, and traditional arts like aromatherapy into an appealing narrative of beauty and health. These were not cosmetics shops; they were partners in a beautiful lifestyle. Consumers liked the experience of the new stores. They were willing to pay a premium for goods that took them up a step on the ladder of benefits.

More and more of BBW's customers were going to these new outlets for their beauty needs. They traded up to more expensive brands, especially for facial creams and makeup, and traded down to less expensive retail brands for body lotions, soaps, and accessories. They also "traded over," which means they were buying goods very similar to BBW's offerings at other locations, such as department stores, just because they didn't want to make an extra trip. Beauty consumers like one-stop shopping and will go where they can get it.

BBW sales flagged, dropping 19 percent from 2000 to 2002. Not only were the new trading-up brands stealing share, the trading-down mass retailers, especially Target, were nipping at BBW's heels from the low end, offering products of similar quality and appeal at lower prices, and with a more sophisticated image. Bath & Body Works was in danger of being caught in the middle. The BBW consumer base was slowly eroding—fewer visits, fewer purchases per visit.

A Chance to Apply the Ideas of Trading Up

In 2003, Neil Fiske accepted an offer he couldn't refuse: to leave his post as a partner at The Boston Consulting Group and become CEO of BBW. As Neil puts it, "Les Wexner said to me, 'We've been working together for a long time. People are talking about trading up. Here's your chance.' I was very happy at BCG. I had learned a lot, and we were having fun, but I really thought that this was an opportunity of a lifetime to put theory into practice and to see if we couldn't turn it around and make it better."

Neil's charge was to find a new way forward for the company and, in particular, to apply some of the ideas we had presented in *Trading Up*. Working in collaboration with Wexner and a team of executives whom Neil calls co-leaders, and with the counsel of Len Schlesinger, COO and vice chairman of Limited Brands (and a former Harvard Business School professor), Neil set about transforming almost every aspect of the Bath & Body Works business—including product sourcing, packaging, merchandising, training, and service.

Neil knew that BBW was in a tough situation, but he didn't realize quite how precarious and fragile a business he was inheriting. Neil identified five critical hurdles. "First, Bath & Body Works had an incredible customer base, fifty-five million people, but it was splitting in half," Neil told me. "Second, the emotional equities of the brand were slipping. No longer was Bath & Body Works seen as distinctive, special, a 'brand for me.' That became very clear with the long-running conversations that we've had with the customers in the store. Third, Sephora, Aveda, and better department store brands out-flanked our position and took our commercial space. And the mass brands started to get better at an alarmingly rapid rate, including product that knocked off BBW at Target and Wal-Mart. Fourth, to counteract the slowing sales, the BBW stores relied more and more on promotions, sales, and discounts—and they had become rampant throughout the stores. In 2002, during our critical holiday time period," Neil said, "there were twenty-two in-store deals at Bath & Body Works. It was like a garage sale with deal signs all over." Finally, and perhaps most important, the Bath & Body Works brand was no longer distinctive and relevant enough to make it into the customer's "inner circle" of brands, as Neil calls it—that handful of brands that the consumer holds particularly dear and close.

As a result of all these factors, the Bath & Body Works brand was stale, reliant on promotions, and delivering ordinary product at higher than market prices. "In specialty retail, there is a life cycle of a brand concept that is seven to ten years, and then it needs retrofitting," Neil said. "Sometimes it needs a little bit of reinvention, sometimes it needs a lot of reinvention. Bath & Body Works was a brand that needed fundamental redefinition. What does the brand stand for? What is the proposition? What's the imagery? What's the marketing? What's the collateral? What's the product? We needed a reinvention as successful as the one at Banana Republic in the 1980s. The Banana Republic brand had been about tropical clothing, safaris, and Jeeps in the windows. Somehow they took that brand of safaris and Jeeps and migrated it to upscale men's and women's clothing—and they did it fast and created a totally new image."

By the numbers, Bath & Body Works hardly seemed to be in trouble. "With the exception of the deals that were proliferating," said Neil, "none of these signs was evident yet in the financials of the company. It was still growing. It was highly productive. The margins were rich. And the attitude continued to be, 'We were the most successful specialty brand ever launched. What do you mean, we're losing our personal connection? What do you mean, our customers are trading up to other brands?' There was a lot of denial and a lot of 'wait till next season.' 'What do you mean, we are no longer special and distinctive enough to be in the inner circle?' There was a fundamental disbelief that something was wrong. That is, with the exception of Les Wexner, who had, thankfully, enough distance from the brand itself to see the pattern."

Then came the bad news. "November of 2000 was a peak month for Bath & Body Works in terms of profitability," said Neil. "The year 2000 was, in fact, the best year that we ever had. In 2001, the bottom fell out. For the next two-plus years, the transaction base of the brand eroded by almost 40 percent. We lost 40 percent of our pretax income in a two-year timeframe. That's how quickly the forces of trading up and trading down can help to build a brand and then just take it away."

Inner vs. Outer Beauty

The value calculus, as it relates to beauty products, had changed. "Bath & Body Works had been focusing on 'fun and fragrance,'" Neil said. "Surface treatments. Specific solutions for particular needs." He and his team began to explore the current thinking about women's health and beauty. "We were most influenced by the scientific evidence that suggests that the women who age most beautifully are those who take care of their inner spirits first and their outer beauty second."

Fear of aging and the desire to look eternally young have always been dominant factors in the value calculus when it comes to beauty products. But the original Bath & Body Works solution had been to cover up the age and present a veneer of youth. "We now approach beauty as the result of how you feel and how you live. The result is how you look," said Neil. "How you feel comes from how well you sleep, a happy and fulfilling day, your essential spirit. How you live is determined by your home, your rituals, your moments of relaxation. We have moved away from 'fragrance and fun,' which is all about creams and topical applications, to a focus on inner *and* outer beauty. There's real science behind our conclusion that the women who age most beautifully are those who take care of their inner spirits first and their outer beauty second."

The change in the brand had to begin with the technical, functional, and emotional benefits of the products themselves. But, while the brand had been building its strong emotional position with customers, it had fundamentally lost its differentiation on these technical and functional benefits. "We had to get back to the basics," Neil said. "I went through the product portfolio and said, 'Are these products good enough to support and create my strategy? Do they have technical advantages? Do they have functional advantages?'"

In *Trading Up*, we wrote about the guiding principle of Ely Callaway, founder of Callaway Golf: that every product should be Demonstrably Superior and Pleasingly Different. "That turned out to be a great mantra for Bath & Body Works," Neil said. "Because what it says is that every product we've already got has to have some attributes that we can find where it's better than the competition. We're going to test it with consumer research, we're going to test it in the market, and we're going to make sure that on that dimension we have the best products. And they can't just be 'Demonstrably Superior'; they also have to be 'Pleasingly Different.' They have to be a joy to use. They have to engage all five senses. That requires thinking about quality in a fundamentally different way than we had been."

And, while going back to basics on the technical and functional differences, the emotional benefits had to be adjusted to fit the new value calculus, the search for a balanced life. "Women, whether they're married or single, working or staying at home, are trying to figure out how to spend enough time taking care of their own physical and emotional needs and also devote enough time and energy to people they love and care about," Neil said. "Women are involved in so many activities, and there are so many demands on their time, it's very easy for life to get out of balance. Women can forget to take enough time for themselves. Or they can become obsessed with their own health and beauty routines and neglect others. Our products are about the 'taking care of me' impulse, but also about 'connecting' with others— by looking and feeling your best. Those are both very important emotional spaces." That's why BBW will participate more in the ritual of sleep, encouraging women to take a bath in a lavender and Dead Sea salt soak, misting a pillow with fragrance, and using topical applications of aromatherapeutic products. Personal care products from Bath & Body Works and other providers also have an element of questing to them. Women like to change the environmental feel and fragrance of their living spaces periodically. "We wanted to give women more opportunity to refresh their environments and experiment with new colors and scents, looks, and arrangements," said Neil.

Attacking Like an Outsider

Neil decided that the reinvention of the brand would be difficult to achieve with only BBW internal capability, and certainly not within the time he wanted to achieve it. "How do you take this organization that's existed the same way for twelve years and try to teach it how to do trading up? You can't. It's not in their realm of understanding," Neil said. "But you can't change everything. So I decided to pick a single area of focus on the belief that if I proved the theory to the organization, they would come around, and they would start to see how to do business in a different way."

For this test-case product, Neil decided to bypass the internal design group at Bath & Body Works, and hire an outside team instead.

"The designers had to have the sensibility and the vision and be un-constrained by the way we'd always been doing business," Neil said. "That was kind of scary to some people. But one of the fundamental principles for succeeding in this market is to attack the category like an outsider."

Neil and his team decided to focus on the premium candle business—a trading-up move. In the market, scented candles sell for as much as $50 and, at the low end, go for as little as $8 (with, of course, some superpremium candles selling for as much as $200 and some votives going for as little as $1.69). Bath & Body Works had been selling its scented candles in the low end of the masstige segment, at around $12.50. "We said, 'We're going to have candles with a higher price than everybody else, except the most exclusive ones on offer. To do that, you have to think about where to make the investment in the technical and functional differences. One fragrance we considered, for example, would have cost about $25 per candle, up from the fifty cents we were used to paying." In addition to fragrances, Neil and his team explored different kinds of waxes and a variety of sophisticated packaging options.

BBW's fig-scented candle was launched in September 2003 at $25. "We humbly called it the 'World's Best Candle,'" said Neil. "It became a mantra for the organization. 'We are going to be the best in the categories that we choose to compete in.' At $25, we can create the best candle in the world. And that's kind of a remarkable idea. Most Americans can't afford the best car in the world; most Americans can't afford the best house in the world; but most Americans can afford the best candle in the world."

The candle was initially made available only at Henri Bendel, the New York boutique that is also a part of Limited Brands. "We launched selectively," said Neil. "We placed it with the very best customers in the world. We had Cher, Goldie Hawn, and all of these celebrities coming in and buying these candles. It just took on a life of its own.

Of course, we didn't make nearly enough of them, so we were sold out and scarcely got it placed back into the stores. It was on eBay. We sold a lot of them, and we made a fair amount of money." *The New York Times* did a feature story on the candle, calling it, "the only must-have item of the holiday season."

According to Neil, the most important impact of the success of the world's greatest fig-scented candle was the motivational impact in the organization. "We had been trying to get PR for our products for years. Nothing like this had ever happened at Bath & Body Works, and people were shocked. And it really started to change the quality of work they were doing."

More Partners

Buoyed by the success of the premium candle, BBW started looking for other concepts and partners to help create them. "Great brands are about things that you believe in with great intensity," Neil said. "We can't replicate that on the inside of the company, but we can partner with people who have it."

Neil conferred with a variety of experts, including health specialists like Dr. Pamela Peeke and Dr. Tieraona Low Dog. Dr. Peeke helped BBW think about the role of women and how they balance their own needs with those of their family and friends. Neil and his team also spoke at length with dozens of consumers. "Our best customers told us two important things, both of which supported what the experts were telling us, and what we believed from our own experience and analysis." First, the customers said they wanted more from Bath & Body Works. They wanted products that were affordable enough so that the women could treat themselves to a beauty experience every day, not just on special occasions. Second, the customers agreed that beauty was not just about self-indulgence and self-care. It's about connecting with others. "These women like to connect through beauty," said Neil. "Women like to give our products to each other. They have beauty parties. In a world where those kinds of connections are fraying, that ability to form human bonds, to take care of yourself and of others is more important than ever."

One of the first partnerships was with Ian Ginsberg of C.O. Bigelow, and resulted in the idea of the "modern apothecary." Neil explained, "The apothecary is a place to go for healing and restoration and caring. The idea of the apothecary is that you connect with the apothecarist on a one-on-one basis. The customer knows him. He knows the customer. In a store that presents itself as an apothecary, we can offer brands that do different things and have very distinct positions. That's a sharp contrast to where BBW has been historically, where the store offered a single brand and it was pretty much one size fits all." The C.O. Bigelow product line was first rolled out within 1,600 BBW units and then in a pilot standalone store in the Easton Town Center in Columbus, Ohio. The company expects the store to grow into its own, freestanding chain. At first, Ginsberg was nervous about the partnership with Limited Brands, but he has come to see that the partnership adds value to his brand, dramatically increases distribution of his product, and offers great potential for growth.

The Bigelow partnership was the first of many. BBW has also developed a line of products with L'Occitane, the well-known French retailer of personal care goods. Called Le Couvent des Minimes, it is a collection of bath and body products inspired by the materials, colors, scents, and values of Provence. Other partners include Goldie (a small producer of color cosmetics), American Girl (makers of educational dolls, books, and accessories), and Canyon Ranch (the spa services company).

Because there are so many purchasing patterns and mosaics of personal behavior, especially when it comes to beauty products for women, BBW is also working to broaden its offering of brands. Shoppers can now purchase many non-BBW brands in the stores, including Molton Brown and L'Oréal, transforming the company from an exclusive own-brand store to a multidimensional third-party retailer. Bath & Body Works is taking on aspects of the bazaar—an unpredictable marketplace that brings together all kinds of offerings at many price points to appeal to a wide variety of consumers while still retaining unifying elements of the brand.

As a result of these efforts, Bath & Body Works has a broader portfolio than ever before, with goods that sell at a much wider range of price points. "We offer quality, innovation, individuality, and tremendous emotional content, at prices that most women can afford. Our goal now is to keep our core customers, add new ones, and entice them all to increase the size of the basket when they visit a BBW store."

In late 2005, BBW opened a C.O. Bigelow shop in Chicago's Water Tower Place and it provides a preview of how the chain will evolve. The 3,500–square-foot store, in one of Chicago's prime shopping areas, is a one-stop shop for skin and body care, beauty, and a variety of health, wellness, and beauty accompaniments. Within the sleek design is displayed an abundance of product—thousands of SKUs from BBW's many suppliers, including C.O. Bigelow—without the store seeming overstuffed or overdone. Three other Bigelow stores are now operating, with more in the planning stage.

By defining beauty holistically, Bath & Body Works gave itself a much broader field to play in. In addition to its core offerings of makeup, skin care, fragrance, and body care, the company could expand into health and wellness products and services, including spa treatments and spa products, yoga, and exercise. "When analysts look at the beauty business, they usually estimate its size at about a $35 billion or $40 billion business," Neil said. "But if you redefine the business as being about inner and outer beauty, it's much bigger. We estimate it at more than $120 billion. And we want Bath & Body Works to be the category killer. We think we can grow from $2 billion, where we are now, to more than $6 billion or so in five years."

Defined that way, it's easy to see that the beauty business is booming. There were nine million cosmetic procedures performed in the United States in 2003. Botox and surgical procedures have risen by

32 percent since 1993. The number of health clubs has grown from twelve thousand in 1993 to twenty-two thousand in 2003. Vitamins, minerals, and dietary supplements are now a $12 billion business and growing at 18 percent per year. Spas are also a $12 billion industry and growing at 23 percent per year. Some fifteen million Americans practice yoga, up 30 percent since 2002. American women are into the idea of holistic health and pursue it in a wide variety of ways.

So far, the reports on BBW are encouraging. One financial analyst wrote,

> The BBW division wins our "Most Amazing Transformation" award. Arguably one year late, but easily the most innovative and improved personal care store we have ever seen. The traditional BBW incarnation reveals a "Hallmark meets Heartland" image. It's a frenetic space, with a mass of products stacked cheap and deep, many placed inside red tablecloth-lined barrels and crates. The new prototype store takes a completely opposite tack, employing a residential design with a modern twist which we call "Waterworks meets Canyon Ranch." The store lays out in multi-lifestyle spaces, with sounds and fragrances unique to each room. White-board walls and clean fixturing portray an upscale "21st Century Apothecary" image. The Spa line, launching for the Holiday season, could help invigorate the business . . . [and] evokes a sense of health and well-being, on a par matched only by some of the more upscale brands. Not only do the stores look visually strong, the assortments seem to us an enormous improvement over past years. The aromatherapy space is not just visually stunning, the products themselves are upscale and authoritative. The accessories are a major improvement and the price points are more varied than in the past. In summary, Limited Brands is transforming the Bath & Body Works

brand. The new store is more upscale, modern, sensual, natural, and interactive.

Not bad. When Neil started at BBW, the business seemed to be in an inexorable decline, with company store sales down 20 percent. The company was losing money in a significant number of its stores. Since Neil joined in the first quarter of 2003, BBW has posted year-on-year earnings growth in eight of the subsequent nine quarters, with earnings at a rate of 16 percent operating profit. Neil says the company is about a third of the way through with this initial journey of change, and on its way to becoming the $4 billion category killer he envisions.

And there appears to be substantial upside for sensory experience providers like BBW. Currently, only 52 percent of women take an "extralong, indulgent" shower once a week or more. Only 28 percent of women take a bath once a week or more. Only 53 percent of women moisturize their body daily. Only 55 percent moisturize their feet. The universal wants include "more time for me," "less stress," "look beautiful," and "feel beautiful."

Unfortunately, BBW, for all its aspiration, can't provide the consumer with more time.

Risks of Reinvention

There are always risks in reinvention and attempting to shift a brand toward an evolving value calculus. For example, it may be that bringing in distinctive partners such as C.O. Bigelow and L'Occitane will not pull Bath & Body Works out of the middle, but will rather plunge the partners into it. Although the Bigelow products are genuine and the brand is venerable (it claims to be "the Oldest Apothecary in America"), the products may seem out of place in the context of a Bath & Body Works store, as if the store is simply copying other venerable "apothecary" brands such as Kiehl's. The gravitational pull of the middle is very strong. Even when a product offers real technical differences, they may not be enough to produce an emotional result, especially in retail surroundings the producer can't control. But Neil believes that the brands will appeal to a wide range of women (and men, as well) and bring in new consumers who are looking for apothecary solutions at affordable prices.

What's more, the move toward third-party retailing may put Bath & Body Works in greater competition with discounters and big-box retailers, which also offer a wide range of brands and products. Neil does not worry about that. "Discount retailers allow consumers to cut back in the categories of spending that are unimportant to them emotionally," he said, "so they have more money to spend on products that help them take care of themselves and connect with their friends, family, and lovers."

It may also be that some customers will question the Bath & Body Works commitment to inner beauty. Outer beauty is a much more straightforward and tangible concept, and the emotional content is far less subtle and individualized. Inner beauty enters into the realms of psychology, mythology, and spirituality. Women may take some time to trust that a store known for fruity fragrances, seasonal colors, and a heartland sensibility can really deliver the promise of holistic health and inner beauty.

"We are in the middle of a multiyear process, a transformation, a work in progress," Neil says. "We have already moved beyond simply fragrance and are starting to see results in the inner/outer beauty story. We are seeing that consumers want rituals, interruptions in the day, that help them to feel more beautiful and enjoy their lives more fully. It's a change that takes time for both consumers and sales associates to understand and embrace."

Infallibility

Some readers may be reading the Bath & Body Works story and saying, "The value calculus may apply to women and personal care products, but does it apply to a broader demographic or a wider range of goods and services?"

The answer is yes. The challenge comes when a company seeks to change in order to accommodate new factors. The value calculation is so instinctual and unerringly right and has so much to do with emotions and instincts, there is plenty of room for the retailer to misinterpret and go wrong.

Think about Sarah and Rick Montfort, the couple who moved for better schools and now live on a very tight household budget. You could argue that Rick is a profligate spender—given the household income—on his hobbies of poker, computers, and golf. We know that the Montfort household income is seriously distorted in those categories. But, according to Rick's value calculus, the balance is right. He is the sole wage earner in the family. He gets one week of vacation per year. He works two or three additional jobs in order to boost the family income. He brings in a very respectable annual income of $85,000. If he spends about $500 a month on his pleasures—$6,000 a year, or about 7 percent of the gross—that fits his value calculus. He's not jeopardizing the well-being of the family. In fact, he's contributing to the well-being of the family by taking care of himself. Poker and golf are ways for Rick to make connections with friends, just as the Bath & Body Works consumers spend on personal care items to share with their friends. Many consumers see such expenditures not as personal self-indulgence but as ways to facilitate connecting. Rick thinks he has the balance right.

What's more, and this is a little strange, Rick's spending does not throw Sarah's value calculus out of whack. The monthly amount he spends on leisure activities may seem a little high to her, but not dangerously so. After all, they have no credit card debt. Their house is appreciating in value. They have a $110,000 investment portfolio. Rick works very hard and is a faithful husband and loving parent. Sarah values family above all, and if Rick's indulgences help to keep the family happy and together, then they're okay. Besides, Rick's trading up gives Sarah a little bit of cover for her own occasional indulgence. If he's spending $100 or more a week on poker and golf, how can he begrudge her an occasional $50 Victoria's Secret bra and lunch out with friends? He can't. And he doesn't.

You could also argue that Sarah makes a fetish of her thriftiness. She made the decision to be a stay-at-home mom and pursue bargains and deals with an almost religious fervor. But does it really make sense for her to drive all the way across town to save a few pennies on a pound of chicken? Doesn't that actually cost more in gas than she will save on the chicken? Doesn't it add wear and tear on Sarah and the kids? All I can say is that it makes sense to Sarah's value calculus.

"I try hard to find values that allow us to make ends meet," Sarah says. "It's a struggle, but we're getting by. And we have lots of love."

7.

IN A PICKLE

When Jim Cantalupo became CEO of McDonald's in late 2002, the cracks in the company's foundation were already visible. Same-store sales were down. Franchisees, who were used to earning $250,000 or more per year, were being squeezed by cost increases they could not pass along to consumers. The number of customer visits had declined. Competition came from traditional competitors and a myriad of newcomers. There are few barriers to entry in the fast-food industry. Virtually anybody with a "concept" and a few hundred thousand dollars to invest can open a fast-food shop with either a generic specialty—burgers, soup, salad, pizza, chicken, dogs, waffles, fish, potatoes, ribs—or an international basis, including Mexican, Caribbean, Chinese, Japanese, Thai, Korean, Greek, Indian, Middle Eastern, Vietnamese, and more.

McDonald's had experienced a fantastic climb to the top of the fast-food industry and $40 billion in annual sales. Ray Kroc opened his first store on April 15, 1955, in Des Plaines, Illinois. For forty-five years, growth was heady. The world's appetite for hot, delicious, salty french fries seemed never-ending. The original menu of simple hamburgers, milk shakes, and fries created an army of franchise millionaires. Most of us can remember in great detail the first time we went to a McDonald's restaurant. We can remember who we were with, what were the circumstances, and how it felt to be there and chow down on a Big Mac or an order of Chicken McNuggets. Unfortunately, as the chain grew, it lost its specialness.

Cantalupo had served McDonald's for twenty-eight years, mostly in international markets, first in Europe, then in Asia and South America. He was an unabashed McDonald's cheerleader—a man who liked to say he had "ketchup in his veins"—but in a tough-minded and serious way. A man of medium stature and mild appearance, he liked to stab his fingers toward the person he was talking to, as if to drive home his points.

When the McDonald's board tapped him to resuscitate the company, he had been happily retired for a year, serving on corporate boards and enjoying life. "But when they called, I knew I had to help," he told me shortly after he accepted the assignment. "Besides, my share values had sunk so low that I practically had to go back to work." Cantalupo took the top job with some trepidation, however, because he knew that McDonald's had lost its momentum and that too many customers were saying to their friends and family members, "Let's try something else for lunch."

One reason for the disaffection with McDonald's was obvious. In an effort to improve profitability as costs spiraled upward, many franchises had cut back on service, training, cleanup, and speed of food rotation. By 2002, in consumer surveys, McDonald's ranked the lowest of the major fast-food companies in product quality and restaurant experience.

Any company, like McDonald's, that achieves significant success and becomes a leader in the trading-down market will inevitably be challenged in one of two ways. A smart, aggressive competitor will begin to steal business by offering more value at the same or a lower price point. Or the leader will fail to respond to changing consumer needs, its products will lose relevance, and new types of competitors will begin nibbling at share. Retail is a particularly primal form of business competition. Success breeds imitation. Competitors can easily attack the leader on price. The leader is generally slow to respond.

When Cantalupo returned as CEO, McDonald's had been facing this unsettling set of issues for at least three years. While McDonald's share and customer satisfaction ratings had been slipping, Wendy's had achieved market share growth for seven straight years, with a 7.2 percent increase in sales in 2000 over the year before. And Jack in the Box, although a $2 billion company with just over 4 percent market share, had boosted its sales by more than 10 percent.

McDonald's still sat at the top of the quick-service restaurant (QSR) heap, commanding more than 40 percent of the market. But according to Technomic, the restaurant industry share gauge, McDonald's share had remained "dead even" with the prior year, despite a 3 percent rise in sales. Burger King, McD's closest competitor, had lost sales and share and its perennial position as number two in the burger battle now translated to 18 percent market share.

Over the next two years, things continued to get worse for McDonald's. Average sales per restaurant peaked at $1.6 million in 2000 and then stalled and refused to budge. In 2001, Subway surpassed McDonald's as the fast-food chain with the most outlets in the United States. McDonald's share price continued to fall, dropping to around $13 in 2002, 40 percent lower than its trading price five years earlier. In the first quarter of 2002, the company also reported the first quarterly loss ($343.8 million) in its 47-year history. In 2002, 126 franchisees left the system, 68 of whom were forced out for poor performance. The rest left voluntarily, seeking greater growth potential and higher profits elsewhere.

How can a trading-down leader—usually a large, established, and often slow-moving company—respond to such threats? Is it true that, once it begins to lose share, it's too late to recover? Must it accept that it will never recapture the glory days of dizzying growth? Must it learn to live with declining market share and find ways to explain it away? Must it ready itself for cost cutting and discounting?

No. It must gird itself for reinvention and revitalization. That's the only way out of the pickle. And that's just what Jim Cantalupo intended to do.

He knew that McDonald's was a company squeezed by competition and ruled by its franchisees. The franchisees found it easier to manage their individual stores to a profit target (by which they could calculate their take-home income) than to a store or company growth target. It was easier for the franchisee to inch prices up, cut back on a cleaning crew, or deliver slightly slower service than to invest. When it became obvious—well before Cantalupo came in—that the middle-aged chain needed to go on a program of renovation, there had been resistance to the idea at headquarters, in the field, and in the restaurants. To get the company to change, a burning case would have to be made for it by an impassioned leader, and the board believed that Cantalupo was the perfect man to lead the charge.

Time was not on his side. When retailers go into a tailspin, as McDonald's had, they often spiral downward, with the speed of the fall increasing exponentially. Loss of volume causes further cuts in service and investment that cause another round of decline. Consumers will tolerate only one or two failures before they take their business to your competitors. Demoralized franchisees rarely invest the time or the incremental cash to fix the problems. There are too many opportunities elsewhere.

Understand the New Consumer Needs

The first task in the revitalization process is to determine what's really going on with the consumers. What are they doing? What are their needs? Whom do they like and why? And how do they think of your products and services in comparison to those of your competitor?

For years, McDonald's had been blaming its slowing growth rate on a variety of factors, many of them external and, supposedly, beyond the company's control. McDonald's execs had cited the strong U.S. dollar, mad cow disease and hoof-and-mouth scares, and the saturated U.S. fast-food market. But, much more important than any of those factors, consumer needs had fundamentally changed and McDonald's had failed to respond to the new calculus.

It is not difficult to determine what drives the consumer. Top on the list of the tools of discovery is the shop-along or, in the case of McDonald's, the eat-along. This fundamental activity requires going along with real consumers to eat real meals in real restaurants. No focus groups or test kitchens or observation through one-way glass. The observer, who should ideally be a company executive, drives to the restaurant with the consumer, orders with the consumer, eats the meal with the consumer, and talks with the consumer about all aspects of the experience. If the food is consumed in a minivan with three screaming children in the back seat, that's where the research has to take place.

You would be surprised how many executives of large companies (especially those in "pickles") have never experienced their product or service as their consumers experience it. This simplest of acts—joining the people who use your product in the process of consumption— usually delivers the most powerful insights and the clearest, most gut-felt imperatives for action. Eat-alongs provide key information that enable you to make a number of important analyses.

Define the Experience Train

Fast-food eaters are not fools, nor are they desperate. They're hungry and knowledgeable about their options. They approach the quick-service restaurant with relatively low expectations for meal quality, service, and environment, but that does not mean they have no expectations at all. Nor does it mean that they don't have varying expectations of different QSRs. McDonald's, as the largest fast-food chain, with the best-known brand name, is held to a slightly higher standard than its rivals. To define and understand these expectations, it is necessary to break the experience down into its component parts. (This exercise pertains to any consumer experience, not just the consumption of fast food, although each experience will be different.)

Here's what the consumer is looking for in a visit to a fast-food store:

1. *Entry.* A sense of welcome. An environment that both looks and smells clean.
2. *Waiting.* It should be easy to see who is in line to order, who is in line to pick up an order, who is not in line, and the length of each individual line.
3. *Crew engagement.* Are the order taker, manager, and order delivery person able and willing to engage with the consumer even in minor ways—with a greeting, a smile, or an exchange of information about the order?
4. *Flexibility.* McDonald's consumers arrive at the restaurant with varying amounts of money in their pockets and, since many McDonald's stores don't take credit cards and many people don't carry them anyway, consumers want enough menu choices and price options to be able to align their hunger with their ready cash.
5. *Order accuracy.* McDonald's customers have learned that it's wise to check the items in the bags before leaving the line to make sure that everything that was ordered actually got into the bag.
6. *Presentation.* Yes, fast-food eaters care about how the food looks. They dislike errant fringes of shredded lettuce. They like the pickle to be centered. They hate globs of milkshake running down the side of the cup.
7. *Trash disposal.* Can the consumer dispose of trash conveniently, without having to come in contact with others' messy trays, greasy bags, or ketchup spills?

8. *Bathrooms*. Is the bathroom clean and stocked with soap, towels, and toilet tissue? Do the toilets actually work? If a child falls, does the mother panic about germs, urine, and dirt?
9. *Exit*. Can the consumer get out of the parking lot with relative ease and without getting, or causing, any new dents or scrapes in the sheet metal?

By understanding the actions and expectations of the consumer in each phase of the experience train, problems with execution and solutions for improvement quickly become clear.

Define the Needs States of Heavy Users

Mothers with young children represent the prime McDonald's user. They want to spend some time together and give themselves a little relaxation and self-indulgent time away from other responsibilities and activities. A meal at McDonald's is, therefore, primarily a connecting experience. Beyond that, however, their needs diverge. The mother focuses on health, safety, cleanliness, value, and convenience. The kids look for fun, empowerment, specialness, and affiliation with other kids.

The McDonald's experience has long been successfully geared toward the kids' needs, but in the past few years, the moms have been rethinking their visits. Eat-alongs revealed that moms often do not order a meal for themselves at McDonald's. They will pick at the child's leftovers, sip a drink, wait till they get home to eat, or skip the meal entirely. What's more, because the mother has become less and less enamored of the McDonald's experience, she usually wields the "veto vote." As the family cruises along, debating the possible choices for lunch or dinner, a "no" vote from Mom—no matter how many "yes" votes may be registered—knocks the restaurant out of contention.

Revisit the Rules of Engagement

When Jim Cantalupo began visiting restaurants in 2003, he was not pleased with the state of the experience train. He believed that the "rules of engagement" that had guided McDonald's for decades—a kind of company "Ten Commandments"—were still valid (even if the language was a little outdated):

1. The customer is the most important person in our business.
2. The customer is not dependent on us—we are dependent on him.
3. The customer is not an interruption of our work—he is the purpose of it.
4. The customer does us an honor when he calls—we are not doing him a favor by serving him.
5. The customer is part of our business, not an outsider—he is our guest.
6. The customer is not a cold statistic—he is flesh and blood—a human with feelings and emotions like our own.
7. The customer is not someone to argue with or match wits with.
8. The customer is the one who brings us his wants—it is our job to fill them.
9. The customer is deserving of the most courteous and attentive treatment we can give him.
10. The customer has the right to expect an employee to present a neat, clean appearance. The employee should have trim, clean fingernails, be clean-shaven and keep his hair cut.

What's more, the business practices and policies that had been so clearly defined and closely followed since the original owner/operator manual had been published in 1958—and that Cantalupo had so strictly enforced in his international markets—seemed to have gone by the board at many franchises.

Cantalupo had always enjoyed eating McDonald's food himself, and was a stickler for McDonald's specs for food preparation. The french fries had to be cooked at precisely 340 degrees Fahrenheit for three minutes, sprinkled with salt, and served hot. He did not ap-

McDONALD'S OWNER/OPERATOR MANUAL—CIRCA 1958

prove of an operational "improvement" that many franchises had adopted, which called for hot storage of meat at various stages in the process of cooking, because he felt it had a negative effect on taste and texture. He believed that McDonald's could only achieve success by returning to the basics of value, speed, and cleanliness.

Based on the initial consumer research, the urgent issues became blindingly clear:

- *Quality*. Consistent standards and measurement were required.
- *Frequency*. Current customers were visiting McDonald's less often.
- *Service and training*. Upgrading was needed.
- *Taste*. Improvement was necessary.
- *Options*. People wanted a broader choice of healthier foods and meals.
- *Loyalty*. Consumers had lost their brand loyalty.

Cantalupo would tell anyone and everyone that McDonald's wasn't working the way it had been designed to work. Many other McDonald's executives, with similarly long experience and successful track records at the company, agreed that the company could get back on track with a combination of "back to basics," discipline, and an engaged, empathetic response to customers.

According to Fred Turner, number two at McDonald's behind founder Ray Kroc, the success of McDonald's had always come from this basic approach. "It wasn't because we were smarter," he said. "The fact that we were selling just ten items, had a facility that was small and used a limited number of suppliers created an ideal environment for really digging in on everything."

The good news about big, embedded leaders like McDonald's is that a sense of urgency, clear direction, and fierce continuous customer visits provide an opportunity for a new chapter in the company story. Most companies—including Kmart, Sears, and Burger King—have squandered this opportunity.

Explore Cultural, Economic, and Demographic Trends

Eat-alongs—along with a number of other consumer discovery tools—provide insight about the experience and the expectations, needs states, and behaviors of individual consumers. These become much more meaningful and relevant when understood within the context of economic, demographic, and cultural trends. As Cantalupo and his team knew, four big ones affect the McDonald's offering.

Changing definition of a meal. When McDonald's opened its doors in 1955, the majority of meals were eaten at home and a family outing at a restaurant seemed like a special treat. The occasion mattered more than the meal itself.

Over the past twenty years, however, people have adopted different eating habits. People snack and graze more. The number of people who eat three meals a day with no snacks dropped from 33 percent in 1985 to under 20 percent by 2004. The number of people who eat two meals and one or two snacks a day rose from 19 to 26 percent in the same period. The percentage of people who eat three meals and also snack once or twice per day also rose.

Meal prep and dining are allocated less time. When people cook at home, they spend less than ten minutes in meal preparation. They make fewer dishes from scratch and favor one-dish meals. When they visit a quick-service restaurant, they define a "fast meal" as a five-minute affair. In 1992, fast meant thirty minutes.

Diversifying tastes/food questing. In the 1990s, with the continued diversification of the population and increased influence of minority cultures came the growth of a wide range of ethnic food specialties. Twenty years ago, a quick ethnic meal meant Italian, Mexican, or Chinese, with relatively bland interpretations of the original flavors and dishes. Now, the possibilities are virtually endless, even in the malls and suburban main streets. Consumers can choose fast and inexpensive cuisine from Cuba, South America, Indonesia, Malaysia, and dozens of other cultures, and they want to experience more of the bold flavors and unusual textures they used to resist.

Health and food safety. Even as Americans snack and spend less time on preparing meals at home, they have become much more focused on the relationship between diet and health. Obesity and its causes have become a subject of national debate. Everybody knows that saturated fats and refined sugars, two McDonald's staples, can lead to all kinds of physical woes. And, a rash of health scares—including mad cow and hoof-and-mouth disease—have made people extremely aware of the dangers of contaminated food. After an e-coli incident at a Jack in the Box restaurant in November 1992 in which three hundred people fell ill and four died, that company recorded a 12 percent decline in sales for the year. (In this sense, McDonald's was justified in blaming external factors for a decline in business.)

The disturbing role of fast-food restaurants in the national health has been explored in a variety of media, including the best-selling *Fast Food Nation* and the hit documentary *Supersize Me*, which chronicles the disastrous health effects on filmmaker Morgan Spurlock of eating nonstop at McDonald's for one month.

What's a family? The family that visited McDonald's in the 1950s and 1960s looks very different from the family of today. Fewer people marry. When they do marry, they do so later than ever. Fewer couples have children and, when they do, they have fewer of them. More families have just one parent, or else two parents of the same sex. More families consist of parents of different races and cultural backgrounds. All of this means that the family no longer manifests itself as a coherent, homogenous, stereotypical unit that seeks a consistent, predictable, stereotypical meal.

Scan the Near and Far Competitive Landscapes

Some two thousand chains compete for consumers and their dollars in the quick-service restaurant industry. McDonald's holds a dominant 43 percent share in the world of burgers, and keeps a close eye on its main burger rivals, including Burger King (18 percent share),

Wendy's (13 percent), Hardee's (4.5 percent), and Jack in the Box (4.4 percent). Then come the nonburger fast-food rivals like Subway, Taco Bell, Arby's, Kentucky Fried Chicken, and Pizza Hut.

But the biggest threats come from QSRs that have found a way to deliver fast food that responds to the demographic and cultural changes we've discussed. More than a dozen of them have established themselves with at least two hundred units in the United States, including:

- *Sonic Drive-In.* The drive-in chain offers malts, burgers, and other standard fast-food fare, but with more current "questing" options like Tuscan grilled chicken with Asiago cheese. Founded in 1953, it has 2,850 units in the United States and recorded $2.7 billion in sales* in 2004.

- *Chick-Fil-A.* These chicken sandwiches have a mission of connection—to serve God and community. The fastest drive-through time of any franchise is a plus for people who think five minutes is a long time to spend on a meal. Founded in 1946, the chain has 1,200 units with $1.75 billion sales in 2004. For Chick-Fil-A apostles, the sandwich is a treat.

- *Del Taco.* Fast tacos are a response to the increasing presence and influence of the Hispanic population. Founded in 1964 in California, Del Taco has 430 units in 14 states, with $470 million in sales in 2004.

- *Cinnabon.* The chain caters to snackers who want flexibility— you can get your gooey bun in a variety of sizes. Founded in 1985 in Seattle, it has 600 units with $208 million in sales in 2004.

- *ICBY (I Can't Believe It's Yogurt).* Founded in 1978, it offers a healthy alternative to ice cream desserts at 1,340 units.

---

*Sales figures are from *Restaurant and Institutions Magazine* and represent all store sales, not corporate revenue, which is largely derived from franchise fees and does not reflect actual sales.

Beyond these rolls another wave of chains that are growing even faster and could pose a serious threat to McDonald's with two thousand or more units by 2010. Challengers include Krispy Kreme, Cheesecake Factory, Dave and Buster's, Miami Subs Grill, In-N-Out Burger, Johnny Rockets, Potbelly Sandwich Works, Chipotle, and Panera.

Even more nerve-wracking, new competitors may emerge from unlikely categories that don't currently look like fast-food providers at all or in markets the company is not currently paying attention to. For example, 7-Eleven—known for convenience foods and take-out coffee—has developed a fast-food offering in Japan. It sells prepared foods and quick meals, including rice balls, box lunches, and deli items. The menu changes for breakfast, lunch, and dinner. In some stores, fast-food items account for as much as a third of total sales in less than 20 percent of the total space. They have achieved CAGR of 9 percent over a period of three years.

Wal-Mart, too, may eventually become a fast-food competitor. The company began offering grocery items in the 1980s and grew to become the largest grocer in the United States by 2003. Given its knowledge and expertise in food handling, wouldn't it see an opportunity in serving quick, standardized meals to its customers?

No company, not even one as large and resourceful as McDonald's, can make perfect sense of a competitive landscape that comprises two thousand identifiable industry competitors and other potential competitors in an unknown number of adjacent categories. Trends can be identified. Winners and losers can be listed. Best practices can be defined and detailed. Threats can be cited. But too much information and too many forecasts can produce analysis paralysis. How can you avoid it?

Evaluate the Opportunities

At McDonald's, Jim Cantalupo and his team determined that the company, despite its size and dominant market share, had several opportunities to substantially grow the business—the possibility existed that they could even double their business within ten years. The opportunities they considered did not require a huge investment of capital, ventures into new categories, or anything particularly radical at all. In fact, the opportunities existed within their current business, grew out of their findings from eat-alongs and data analysis, and connected directly with their original mission. Instead of adding stores to get more customers, they focused on bringing more customers to existing stores.

Expanding Customer Choice: a $5 billion opportunity. The shift in the consumer value calculus had to be addressed, particularly that of the core McDonald's customer: the mother with kids. For years, Mom's need to be with her kids for a connecting time at McDonald's had actually outweighed her desire to eat. Even if it meant picking at the leftover fries or skipping lunch entirely, Mom was willing to make the sacrifice. She placed loyalty to the family above her own hunger. But as more restaurant options became available, offering more types of foods that appealed to her, and as health and wellness concerns grew stronger, she exercised her "veto vote" more often. The family that once visited McDonald's twice a week now might visit twice a month. Getting Mom to vote yes to McDonald's more often could be worth some $5 billion to McDonald's over a decade.

The $10 Billion Drive-Through Opportunity. The drive-through experience at McDonald's had faltered, especially after a corporate decision in the late 1990s to stop grading franchisees on their performance. A McDonald's drive-through, once the most efficient fast-food experience on the road, began to take longer. In time tests conducted in 2002, a consumer could wait six or more seconds longer (sometimes minutes longer) in a McDonald's line than at Wendy's or Chick-Fil-A. That may not sound like much, but when multiplied by the one thousand average visits per day in the twelve thousand units in the

McDonald's system in the United States, a few seconds per customer translates into billions of dollars lost—or gained.

Several factors contributed to the longer wait time at drive-through, from inconsistent training of drive-through associates to packaging that slowed things down—including a pizza box that wouldn't fit through the restaurant window, beverage cups that were too big for standard car cupholders, and condiment containers that were hard to open.

Develop a Plan: Big, Bold, and Breakthrough

Major opportunities require big commitments and significant actions. Most companies, however, shy away from these opportunities. They prefer to go for the promotional effort or the incremental improvement. But such baby steps will not enable the company to regain its way and escape the threats coming from both ends of the market. Only the big, bold, breakthrough plan can do that.

Strategic importance. McDonald's major strategic problem was that it no longer could provide value to the consumer as it once had. Customers had lost loyalty, and they were no longer willing to accept the McDonald's compromise—relative speed and convenience at the cost of quality and experience. So, whatever opportunity McDonald's chose to pursue had to further its fundamental strategic mission: to regain customer satisfaction and rebuild loyalty.

Doability. Being "doable" at McDonald's translates almost directly into "Will franchisees accept, support, and execute the plan?" The franchisee is the ruling body at McDonald's. Senior management has influence, but the operator ultimately calls the shots. By the time Cantalupo became CEO, the typical franchisee was settled in his ways. He would accept change but only if it carried an almost guaranteed return on investment, time, and attention. Franchisees had a short timeframe for return, and it took passion at the top to convince them that "all for one" meant that everyone needed to support a set of common operating standards. They had to be convinced that the poorly performing franchisees were causing a serious degradation in consumer loyalty, frequency of visit, and consumer regard for the brand.

A new approach may also have implications for the current operating infrastructure. Will major changes in organization and processes be required? Will capital investment be needed? Are there gaps in skills and capabilities that will need to be filled (through training, education, hiring, and redeployment of resources)? Based on these considerations, the company leaders must then make a rather simple, nonscientific estimate of the risk involved. Based on their experience and judgment, how likely do they think this venture is to succeed?

Cantalupo and his team chose to go big and bold, with three main initiatives. They called it "McDonald's Plan to Win"—all driven by a goal of improving the customer experience.

The flawless experience. The "Plan to Win" required rethinking the entire experience chain, from arrival to exit. The goals were to make the experience more personal and engaging, and to increase speed and convenience both at the counter and in the drive-through. The key to creating the flawless experience was a focus on the restaurant manager. Although the company had originally become known for its consistent quality and cleanliness through the establishment of corporate standards and rigorous systemwide oversight, this approach was less suited to providing the more personal experience that consumers expect today. Only a well-trained, committed, on-site manager can do that.

In the flawless experience, the little touches mean a lot: parking, entryway, the greeting, order accuracy, order delivery, ease of use of the packaging, waste management. McDonald's committed itself to hiring, training, promoting, and recognizing more "great people" as managers.

It also evaluated ways to increase speed and convenience without degrading the experience. They found an important solution in offering more flexibility in payment options, particularly cashless forms.

Measurement of every aspect of the experience was critical—including dozens of measures of speed, accuracy, taste, and restaurant conditions.

Customer choice. To avoid the "veto vote" from moms, tweens (kids between childhood and adolescence) and seniors would require a broader menu choice, so McDonald's committed itself to food and menu innovation. The Chicken McNugget, despite its popularity and success, was not all that a chicken nugget could be. The standard McDonald's version was made from pressed chicken, which is, in essence, the equivalent of a hamburger—a variety of miscellaneous parts combined and pressed into an easily workable whole. McDonald's introduced the premium chicken nugget made with breast meat only. It rethought its salad offerings, replacing the "shaken salad"—which was composed primarily of shredded iceberg lettuce—with a mixed salad containing sixteen varieties of lettuce. Other new menu items included a selection of fruit and yogurt parfaits, new soup varieties, McGriddles, and several crispy-spicy options for the food questers.

Ubiquity. "When and where you want it" became the mantra at McDonald's. The goal: to provide a "McDonald's option" for the customer, regardless of his or her location. That meant continued creation of traditional stores to increase their density in the locations where consumers expect to find a McDonald's. It also required the development of new footprints, bringing the fast-food leader into small towns, food courts, resort destinations, and other special venues.

McDONALD'S FRENCH FRY SPECS

- Use only #1 Idaho russet potatoes.
- Cut to 7/32" thick.
- Check for 21 percent minimum solids.
- Cure to ensure sugars are converted to starches.
- Preblanch in two-step frying method for optimum flavor and color.
- Fry in mix of beef fat and vegetable oil.
- Pull when oil temperature rises three degrees above minimum.
- Bag with McDonald's-designed metal scoop.

Ubiquity, of course, can adversely affect the brand. So, trading-down brands often seek to add a high-end version of their offering in hopes that it will add luster at the low end. For McDonald's that meant creating flagship stores that offered "retailtainment." McDonald's three flagship stores (in Chicago, in New York's Times Square, and on the perimeter of Disneyworld in Orlando) show the way toward a new idea of the McDonald's environment and experience. They are built around a theme and feature wide-screen televisions, wi-fi connections, comfortable seating areas, and separate shops within shops. At the (newly re-created) Original Rock 'N Roll McDonald's on Clark Street in downtown Chicago, the theme, obviously, is music—celebrating the rock-and-roll hits of the five decades that McDonald's has been in business. In addition to dozens of plasma-screen TVs, there are digital-media kiosks for burning CDs, down-loading cell phone ring tones, and printing photos. While the music and videos play, customers eat their meals in comfortable Barcelona chairs under distinctive lighting fixtures, or hang out at the McCafe, which offers gourmet coffees and fancy pastries. The store is known, to Chicagoans at least, as a "McAttraction."

Cantalupo's journey to resuscitate McDonald's into the new century has been a resounding success. By January 2004, McDonald's sales had catapulted upward. The basic formula—service, value, cleanliness, and quality control—had worked. Franchisees were spirited. The senior management team embraced this revitalization of the McDonald's legacy.

The night before the opening of the annual global franchisee convention in 2004, Jim Cantalupo had a heart attack and died. His successors, particularly Mike Roberts, then head of the U.S. business, continued to drive his agenda. Gradually, the company learned how to innovate, and successfully launched a stream of products over the next two years that caught the consumer's interest and generated lots of trials. Same-store sales continued to grow. Consumers who had long rejected McDonald's as "fat food" and "boring" started to come back and were surprised to find that the quality had genuinely improved.

As anyone who has worked in the fast-food business knows, the war for the title of value leader is not won in a single battle. Cantalupo's first move—back to basics—works when the brand equity is strong, and McDonald's resurgence has been catastrophic for Burger King and Wendy's. Yet the market for fast food is vast and many competitors stalk.

Even Now, the Nemesis Is Out There:
Visit an In-N-Out Burger

Despite the company's gains and improvements, McDonald's has yet to bring the new company completely in line with the value calculus of its key consumer groups, nor has it found a way to make a McDonald's meal competitive with the offerings of many smaller players. Panera Bread and Cosi offer much greater variety and fresher ingredients, if at a higher, trading-up price. Wal-Mart and 7-Eleven could attack from below, with lower-priced meal options with greater speed and efficiency—even if the experience would lack warmth and pleasure. Although McDonald's has expanded its food offerings, with a sharper focus on freshness and health, there's stiff competition from Subway and other chains that bake bread and assemble meals from scratch. McDonald's food has improved, but mostly within the context of its past performance—not in comparison to the amazing variety of choices available to almost every consumer, no matter how much money he or she wants to spend.

McDonald's is a value play. It offers utilitarian food at acceptable prices. It is not the cheapest, but it is the most widely available. Consumers say it has become a predictable experience. That's why many have come to think of the chain as a "utility player." Some even say that McDonald's major asset is not the french fry at all, but the real estate its restaurants occupy. When that kind of talk emerges, a company is clearly not out of trouble. Somewhere lurks the nemesis that can redefine the burger-and-fries meal for the next generation of consumers.

It may well be an up-and-coming chain called In-N-Out Burger. In-N-Out Burger operates about two hundred restaurants in three states—California, Arizona, and Nevada—in comparison to the thirty-one thousand McDonald's restaurants worldwide. Its annual sales of less than $400 million are less than 1 percent of McDonald's $45 billion in revenues. The company is privately held by the Snyder family, who founded In-N-Out in 1948, seven years before the first McDonald's opened.

In-N-Out seems, on the one hand, to be a throwback to mid-twentieth-century American culture and, on the other, to be the perfect manifestation of the burger-and-fries restaurant for today. The restaurant has a number of distinctive attributes. First is an extremely simple menu: cheeseburgers and hamburgers in a number of combinations and finishes, french fries, three shakes (vanilla, chocolate, and strawberry), and a limited variety of beverages, from Coke to coffee to milk. Nothing on the menu costs more than $2.75. There are no complicated combinations of meals.

Second is a maniacal devotion to quality and freshness of ingredients. In-N-Out butchers, hand-cuts, and grinds all the beef used in its restaurants at its own wholly owned facility. It uses chucks, front ribs, and shoulder meat only. The meat is free of additives, fillers, and preservatives. The lettuce is hand-leafed at each store, the buns are delivered fresh from a local bakery, and french fries cut from potatoes delivered to each restaurant from neighboring farms. Fries are cooked in 100 percent pure vegetable oil; no animal fat is involved. (Customers can watch them being cut and cooked while they wait.) The milk shakes contain 100 percent pure ice cream.

Third, everything at In-N-Out Burger is cooked to order. It does not try to be a fast-food outlet or even quick-service restaurant. It takes roughly thirty minutes to order and eat a meal at an In-N-Out and nobody seems to mind. If you go into an In-N-Out Burger at lunchtime, you will find a line that snakes through the restaurant. At 11 A.M., many of the customers are contractors, construction workers, gardeners, and other people who get up early to work hard. You will hear many languages spoken. They will tell you that In-N-Out Burger offers the best hamburger in town, delivered hot and the way they want. Many of the clientele go to In-N-Out Burger every day. They believe it is "better" and "an unbelievable value." When I've asked various friends who live outside of the In-N-Out Burger states, they often give me a smile and say, "I wish I had the franchise rights for New York, or South Carolina," or "It's the best burger joint out there."

In-N-Out Burger meets the consumer's current value calculus, but in unexpected ways. It doesn't obviously cater to the questing consumer, except that the company pushes the limits of freshness and taste in a classic burger-and-fries meal. It doesn't offer "healthy options" and "lighter-fare meals" yet health-conscious consumers happily eat there because the ingredients are natural, pure, and fresh. It doesn't offer much menu choice, yet everything is affordable and the quality is exceptional at the price. It can't get you in-n-out in under thirty minutes, but the experience is satisfying enough that thirty minutes does not seem like a long time.

In-N-Out Burger does not seem to show up on McDonald's radar. Too small. Too regional. McDonald's may be right not to notice or care. But their nemesis is no doubt out there. If In-N-Out Burger doesn't grow to reshape the world of burgers and fries, some other competitor will.

8.

NICKELS AND DIMES

Arnold and Molly: Tight with a Dollar

Arnold Piso, age twenty-eight, is a banker, and lives with his wife, Molly, twenty-six, an entertainment publicist, in Chicago. He is a self-professed skinflint. Arnold says that he does not need a cell phone because he doesn't make that many calls and, anyway, it's "cheaper to use a pay phone." He doesn't drink soda because it's a "waste of money." If he's out and gets thirsty, there's usually a water fountain handy. The Pisos don't own a car because they live in an apartment and can take public transit to work. Arnold figures they save about $6,000 a year on payments, insurance, and gas. And, besides, a car is a depreciating asset. Both Arnold and Molly save the receipts from all their expenditures. Every evening after dinner, Arnold sits down at the computer and enters each cost into a spreadsheet, down to the thirty-five cents spent on a pack of gum. From Arnold's point of view, the world is on a mad dash for cash. "Everyone wants your cash," he said to me. "Wherever you're at, they want to sell you something. Everyone's got their hands out. They all want your wallet."

THE PISOS' ASSETS		THEIR LIABILITIES	
Savings account	$0	Mortgage	$0
Checking account	$2,500	Home equity	$0
Investments	$200,000	Credit card	$0
Home value	$0	Student loans	$0
Other	$35,000	Other	$0

It's not that Arnold and Molly are poor. He earns about $50,000 a year and, at twenty-eight, already has an investment portfolio worth some $200,000. Molly makes about $25,000 a year, so their combined household income totals about $75,000. Their rent is $1,200 a month and total monthly expenses run to $2,500. They have no debt—no mortgage, no student loans, no credit card balances. Arnold strongly believes in not spending on things he doesn't need and is proud of his ability to wring the most value from his money. "I can get through an entire week without a dollar in my wallet," he said. "For people who are always buying their coffee at Starbucks, that would be much harder."

For Arnold, life is a form of banking. It's about deposits and withdrawals, assets and liabilities, cash flows, investments and securities, nest eggs, and futures. Arnold is proof that not all American consumers are dizzy with consumption and brand names, or plunging themselves into debt by overspending on items they don't really need. "I've got that spreadsheet in my mind," he said.

Yet Arnold will spend money, and even splurge, when he thinks he's getting a particularly good deal or making a wise investment. The best example is the leather sectional couch. I asked the Pisos to tell me about the last time they treated themselves. Molly immediately said, "The couch!" I looked at the canvas couch we were sitting on. It was perfectly nice and comfortable, but it didn't look like a splurge to me. "Not that couch," Molly said. "We bought a beautiful couch, the same basic style as this one, but all-leather. It was a great deal. We knew we loved it and could afford it now. But it wouldn't fit in this apartment. Too big. So we're storing it at Arnold's father's house in Minneapolis. It will go into our house when we buy one. Whenever that is." Arnold adds that Molly plans to stop working when they move into a real house. "When we have the income cut," he said, "we won't be able to afford that stuff, so that's why I decided to purchase the couch. It cost $3,700."

Arnold and Molly also splurged on a trip to Europe—$10,000 for a tour through Spain, southern France, and Italy. While on the trip, they stopped at a Pucci boutique, where Molly admired a purse. Arnold took one look at it and said, "That's a great purse." The next thing Molly knew, Arnold had shelled out $600 for a purse she loved but would never have bought on her own.

THE PISOS' MONTHLY EXPENSES		
Item	Spending	Index vs. Average
Income (posttax)	$6,080	1.0
Car/taxi	250	0.2
Mortgage/rent	1,250	1.2
Household utilities and maintenance	170	0.3
Eating out	350	0.9
Groceries	350	1.0
Travel and entertainment	300	1.0
Healthcare/personal health	0	0.0
Home goods	0	0.0
Clothing	300	1.3
Charitable contributions	20	0.1
Education	0	0.0
Personal care services	180	2.4
Life insurance	40	0.6
Other expenses	430	3.4
Total spending	3,640	0.7
Net savings/(deficit)	2,440	2.6

The Pisos trade up in many categories of goods—home furnishings, travel, clothing, and especially premium brand-name foods. They trade down in many other categories, particularly household cleaning products, paper products, hair care, and bottled water. And in many more categories, they simply go without. Molly might like a manicure every week, but their lives are strictly budgeted and, if it doesn't fit the budget, it doesn't happen. If they spend $50 more than planned, they won't go out for dinner at a restaurant, as they usually do.

Why, at age twenty-eight and in a relatively secure financial position, is Arnold so preoccupied with budgeting and saving and being cheap? Why not follow a live-life-to-the-fullest, spend-now lifestyle? Partially, it's in Arnold's genes. "My nature is more of a Midwest mentality, to not spend as much and show off money," Arnold said. Part of it comes from life events. His mother died when he was a child and it's clear that he wants to protect himself from any "shocks" in the future. "With this budgeting system," he said, "we know at the end of the year that we're going to have saved a certain amount of money. It allows for more freedom. The knowledge takes away fear. From our financial models, I can project out the next fifteen years, and I can ask, 'Do I have to worry, or do I not?' The average person isn't going to do this."

Arnold takes great satisfaction in their lifestyle. When I ask him to rate his life on a scale of 1 to 10, he gives it a 10. "Our friends wonder how we buy the stuff we do," he said. "They say, 'Oh, you must make a lot more money than I thought.'" I like the fact that because of planning and organization, we're able to outsmart others who may or may not be aware that they can do the same thing." Even so, he admits that he'd like to own a vacation home, travel around the world, and go out for dinner more often. Molly rates their life at 8.5. She would like to buy the house sooner rather than later, and not to have to live on such a strict monthly budget.

Arnold smiles at his wife. "The material things mean more to

Molly than they do to me. For me, it doesn't matter, I'm happy living just like this."

The Pisos—with no children, low expenses, no debt, and above-average household income—are frugal by choice. But they really are no different from millions of American consumers who always feel that the good life, the truly perfect 10 (despite Arnold's current rating), is just slightly out of reach, that others have more wealth and more possessions than they do, that they have to work constantly to achieve all they want to and to keep up with people who are more successful (or at least appear to be), and that disaster is always right around the corner.

The Beauty of Retail Banking

It's not surprising that Arnold believes that the world wants his wallet. He works in an industry where getting an increased "share of wallet" is, in fact, always the goal: retail banking.

A secret of the financial-services world is that retail banking—providing services to individual consumers through branch offices—is a hugely profitable business. You might think that retail banking, with its millions of small depositors and billions of relatively tiny daily transactions, would be a high-cost, low-margin business, especially in comparison to corporate banking. Not at all. The difference between the interest paid on deposits and the interest charged on loans—known as the "spread"—is deliciously large and the primary source of a retail bank's profits. A standard savings account may pay the consumer 3 percent interest, while the consumer pays 6 percent for a home equity line of credit and as much as 18 percent on a credit card balance. In addition, the bank charges consumers various fees for the privilege of accessing and using their own money—from per-check fees to penalties for not maintaining a minimum balance to "account analysis" fees.

The profitability of retail banking is not, of course, a secret within the financial-services industry. The lure of high margins achieved with little investment and the fast growth possible through mergers and acquisitions have attracted the attention of many entrepreneurs seeking to create banking empires. The danger for financial-services companies is that retail banking is located squarely in the middle of the market. Competitors grow by stealing share. They often "bait" away each other's customers with low (and unprofitable) introductory rates. Interest rates are regulated and there is only so much consumer tolerance for differences in fees from bank to bank. In most areas, the customer base is inherently sticky. Plus, people do not buy banking services as they do coffee or clothing—discretionary dollars do not get spent on additional checking accounts or home loans—so the introduction of new products will not reliably attract new business.

As a result, consumer banks have generally sought to grow through mergers and acquisitions, rapid branch build-outs, expansion across regions, and grabbing competitors' customers. Because very wealthy consumers often manage their money through private bankers, and because low-income families may not deal with banks at all, retail banks get their customers primarily from the middle class. So, when a bank enters a market where competitors already are firmly entrenched, the interloper usually encounters a fierce response, and a battle for customers may ensue.

It's ironic that retail banks, which cannot survive without middle-market consumers, generally treat them so poorly.

The Fleet Juggernaut

FleetFinancial, in fact, had an almost pathological inability to interact with everyday consumers. When the huge bank found itself under attack by a scrappy competitor with a consumer-centric approach to retail banking, Fleet had to find a way to change—or lose customers and share. In 2002, Bradford H. Warner, CEO of the consumer business of FleetFinancial, was tapped to lead the "turnaround." That's a bit of a misnomer, since Fleet was fabulously profitable. However, it was essentially true that Fleet needed to fundamentally refresh its approach and revitalize a business that had grown stale.

FleetFinancial (now part of Bank of America; more on that later) began as a small retail banking operation in Rhode Island. Driven by an aggressive entrepreneur, Terence Murray, Fleet Bank grew through a series of some fifty mergers and acquisitions, made over two decades, to become one of New England's major banks. In 1999, Fleet Bank merged with the larger, but slower-moving, BankBoston to become FleetBoston Financial, the seventh largest bank in the United States, with some $196 billion in assets and deposits. Effectively, the smaller Fleet Bank acquired the larger, slower-moving BankBoston. Most of the senior team came from Fleet and had an aggressive, hungry growth orientation.

Although it had begun as a consumer bank, as the company mushroomed in size, it took its eye off the relatively simple joys of profitable consumer banking and got more and more involved in nonretail activities. Fleet made so many loans to corporations and other large institutions that, at the time of the Fleet–BankBoston merger, nearly two-thirds of its profits came from corporate lending. Fleet also ventured into investment banking, with the acquisition of Robertson Stephens, a San Francisco–based underwriter of technology- and Internet-related companies. Fleet and BankBoston looked abroad, too, beefing up their operations in Latin America.

From the earliest days of the merger, things did not go smoothly for the newly bulked-up bank. Some of its corporate loans went sour, including some $700 million in charges related to financial dealings with Enron. Big investments in Argentina took a dive. The business of Robertson Stephens virtually evaporated after the Internet bubble burst. Fleet tried to sell the unit but could not find a buyer. To make matters worse, the transition from BankBoston to Fleet was plagued by technical difficulties, many of which had been festering from Fleet's 1996 merger with BayBank. With its nonretail operations in disarray,

FleetFinancial looked to its retail network to fill earnings gaps. The bank held down interest payments, jacked up fees, trimmed services, and reduced investment. As a result, customer satisfaction plummeted.

Fleet could hardly afford a drop in its ratings, because the level was already quite low. While the bank had been focusing on corporate lending, investment banking, overseas operations, and acquiring one bank after another, it had paid little attention to improving its retail banking operations. So, although Fleet maintained more branches (1,500) than any competitor and a far more extensive network of ATMs (3,800 in 2001), it had done very little to create relationships with consumers. It seemed that the bank was always undergoing a postmerger integration and that its energy was directed at rationalizing the branch network and personnel, trying to fix the problems of changing over accounts from one system to the other, replacing signs, and dealing with all the other internal tasks of accomplishing a big merger.

Following the acquisition of BayBank in 1996, the voice of the middle-market consumer had grown faint. After the creation of FleetFinancial, it had almost completely been lost. Enter Brad Warner, career banker, eager to learn, and ready to engage consumer finance with vigor.

A Challenge from the McDonald's of Banking

Fleet might not have noticed that its consumers were less than happy—or, if it had noticed, been able to ignore the fact—had it not been for the rapid rise of a competitor, Commerce Bank, in Fleet's own backyard of New Jersey, New York, Pennsylvania, and Connecticut.

Commerce Bank, founded in 1973, grew very differently than Fleet, BankBoston, or any of the other banks that had been subsumed into the Fleet system. Commerce had been built on what they call a "chain concept" that features "standardized facilities, standardized hours, standardized service, and aggressive marketing." Commerce calls itself "America's Most Convenient Bank." In other words, it is a banking version of McDonald's.

Indeed, a Commerce Bank branch more resembles a McDonald's than it does the typical New England Main Street Fleet branch. FleetFinancial inherited much of its character from the old-line Boston banks it swallowed up, with their high-ceilinged rooms, ornately carved woodwork, hushed atmosphere, short hours, and sense of discreet banking "professionalism." Each Fleet branch was custom-designed and the build-out expense was usually high.

Commerce has none of that. If you had never visited a Commerce Bank branch and were looking for one along the highway, you might not recognize it as you approached, because it looks more like a fast-food outlet or dry cleaning establishment than a bank. It is identified by a large, internally lit, plastic sign that makes its claim for convenience very evident in the tagline "OPEN SEVEN DAYS." The branches sit on nicely landscaped plots in easily accessible, high-traffic locations. The windows are large (and frequently washed) and the interiors well lit, so that the office looks warm and welcoming, and staff and customers can be seen within. No stuffy, bank-vault mentality here. No pomposity and posturing.

The building design is modular, just like a fast-food chain, so there can be some variation in configuration, but each branch is unmistakably a member of the Commerce family. Each location offers a drive-through window, a feature that many other banks have discontinued. The ATMs are located in the warm, well-lit foyer, rather than mounted on an exterior wall, allowing customers to do their banking sheltered from the elements and scrutiny of passers-by. Carpets, furniture, and fixtures all look new, thanks to an aggressive continuous renovation program. Customer service representatives sit at open, clean, uncluttered desks in a large, open space. There are public restrooms and another novelty: a free change-sorting service. The standardization makes it possible for a new building to be constructed in just twelve weeks.

Convenience at Commerce is further manifested in customer service. Rather than cutting back in branch personnel, as many banks have done, Commerce branches seem unusually well staffed, which means few lines and short wait times. Offices are open seven days a week: from 8 A.M. to 8 P.M. Monday to Friday, 8 A.M. to 6 P.M. on Saturday, and 11 A.M. to 4 P.M. on Sunday. Fleet branches, by contrast, close at 4 P.M. Monday through Saturday and are closed on Sunday.

At Commerce University, from which all employees must "graduate" before taking their positions and return to regularly for additional training, new hires learn about Commerce Bank products. "But they really make sure we know it's all about serving the customers," said one teller. The VP and director of training at Commerce said, "We want employees who are outgoing and aren't afraid to talk to other people . . . someone who will engage the customer."

Founded in 1992, Commerce University is modeled after Walt Disney's "Disney University" and McDonald's "Hamburger University." It offers nearly seventeen hundred courses with over fifteen thousand enrollments each year. The university is organized in seven "schools" related to specific areas of operations at the bank. Students can earn college credit through the training program; employees who earn certificates or degrees or complete the advanced training program are rewarded with stock options.

The curriculum emphasizes the customer-focused culture of Commerce Bank and its service philosophy. Students are given "shopping" assignments at other retail banking chains to observe and evaluate various types of retail experiences, with an eye for consistency of delivery and exceptional customer care. Courses address the needs of both new employees and those working toward career advancement. This helps to ensure the success of Commerce's "promote from within" policy.

On the job, Commerce employees are rewarded for their efforts to improve customer service. When a branch manager observes an employee who engages in some exceptional instance of good service, she can reward that person with stickers redeemable for clothing and other prizes. When a branch succeeds well enough to put a competitor's branch out of business, Commerce pays a "branch bounty" of $5,000 that is distributed among all staff members at the winning branch. Commerce's attention to its employees is reflected in its high employee-related expenses—32.5 percent of revenue versus 29.9 percent for a typical regional bank.

Customers we spoke with gave Commerce high marks for service and products; they especially liked the lack of fees for regular transactions. No monthly fee. No per-check fee. Free ATM transactions at non-Commerce banks and at foreign ATMs. These differences may seem cosmetic and trivial, but they reflect a unique philosophy of banking and are fundamental to Commerce's success. Traditional bankthink is that loans generate profits and that deposits are virtually irrelevant. As a result, most banks look at their branches as a cost drain and not an income center. Their goal is to cut costs in the retail network and to develop systems that keep consumers out of the branches whenever possible. For them, the best customer is the one who shows up the least and makes the fewest transactions.

Commerce, however, sees the branch as the center of the business. It believes that deposits are important and its deposits have steadily grown—despite the fact that Commerce does not always pay the highest interest rates in their area—simply because depositors value the service they get at Commerce.

Commerce's fast-food approach to financial services has produced strong results, although the profits stack up differently for Commerce than they do for other banks. Overall, the company has posted strong growth since 1997, with a 23 percent CAGR in number of units. From 1997 to 2004, Commerce achieved a remarkable 30 percent CAGR in revenue, while the average revenue growth for regional banks was 9 percent. Commerce posted 30 percent earnings CAGR over the same eight-year period, compared to an 18 percent average for regional banks. And Commerce has significantly higher deposits than competitive regional banks—$86.6 million per branch versus $65.5 million in the average bank.

Perhaps most telling, Commerce has benefited from the rash of mergers and acquisitions that has reshaped the financial services industry. "For every bank merger, and the bank closings that always follow bank mergers," said one Commerce executive, "there are thousands of disgruntled customers coming over to us. Fleet and Summit are going to make our year."

At last, Fleet began to notice that something was amiss in its retail banking operations and that competitors were stealing customers away. But replicating Commerce's model was not an option or an intention for Fleet. As a Commerce exec put it, "Even as we become larger and larger and other banks start to notice us more and more, there's just no way they can match what we're doing. It's a matter of culture and style, and it would mean totally rewriting the way they operate, from the ground up."

Fleet would have to find its own way to meet consumer needs without completely rebuilding itself.

The Financial Trials of Bob and Joyce

FleetFinancial is the primary bank of Bob and Joyce Reilly, whose life seems almost as fractured and complicated as that of their financial institution. Bob, 41, and Joyce, 39, have been married for 18 years. Bob is a partner in a plumbing company, while Joyce stays at home to look after the four daughters, ages 6, 11, 14, and 15. They live in one-half of a two-family home in Malden, Massachusetts, a working-class suburb of Boston.

To visit the Reillys' home is to step into an appealing kind of family chaos. During a two-hour visit, between 6 and 8 P.M. one evening, we counted at least fifteen rings of the phone—or phones, there being six extensions—and could hear various bits of music and dialogue spewing from one or more of the five TV sets. In addition to the two adults and four Reilly daughters who wandered through our conversation, a neighbor girl came to visit, and three family cats got into a noisy fight in the kitchen. "We have a pretty hectic schedule," Joyce said.

The subject of money is never far from the Reillys' minds. Bob brings in around $60,000 a year from the plumbing business. Their tenant pays a few hundred dollars in rent each month. Joyce's brother, who won the Massachusetts Lottery, sends them a check for $5,000 every year and they always save it to fund their vacations. The Reillys have assets of about $70,000, including about $2,000 in a checking account, $3,700 in savings, an IRA of $22,000, and $40,000 in a whole life account and mutual funds.

The Reillys' financial commitments—over $200,000—outweigh their assets. They bought their home six years ago, which required a mortgage of $180,000, and have been renovating it piecemeal virtually since the day they moved in. Bob got so sick of working on the improvements after work hours and during weekends that he hired a contractor to fix the stairs. They bought a truck, taking a loan for $22,000. They owe around $6,000 on various credit cards. "I used my credit card for Christmas gifts last year," said Joyce, "and we're still paying off the balance, eight months later."

The Reillys struggle with their finances and feel that their bank does very little to help them. In fact, they have relationships with nine different financial services institutions—four banks, two insurance and fund providers, and three issuers of credit cards—but the Reillys don't really think of them as relationships at all. "Banks do not care about the little guys," Bob says. "I would like a person to be allocated to me, to start a relationship and go over all my products every three months. You do not get that personalized service at my bank. If I did, I would keep all my financial stuff—my banking, savings, mortgage, and mutual funds—at the same place."

The Reillys have their financial dreams. Bob would love to semi-retire from the plumbing business by the age of fifty-five, buy real estate, and manage it as a source of income. He wishes he could find more time to spend with the kids, before they all leave home for college. And how will they afford tuition—especially when three kids will be in school simultaneously for at least one year? But, for now, it's all the Reillys can do to manage their obligations. For years, they saved virtually nothing. "We would have no savings whatsoever if Joyce's brother hadn't won the lottery and given us some money," said Bob. "It's really hard to save. I know we have to do it, but it's really boring." At last, Joyce put the family on an automatic deposit plan, which guarantees that at least $25 will find its way into the savings account each month. The only other method of control they have is to constantly shop for the best credit card rates and roll over balances when they can.

The Reillys say they would welcome a better way—a "turnkey" approach, that would include solutions to all their financial needs, low fees, competitive interest rates, and a personal relationship. "We're overwhelmed by financial matters. We want an institution that will recognize us, help us toward our goals, and let us in on the secrets about how to manage money better," Joyce says.

Just by listening to the Reillys, six ideas for improvements to Fleet's offering emerged: life-event product bundles, seminars on financial planning, income-tax-refund savings programs, one-stop shopping, value packs on accounts, and simplification of credit transfers.

Fleet Starts to Listen

When Fleet set about determining a new way forward, it began by listening carefully to its middle-market customers like Bob and Joyce to learn what most frequently causes the money arguments. (Middle-class families tell us they tend to fight about three subjects: kids, sex, and money. All three are tough to manage and there is never the right amount of any one of them.)

From their consumer research, which Warner personally supervised, Fleet learned that financial concerns have high share of mind for most middle-market consumers. They feel insecure about managing their finances. They feel they don't know enough about finance and don't have the time or the inclination to learn. "We do not have time to read fancy, complicated offers that come through the mail," said Joyce. "We just throw them out. We just want a nice simple TV ad that lays things out very easily."

In particular, consumers worry about credit. They think of it as a necessary evil, the only way to get many of the good things they want in life and feel that they deserve. Yet they are rightfully wary of the dangers involved. "Credit cards go in like a lamb and out like a lion," Joyce said. "They suck you in and you're charging away, but before you know it, you have a huge debt." Dealing with checking and savings account balances, paying bills, and managing credit card debt become daily worries and a major drain on time and emotional energy.

Fleet learned that it was doing some things right. In particular, their customers liked their online banking system because it enabled them to maintain control of their day-to-day financial activities— checking balances, and monitoring checks and deposits. Consumers felt a sense of pride in knowing the details of their financial situation, being able to avoid bouncing checks, and keeping a close eye on their credit situation.

However, they felt a complete disconnect between short-term control and their long-term goals of financial security and well-being. They felt lacking in knowledge and unsure of where to turn for financial advice. "I don't know what I don't know," said one consumer. "Maybe I'm only happy because I don't know any better."

They also felt that simple issues like opening hours and the design of bank statements and the volume of paper work they had to handle made it more difficult to keep on financial track.

Managing money is an activity that requires skills and experience far beyond what most consumers possess. When we ask consumers to make a collage with images that illustrate how they feel about managing money, the paper fills up with strung-out people juggling many balls at once, a tight-rope walker, a pedestrian blown over by a strong wind, an enormous jigsaw puzzle, and a tiny figure overwhelmed with stacks of paper on a huge desk. The right combination of benefits, however, can take the consumer to a place of security and comfort, dream fulfillment, and systematic movement toward goals.

Like Bob and Joyce, most middle-market consumers juggle relationships with multiple financial services providers—for the mortgage, home equity line, bank credit cards, store credit cards, retirement account, life and disability insurance, stock portfolio, and checking, savings, and small business accounts. They would much prefer to consolidate their accounts, debt, and portfolios with a single provider that has the knowledge and ability to look at their entire financial situation and devise a complete solution for them—without fear of being sold a fistful of unnecessary products or having to live with non-

What manging money feels like   *What I wish it felt like*

Source: BCG Consumer Research

competitive rates. They want help, advice, information, and a personal relationship. But they feel intimidated by most large banks.

As a result of all this, consumers end up making bad choices about how to handle their finances. They don't seek enough information. They don't ask the right questions. They get bad advice from friends and family. Or, feeling guilty and embarrassed about their lack of expertise, they make decisions without consulting anyone at all. They don't have time to read the fine print and don't always pay close attention to their statements. As a result, some end up with excessive finance charges and unexpected penalty fees. When they can, they try to wriggle out of their troubles by switching to different providers— refinancing mortgages, rolling over home equity lines, and transferring credit card debt. They spend far too much time micromanaging the day-to-day transactions and far too little time planning for the future and thinking about long-term issues.

Fleet asked its consumers, "What works for you?" They said, for example, "Strict control of the day-to-day. Absolute certainty of what's in the bank, by using online access to check balances, check clearing, and posting of deposits. That gives me a sense of pride in not bouncing checks and keeping credit to a minimum."

When asked, "What doesn't work for you?" they had many more things to say:

- "Short-term control doesn't enable my long-term goals. I don't have enough knowledge or advice on how to get there."
- "Branch hours force me to plan trips around the bank, which gets in the way of other goals and activities."
- "There's a conflict between the short term and long term. I'll tell myself, 'We've had a good month, and I think I can get those new boots,' but I forget it's taking away from that longer-term saving."
- "I'm overwhelmed by paperwork."
- "The children's education is draining what savings I have."

■ "I'm fearful of creeping credit. I avoid it. I know we won't pay it.
It keeps me up at night."

Finally, Fleet asked customers to answer one simple, telling question: "If Fleet were a person, what would it say?"

One consumer replied, "I'm Fleet. I'm big and important and I'm waving, but I don't know who you are."

Another responded, "Fleet is everywhere but there's no one home. It's just the big green sign."

The Opportunity

What can a retail bank do to make itself more attractive to the middle-market consumer? How can it serve the middle without getting stuck in the middle?

The answer is not to be found in radical transformation; a retail bank cannot move dramatically up or down the value chain. Rather, it must follow the lessons of all world-class retailers and perfect the brand platform. Fleet had everything it needed to grow its consumer banking business; the work was to improve its offering, deepen its understanding of consumers and its response to them, build organizational unity around vision, sharpen its execution, and gain economic advantage from higher throughput.

So, in addition to talking with consumers, Fleet also did its homework into the economics and demographics of its market and discovered, surprisingly, that despite its large network of branches and ATMs, the middle-market consumer was still seriously underserved in its markets. In fact, Fleet had touched only 22 percent of the mass-market households in its geographic footprint. Although Commerce had stolen some customers from it, there was an untapped opportunity, especially given the ease of switching banks or of working with multiple banks, and the obvious proclivity that consumers have to do so. Fleet also found that not all of its products and services were offered in every one of its branches, so there was opportunity to bring in new customers by making more products available. The bank could also capture a larger share of its current customers' wallets by working with them to consolidate their activities with Fleet. In particular, Fleet was underrepresented in credit, which is a highly profitable area of activity for a retail bank and—despite their concerns and wariness— a significant need for middle-market consumers.

The availability of products, however, was not the real problem. The issue was how to make the products easier for the consumer to understand and use. Warner personally supervised the consumer research. The example of Commerce Bank, which retained customers even when its rates were slightly higher than competitors', showed the importance of meeting the consumer's needs for simplicity, convenience, consistency, and speed. However, even with its friendly tellers and focus on in-branch customer service, Commerce did not have the range of services that Fleet offered or could offer. So, if Fleet could improve its branch experience, and take a more holistic view of middle-market consumers and their total financial picture, the bank could take back share and build stronger, more profitable relationships with its customers.

To do so, Fleet would have to come to know its consumers well and build relationships with them. The Fleet branch would have to offer a more personalized experience. The banker would need to know the customer—not just the products he or she held, but something about the composition of the household and something about the customer's needs, hopes, and dreams. Fleet, through its employees, would come to be seen as an enabler of customers' dreams, rather than as a barrier to their achievement.

This meant that the sales force and branch management teams would have to be trained so they could shed the habits of the aggressive upsellers they had been and become comfortable with the ways of relationship bankers. A new system of incentives would have to be devised that rewarded them for serving, retaining, and upgrading current customers as well as attracting new ones.

The bank would also have to improve the appearance of the branch offices and step up its maintenance activities. Brighter, cleaner, newer, nicer. It would still be a New England bank with a sense of colonial heritage, but it couldn't be stodgy or intimidating.

The Fleet brand needed attention, too. For many former customers of BayBank, BankBoston, Shawmut, and other regional banks that had been acquired along the way, the Fleet name had little meaning. Fleet's acquisitions had received a huge amount of press in the New England media—much of it negative—with stories about job losses, huge payouts to departing executives, branch closings, increased fees, system glitches, and more. Fleet's own marketing and public communications efforts had tried to make the point that Fleet's increased size would be good for customers, although consumers we spoke with for this book did not equate institutional size with personal advantage. Quite the opposite.

Fleet, pressed by Wall Street for growth and challenged by faster-moving competitors such as Commerce Bank, set out to solve its problems with customer service, and become a top-notch retailer, a world-class consumer bank, a selling and service powerhouse.

A Transformed Fleet

Brad Warner declared that there would be a "consumer revolution" at FleetFinancial and he laid out a plan for a twenty-four–month rollout. Although he had virtually no experience in retail banking, Warner became the principal advocate of consumer-oriented service. In his personal visits with customers and branch associates, he became a roving ambassador, talking up the importance of creating consumer "chemistry."

At the heart of the plan was the free financial checkup, a face-to-face meeting between a branch manager or customer service rep and the consumer. The purpose was to gain insight into the consumer's goals, review his or her current products, identify any gaps or inefficiencies, and make recommendations for changes and improvements.

The checkups allowed the Fleet financial adviser to demonstrate that he or she had deep product knowledge and financial expertise that the "convenience competitors" like Commerce could not match. The checkups allowed the bank personnel to show that they could actually be friendly and personable, and not the stuffed shirts of old.

The financial checkups were supported with new products and product bundles that the customer service rep could tailor and customize in many ways to best suit the customer's needs. The bank made these products and customized bundles even more attractive by revamping, and in many cases reducing, fees and charges. This gave the financial adviser many tools to work with and benefits to offer, including:

- Simple and transparent pricing options, with discounts and rewards for customers with more than one touch point with the bank (for example, a reduction of the interest rate on a home equity line for customers with existing checking or savings accounts).
- Instant approval for certain products, based on credit reports, modeled demographics, and the customer's relationship with Fleet.
- An incentives program that rewarded the consolidation of multiple credit card balances with Fleet with a lower interest rate.
- The ability to consolidate and repackage debt, whether held by Fleet or a competitor, and transfer the balances from high-rate to lower-rate products.
- A revolving credit line, accessible with a Fleet credit card, with no monthly fees.
- Checking accounts with no maintenance fees.
- Fewer penalties and fees for errors, such as bounced checks or late payments.
- A single consolidated statement of all accounts and positions.
- Warning calls when an overdraft kicks in.

After the initial checkup, customer service reps were encouraged to keep in touch with consumers and offer additional consultations at important lifestage milestones such as the birth of a child, the purchase or sale of a home, or a child's matriculation in college.

For Fleet, the primary benefit of the financial checkups was to cross-sell. The bank had estimated that cross-selling could add some $380 in revenues per customer each year. And cross-selling has greater value the earlier it occurs in the relationship. The value of a credit card account to the bank, for example, is 30 percent greater when sold in the relationship's first year than when sold in the fourth year. Cross-selling also correlates with customer retention, because the more connections a consumer has with the bank, the more likely he or she is to stay, not switch.

In addition to the checkups and product improvements, Fleet continued to improve its online banking operations with the intention of being known as the bank with the best network.

And, even with its new focus on customer service, Fleet did not forget the importance of ubiquity. The bank continued to build out its network of branches and ATMs, with the goal of increasing its presence throughout its area. Commerce was continuing to expand, and Fleet had no intention of losing its advantage as the most available financial services company in its region.

The program worked. As relationships improved, customers agreed that the technical and functional differences had changed how they felt about Fleet. They began to agree that:

- "The customer service reps at Fleet know me well and can develop the best financial plan for me."
- "Fleet makes me feel more secure about my money."
- "I feel that Fleet cares about me, my family, and my money."
- "I trust Fleet; it is my first-choice financial provider."
- "I feel smart that I bank with Fleet."

Conclusion: But That's Not How It Played Out

The program worked. In short order, the operating profits of the consumer bank doubled, and Fleet's retail operation had the power of a growth trajectory.

Nevertheless, in April 2004, FleetFinancial was purchased by Bank of America in a share-transfer deal valued at about $48 billion. The combined operation became the largest retail bank in the United States, the second largest bank in total assets, controlling, at the time, nearly 10 percent of the nation's deposits, and operating in twenty-nine states from 5,700 branches.

According to Fleet's management, they had not rushed into the sale and only made the deal because it brought a significant premium to shareholders. "We had no need whatsoever" to do the deal, Fleet-Boston's president, Eugene M. McQuade, told *The New York Times*. One of the main reasons that Bank of America was attracted to Fleet, beyond its geographical position in the Northeast, was its vastly improved consumer banking operations. Even so, Brad Warner felt that more could have been accomplished. "In retrospect, we could have moved faster. My only regret is that we were not as aggressive as we could have been," he told me. "When you have a great franchise, you can do more faster. But change in a big company is so hard."

It took virtually no time for the press, analysts, and shareholders to comment on the deal. From the time of the announcement in October 2003 through the transition period, which lasted through 2005, came very familiar postmerger news of layoffs, branch closings, increased fees, consumer defections, and more.

Here's the lesson: FleetFinancial was on the right track. What's sure is that, for Bank of America to retain its leadership as a retail banking institution, to achieve growth when acquisitions don't make sense, and to keep ahead of the still-expanding Commerce Bank, it will have to continue the learning that FleetFinancial began: how to understand the hopes and dreams of the consumer and shape its offerings around them.

Banks operate retail branches that behave like stores. A properly defined consumer experience can improve the consumer's loyalty to the bank, increase referral rates, and boost their product purchases. If appropriately served, consumers will choose a bank and buy financial services just like any other product, although with perhaps a little more trepidation and a little less confidence.

As Bob Reilly explained, "Big banks are starting to get better at treating the little guys because all the rich guys have left and gone to investment places. The big guys don't put their money into savings accounts. The little guys are all banks have left."

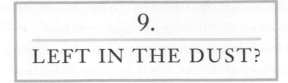

9.

LEFT IN THE DUST?

Peter Kim: A Waiter

Peter Kim, a thirty-year-old waiter, believes that he has been left behind. The realization came over him quite suddenly. In fact, he can pinpoint the moment. About a year ago, Peter's best friend from high school called to say that he and his wife were moving out of the city and buying a $1 million home in the suburbs of Chicago, so they could have more room for themselves and their two young children. Peter lives in a tiny apartment in the city. His mother and father live in an apartment two blocks away. He's single, has no significant other, and is uncertain about building a family. With that call from his old friend, a lot of the concerns that had been lurking in the background for Peter leaped into the foreground. Why was he still living in the city in such a small place? Where was he headed professionally? What about a family? How would he spend the rest of his life?

Peter works at the main restaurant of a high-end hotel in downtown Chicago. He is a perfectionist who truly cares about food presentation, wine selection, and delivering spectacular service. It hurts him personally when one of his dinner guests doesn't finish the food on the plate, so much so that he will offer to substitute a dish that might be more to the customer's liking. He finds it hard to understand that most of the unfinished portions are on the plates of women who are not dissatisfied with the food but, rather, are dissatisfied with their weight.

Peter was born in and spent his early childhood in Korea and moved to Chicago with his parents when he was five years old and his sister, Julia, was seven. His father worked in a factory and his mother owned a coin-operated laundry. Peter attended public high school and the University of Illinois, where he earned a bachelor's degree in Asian studies and economics. After graduating, he spent three years in Japan in a teaching exchange program. There he learned Japanese and brushed up on his Korean. He returned to Chicago and decided he would go back to school to earn his MBA, as his father had always hoped he would. But Peter found that business school was not for him. He preferred a less structured lifestyle, one that would give him time to pursue his real interest: art and design.

Peter quickly found work in the food service industry, and discovered that he enjoyed being a waiter. He liked the fact that it was so flexible that it was not really a job at all. It required no planning ahead. It was like living totally in the moment. Besides, he loved food and wine and talking with people. He did stints at a variety of fancy restaurants in Chicago, including OxCho, Vong, and Mod, before settling in at the hotel restaurant. As his skills improved, he became known throughout the city as one of the best and most reliable waiters in town. His earning power increased, and he found he could easily make $50,000 a year and, if he worked extra shifts, as much as $75,000. He didn't save any money because he didn't think he needed to. If he did pile up a little cash in his savings account, he'd use it to take a trip somewhere. He got comfortable with his life as a waiter. He had no desire to work a nine-to-five job in a big company and he wasn't ready to open his own restaurant, which he knew would require raising lots of capital and working long hours. He had a core group of about six good friends, and none of them was on any of the traditional career or family paths. For five years he cruised along and thought he was doing just about as well as everybody else he knew. "I didn't feel envious of anybody," Peter told me. "I could travel when I wanted. I could move at will. I could pursue my hobbies."

After all, Peter felt that he had plenty of money and that he didn't need to be particularly frugal. He traveled regularly, visiting Thailand, France, Mexico, and the Caribbean. He ate out several times a month. Most of the time, he would eat at inexpensive restaurants where he could hang out with his friends and spend $20 or less on the meal. He would also occasionally dine at one of Chicago's upscale restaurants, like Charlie Trotters or Tru, primarily as a form of professional development. "As a waiter, I have to know what's going on," he said. "But I just go once." He bought a Jeep Cherokee just for the freedom of being able to drive anywhere he wanted. Even though he loves the car, he thinks it is "horribly made."

PETER'S ASSETS		HIS LIABILITIES	
Savings account	$2,000	Mortgage	$0
Checking account	$1,000	Home equity	$0
Investments	$12,000	Credit card	$500
Home value	$0	Student loans	$0
Other	$40,000	Other	$0

A Spending Distortion

It would not be fair to say that Peter was a profligate spender. His expenses were not particularly out of line with his income—except in one area: art supplies. About ten years ago, Peter began to put more and more of his energy into painting. He works only in oils. His canvasses are big, some as large as 6x8'. They all are abstract, and many have been created with a strictly limited color palette. They hang, like Stephanie's scarves, all over the walls of Peter's apartment. He has also created a storage space in the back, behind the kitchen, where he keeps another fifty or sixty canvasses.

Gradually, as Peter studied his craft and learned about the best art-supply brands and where to buy them, he spent more and more money on his painting. In fact, he has spent as much as $5,000 a year on paints, canvas, and other art supplies. He will work only with Old Holland, which he considers to be the best brand of paint for his work. But he never sells any of his paintings and has no desire to. "I have given a few away," he told me, "but it was very painful to do so. Each piece means a lot to me." Yes, $5,000 a year out of a total income of $75,000, tops, is a large distortion. But, to Peter, it fits the value calculus. He considers painting to be much more than a hobby. "It's about possibilities," he said. "About achieving mastery over something."

As distorted as his value calculus may seem to the observer, Peter didn't question it until he approached thirty, and he began to see that things were shifting around him. His sister had gotten married and moved to Los Angeles. He learned that she was earning at least $200,000 a year as an executive at a large philanthropic organization, and that her husband, a telecommunications executive, was making about the same. Their house was worth $1.3 million or more. Suddenly, Peter's $75,000 income looked puny. Everybody he talked to seemed to have a 401(K) plan or some kind of nest egg or safety net. Peter didn't. Everybody seemed to be buying an apartment or a home and they all cost at least $400,000. Some of his friends had moved out of the city. Peter was living right where he had for the past eight years, only a short walk from where his parents had lived for the past forty-five years. He had no steady partner and wasn't sure he wanted one. Although he had never aspired to a conventional life, and still had friends who felt the same way, now he began to wonder if he had made the wrong choices. Then came the call from his high school friend, and it hit Peter very hard. "I think of most of my peers as upper-middle-class, but I began to feel very lower class," Peter told

PETER'S MONTHLY EXPENSES

Item	Spending	Index vs. Average
Income (posttax)	$3,950	1.0
Car	280	0.4
Mortgage/rent	600	0.9
Household utilities and maintenance	150	0.4
Eating out	50	0.2
Groceries	200	0.9
Travel and entertainment	200	1.0
Healthcare/personal health	0	0.0
Home goods	50	0.3
Clothing	50	0.3
Charitable contributions	0	0.0
Education	0	0.0
Personal care services	30	0.6
Life insurance	0	0.0
Other expenses	500	6.1
Total spending	2,110	0.6
Net savings/(deficit)	1,840	3.0

me. "I'm not upwardly mobile. My friends from high school and college are leaps and bounds ahead of me. I felt like I woke up one day and the world had left me behind."

Trading Down to Get Back on Course

Peter decided that he was just in a phase and that he could take action to change his life for the better. He wanted to start by getting control of his finances and saving some money. Rather than cut back on the art supplies, which might have been the obvious thing to do, Peter looked for other places in the budget where he could trade down. He started shopping more at Costco because he could find high-quality goods there at very low prices. One of his favorite purchases is the four-pound can of tuna fish. It costs $4.00 at Costco, in comparison to $2.00 for the 6-ounce can at the supermarket. Peter likes to entertain and he can stretch a four-pound can of tuna fish a dozen different ways and over many days. He develops elaborate recipes for tuna salad, involving pickle brine, hard-boiled eggs, and chopped herbs. In Peter's mind, the savings on food offsets some of his extravagant spending on paint.

Peter has also become very careful about his spending on clothes. In fact, that was one of the first categories where he cut back. His work uniform is a tuxedo and he owns four nice ones, along with about twenty-five ties, but everything else is fair game for trading down. He shops at the trendy trading-up specialty shops that he has always favored—like Diesel, Club Monaco, and Banana Republic—but he only shops when there is a sale or end-of-season closeout. He looks for styles that he can wear all year long, rather than worry about seasonal wardrobes. In a pinch, he'll buy black socks at Walgreens for $3.99. But his best trick is to buy clothing on sale that he doesn't necessarily need and then carefully pack it away in special storage containers. When he needs something new or just wants a lift, he takes the shirt or pair of pants out of the box—still in its original packing and with tags flying—and treats himself to something "new." He figures he has at least $1,500 worth of clothing salted away.

Peter has also cut back his spending on dining out and entertainment, and held his other expenses in check. The rent on his apartment is only $600 and utilities run about $150 a month. The car costs about $280 a month. Another $200 a month goes for groceries. His clothing expenditure is down to about $50. In the past two years, Peter has been able to save $12,000, more than he has ever saved before.

But Peter's value calculus has not fundamentally changed. He does not aspire to wealth. He doesn't really worry about his finances. He cares more, as he puts it, "about the beauty of things." He has thought a lot about his life and what he wants to accomplish. He has four main goals: to leave a "legacy of art," to write and publish a book, to start up his own business, and—although he says it rather tentatively and almost as an afterthought—to have "a family."

Even so, Peter has to earn a living and he wants the freedom that having money can bring. He is considering changing careers, or at least adding another skill to the mix, and is focusing on graphic design. He has been taking classes in computer graphics at a community college. And he made a major financial commitment by purchasing a high-end, graphics-oriented computer for $3,500. He had to use a credit card to make the purchase, which he didn't like to do, but he saw it as an investment in his future and his ability to achieve his other goals. He may transfer to a hotel restaurant in Los Angeles so he can be closer to his sister and where he thinks he can get better instruction in painting. He may even work toward another academic degree. "I consider myself a student," Peter told me. "I'm still trying to figure out the meaning of life."

It is very difficult to get back in the action once you've been left behind, as Peter feels he has been. Peter's solution is to move and to gain new skills—to reinvent himself.

Retailers Who Wait Can Also Get Left in the Dust

Peter Kim is not the only one who feels left in the dust—the trading-down/trading-up phenomenon also has created much turmoil for retailers, and the ones who most often get left in the dust are those in the middle of the market. As Wal-Mart and other winners have led a retailing revolution—achieving 20 to 40 percent annual growth and shareholder return two to four times the market average—the traditional grocery chain has lost thirty share points and the traditional department store has lost as many as fifty share points. Zayre, Ames, Bradlees, Caldor, and Venture Stores have all been left in the dust.

These stores were unable to adapt to shifts in the market. They lost price advantage, could not retain their core-customer share, and provided insufficient service. They often gave up volume to specialists who built preference among younger consumers, provided faster product rotation, and emphasized emotional connections. The losers failed to permit consumers to trade down and save, or trade up and gain emotional benefits. The worst offenders of all were the conventional department stores. They just kept offering more of the same— goods at the same price point, with identical merchandising, offered at a high initial mark-up but generally sold at an end-of-season markdown.

Retail has long been among the most Darwinian of industries. Consider the list of the largest retailers in the United States in 1970. At the top was Sears, followed by JC Penney, Kmart, Woolworth, and McCrory. Also on the top list, but now gone, are Grant Co., Genesco, Allied Stores, May (now part of Federated), Dayton Hudson, Associated Dry Goods, Broadway Stores, and Cook United.

RETAIL SUCCESS DIFFICULT TO SUSTAIN
Few Players Stand the Test of Time

Top U.S. retailers 1970		Top U.S. retailers 2004	
Retailers	Sales ($B)	Retailers	Sales ($B)
Sears, Roebuck & Co.	43.3	Wal-Mart Stores	288.2
JC Penney	19.4	Home Depot Inc.	73.1
Kmart Corp.	12.2	Kroger Co.	56.4
Woolworth F.W. Co.	11.8	Costco Wholesale Corp.	47.1
McCrory Parent Corp.	10.7	Target Corp.	46.8
Federated Dept. Stores	9.8	Albertsons Inc.	39.9
Grant Co.	5.9	Walgreen Co.	37.5
Genesco Co.	5.8	Lowe's Co.	36.5
Allied Stores	5.7	Sears, Roebuck & Co.	36.1
May Dept. Stores Inc.	5.5	Safeway Inc.	35.8
Dayton Hudson Corp.	4.6	CVS Corp.	30.6
Macy & Co.	4.2	Ahold USA	27.5
Spartans Industries Inc.	4.0	Best Buy Co. Inc.	27.4
Associated Dry Goods Corp.	3.7	Kmart Corp.	19.7
Woolworth Pfc. Adr.	3.6	Publix Super Markets Inc.	18.6
Walgreen Co.	3.5	JC Penney	18.4
Interstate Stores Inc.	3.2	Rite Aid Corp.	16.8
TJX Companies	3.2	Gap Inc.	16.3
Broadway Stores Inc.	3.1	Delhaize America	15.8
Cook United Inc.	2.9	Federated Dept. Stores	15.6

1970 sales are in 2004 dollars.
Source: Holt database; IMF International Financial Statistics; STORES; BCG analysis.

The scale of operations of the new retail leaders has increased sevenfold since 1970, in comparison to a doubling in size of the entertainment, consumer-products, and transportation industries. To be in the top rank of retailers in 2004 required at least $15 billion in revenue, versus just $2.9 billion (in constant 2004 dollars) in 1970. The vast majority of the fallen retailers served the middle market. They competed supply chain versus supply chain but were unable to adapt or generate sufficient cash to reinvent themselves.

The rise of the consumer-driven economy drives this retail turmoil. Consumers believe there is no meaningful difference among a wide group of categories. They have drained grocery stores of volume, have forced a wholesale reordering of the department store industry, and have caused the closure of many small independent stores in a variety of categories.

The result has been a dramatic reduction in gross margin in most areas of retail, as well as real price declines. The savings from trading down, more than $100 billion, has mostly been spent on the goods consumers really want—bigger homes, luxury cars, adventure vacations, exotic food ingredients, and meals at better restaurants. The trading-down wave has swept such categories as canned food, dry goods, snack foods, paper products, condiments, cereal, laundry detergent, bottled water, frozen foods, and bakery products.

Turmoil in the Grocery Industry

Of all the retail segments, the conventional grocery industry, to a very large degree, has been most transformed. It built an extensive network of 40,000 to 60,000 square-foot stores. Competitors offered very similar products and services. They generated positive cash flow in their home markets and used the money to replicate their operations in new markets. They viewed competition narrowly and, as a result, failed to see that a lot of their volume was being siphoned off by discount stores, supercenters, warehouse stores, hard discounters, and dollar stores. Our research suggests that the majority of U.S. consumers are trading down in grocery basics such as paper goods, canned products, and items in the "glass" aisle, such as mayonnaise, pickles, ketchup, and cooking oil. The conventional groceries also failed to realize that they were being threatened by specialist category experts—those who offer fresh bread, gourmet foods, or speciality takeout, for example. The result is that the traditional grocery industry is suffering from overcapacity, price deflation, share loss, and a new industry order.

Wal-Mart is responsible for much of the shift in the grocery industry. Over a period of fifteen years, Wal-Mart grocery sales have increased from just $10 billion to over $70 billion, making Wal-Mart the largest grocer in the United States. The Wal-Mart superstore value proposition is compelling. Prices are 10 percent lower than most supermarkets and the company's global network delivers sourcing scale, technology advantages, lower logistics cost, and sophisticated analysis on all the major elements of store operations. A Wal-Mart superstore is typically at least 100,000 square feet in size and is designed to sell up to $100 million in merchandise per year. The superstores have steadily taken share from conventional grocers, leaving them stranded with the fixed costs of an infrastructure built for much larger operations. A Wal-Mart supercenter will deliver twice the labor productivity of an ordinary supermarket, through a combination of lower prices that drive high traffic, engineered logistics, and a unique mix of food and general merchandise. The supercenter delivers higher store traffic, drives general merchandise sales, and increases per-customer visits to the store. The typical supercenter will provide twice the space per SKU. The Wal-Mart supercenter is one of those very rare examples of a return to an earlier retail concept that dramatically improves the earnings of the original.

When a retail company wins big in the trading-down segment, it delivers huge space velocity advantages, which simply means that it sells more dollars of goods per square foot of store space than its competitors do. This is a function of low prices that drive turn, replenishment that avoids out of stock, and high traffic. When you earn gross margin 50 percent higher per square foot than a competitor, that can translate into four times the profits per store. The cash can be taken to the bank or reinvested in the business. If reinvested in the business, that can translate into more and better service, wider inventory, higher in-stock rates, more frequent replenishment of product offerings, more advertising, and better locations—all of which can bring still greater profit.

The supercenter provides a new shopping tool to the middle-market consumer. Sarah, our Arlington Heights stay-at-home mom, uses her trips to the supercenter as a budget balancer. "At the beginning of the month, I plan my food purchases to maximize our dollars," she says. "It's worth the extra time because I save ten or twenty dollars on every visit." Sarah says she has practically given up on Jewel, which was once the dominant Chicago grocer. She used to purchase all of her groceries at Jewel, and the chain took in more than $700 a month from the Montforts. Now Sarah prefers the everyday low prices she gets at Wal-Mart and Sam's Clubs, and views Jewel's high low pricing as deceptive. Jewel has become her secondary supplier. "When I do go there," she says, "I only buy items on sale. All of my household products are bought in bulk. National brands are generally more expensive, so we buy off-brands except for where it really matters in quality, like paper towels."

H.E. Butt: Prospering Where Others Don't

Even as the grocery industry is being reconfigured, a few smaller chains, like H.E. Butt, have found a way to compete and prosper. This 100-year-old San Antonio, Texas, chain operates 300 stores, primarily in Texas and northern Mexico, with extraordinarily high local market shares. The company is the largest private employer in Texas. Charles Butt, grandson of the founder, has led the company since

1971. He is a Wharton School grad with an MBA from Harvard. His success at H.E. Butt places him ninety-seventh on the Forbes 400 list, with an estimated net worth of $2.2 billion.

Butt told me that the key to success in grocery today is "innovate or die." He has continuously challenged his management team to take food retailing to the next level. The company has pursued a high degree of vertical integration with milk, meat, ice cream, pastry, and even its own chip-making facility. (Authentic Texas-style tortilla chips, that is, not silicon.) Butt knows the chain must compete on price and perishables. The chain, which is actually a collection of stores under several different brand banners, is managed to create produce and meat sections that offer fresh goods, to offer fast service, and so its stores can be customized to the local market.

One of H.E. Butt's boldest moves was the introduction of the Central Market brand, which is essentially a trading-up grocery. The Central Market stores are pavilions that celebrate food. They have an executive chef, provide their customers with online recipes in seventeen categories, offer cooking schools, and conduct cheese and wine tastings. One of their innovations is a takeout "dinner for two" menu, featuring a variety of dishes available at $13.99. A wine expert is on hand in the store to suggest wines that will complement the chosen meal. In 2005, Central Market partnered with the Culinary Institute of America to introduce twenty-five new pastry items, including raspberry mousse, chibouste lime tart, and red velvet cake. Central Market also offers prepared sauces, salsas, and dips in bulk. There are 700 types of produce, 80 varieties of fish, and 600 kinds of cheese. At the chain's San Antonio location, consumers can sit on the patio each weekend and enjoy live music under the stars. It's almost as if Central Market is providing an answer to a personal ad: "Attractive single parent, 35 to 40, seeks leverage at moderate cost at Central Market."

The H-E-B stores understand their middle-market consumer very well. They know that the majority of working women ask themselves the same question at the end of every work day—"What's for dinner tonight?"—and that the answer is usually "I have no idea." That's why the H-E-B Web site offers a variety of recipes to browse, along with daily grocery specials. If the "Couscous Casablanca" looks good, you can print out the recipe and the shopping list of items you'll need to buy (preferably at H-E-B) in order to prepare the dish: 1 (10 oz.) pkg. couscous, 1½ cups frozen onion seasoning blend, 1 bulb garlic, curry powder, butter, H-E-B fully-cooked roasted chicken breasts, 1 (11 oz.) can mandarin oranges, 1 (8 oz.) pkg. crumbled feta cheese, fresh apple slices, and a fresh express spinach salad kit.

Many of H-E-B's consumers are Spanish-speaking Mexican-Americans. Unlike many grocery companies that practice a rather undifferentiated style of "Hispanic marketing," H-E-B understands that recipes, flavors, and ingredients vary widely in different regions of Mexico. It offers, for example, more than a hundred types of potatoes at stores that serve Mexican-American consumers. Most varieties cost H-E-B about a dime per pound when purchased at wholesale, but sell briskly at retail for $.99 a pound. H-E-B is the only grocer to provide so many different kinds of potatoes, and the variety attracts consumers.

H.E. Butt has also developed an answer to the Wal-Mart supercenter: its 109,000 square-foot H-E-B Plus stores. These stores carry a very broad line of products—both premium and basic—and deliver similar economics to those of the Wal-Mart supercenters. There is also a designated space for "surprise buys" that offer shoppers H-E-B's version of the treasure hunt.

In the face of some of the toughest competition from Wal-Mart, Target, and other nearby intruders, H.E. Butt has continued to grow. When Charles Butt was named president, the company had sales of $250 million. H.E. Butt closed 2005 with sales above $11 billion.

Avoiding the Seemingly Unavoidable

Trauma and turmoil, when they occur, generally sneak up on the retailer, whether it is in groceries or general merchandise. The retailer buys goods, expecting a strong season, but then is disappointed by the results. The company is forced to sell the remaining products at a discount and carry the inventory much longer than it had expected to. The economic formula that made it successful starts to lose its relevance. It's easy to feel the effects of these problems when you walk the aisles of traditional retailers. The number of employees has been cut. Specific items and sizes may be hard to find, generally as a result of poor or limited buying, slow rotation, or inadequate labor spent on organization.

The single most important early-warning signal that you may be in danger of getting left behind is a drop in share of "primary shop." When a consumer ranks you as their first choice for purchasing goods in a particular category, you enjoy the bulk of the sales and margin that that consumer has to offer. This is important because retail is a very leveraged business—space occupancy, staffing, and inventory are essentially fixed costs—and a loss of as little as 10 percent of volume can cut profitability in half.

Many of the retailers that succumbed during the last forty years failed to respond to such signals. They focused too narrowly on their core businesses and were blind to threats and opportunities beyond their normal range of vision. They displayed characteristics typical of the dinosaur in any industry:

- An inability to see shifts in the market, including trading up/ trading down, and death in the middle.
- An unwillingness to confront competitive initiatives that have "germs" of ideas that can be adopted, brought front and center, and executed by the established competitor.

- A desire to protect today's market definition and market share and not attack boundaries that provide expansion.
- Increasing complexity costs, resulting in inflexibility and slow decision making.
- A tendency toward internal conflict and organizational stratification.
- A leadership that emphasizes capital investments as a solution to all problems.
- Centralized control with limited coordination among divisions and a weakened sense of market trends and consumer needs.

But decline is not inevitable for retailers. Successful, but threatened, companies can overcome complacency, competitive threats, and shifting markets. H.E. Butt, for example, was able to do so. When Wal-Mart, Target, and Kmart attacked H-E-B in Victoria, Texas (population 60,584), the company took the invasion as a challenge and declared that it was going to stand and fight. H-E-B cut prices, added variety, expanded capacity and operating hours, and grew its local share. Ultimately the lessons from Victoria became H-E-B's statewide victory formula.

The work needed to see big market shifts and spark a renaissance is usually time-consuming, complex, difficult, and uncomfortable—and can overwhelm even the most capable management team. It requires a leadership team that is willing to take on the analysis of root causes and has the skills and will to initiate a massive effort to change. Typically this begins with a three-step process of rethinking the business. Step one is to develop a fact-based assessment of economics and competitive position. Step two is to get a deep understanding of what the core customer and the potential core customer want and need. Step three involves a fundamental reinvention of the concept as a whole. During this process, managers must ask fundamental questions, such as:

- How do we compare to our major competitors?
- What is the economic driver of our future success?
- Who are our heavy spenders? How do we attract more of them?
- What are the functional compromises in our business, the rules that prevent optimization, the dysfunctional operations?
- Where is our market going?
- How do we participate in the next round of growth?
- Can we anticipate the market change and get there first?

The Consumer, as Always, Is Key

Understanding how consumer needs are changing is an art, not a science. It is not a one-time action, but rather a continuous effort to build a platform of knowledge. It requires conducting research at the store level and developing expertise in listening to consumers and interpreting what they have to say. It involves:

- Shopping along with consumers. You should be able to describe their experience from purchase to repurchase, their biggest dissatisfactions, and when and why they defect to your competitors.
- Understanding your competitor's consumers to the same degree you understand your own. You should gather data on how often those consumers buy your products and their intentions to repurchase. You should carefully analyze the consumers' value calculus.
- Knowing your competitors' best sellers. You need to track your competitors' test markets and adapt or improve on the profitable ideas at the earliest sign of success. You need to look beyond your normal set of competitors to see what other stores may be doing to entice consumers to trade up or trade down.

We often visit retail locations to conduct interviews with shoppers, and we're especially interested in those who leave the store without having made a purchase. There are four main reasons for such "no-purchase" exits: the item they wanted was out of stock, the product selection was poor, items were hard to find, or the service was poor.

How does this happen? In retail companies, operating systems are often developed for the needs of the store rather than for the needs of the consumer. Stores want to drive out cost by reducing the number of SKUs, eliminating low-productivity operating hours, decreasing promotional activity, and eliminating experimentation. The consumer, by contrast, wants a wide range of product SKUs, long opening hours, lots of promotional opportunities, and a constant stream of exciting new products and services to try.

The solution is to get at the root causes of consumer dissatisfaction by applying statistical process control (SPC) to the store envi-

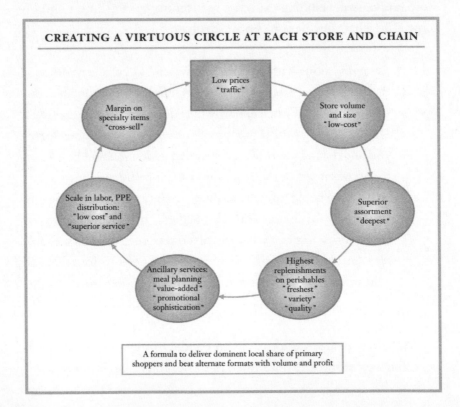

CREATING A VIRTUOUS CIRCLE AT EACH STORE AND CHAIN

Low prices "traffic"

Store volume and size "low-cost"

Superior assortment "deepest"

Highest replenishments on perishables "freshest" "variety" "quality"

Ancillary services: meal planning "value-added" "promotional sophistication"

Scale in labor, PPE distribution: "low cost" and "superior service"

Margin on specialty items "cross-sell"

A formula to deliver dominent local share of primary shoppers and beat alternate formats with volume and profit

ronment. This involves breaking complex problems into manageable components. The process can be useful in understanding such issues as why items are out of stock, consumer exits without a purchase, and appropriate staffing levels by time of day, among other concerns. The problem-solving process can result in improvements to store operations, performance control, service levels, and labor management.

To avoid being left behind, retailers need to do this kind of major renewal effort regularly. To succeed, the management team must help the company adapt to new realities without discarding the wisdom it has acquired through experience. It must respond to intruders while seeding the organization with the intellectual diversity and vitality necessary for its continuing evolution.

Just as Peter Kim did, retail companies need to recognize the importance of learning new skills, trying out different concepts, and periodically reinventing themselves.

TAKING ACTION

Lessons from a Master Innovator

Leslie Wexner, founder of Limited Brands, has an extraordinary ability to understand the consumer and the consumer-goods market, and to put his understanding into action. He has a remarkable record of success in the world of retail; he's the man behind The Limited, Express, Limited Too, Victoria's Secret, the reinvented version of Abercrombie, and Bath & Body Works. He has a keen ability to observe people and their behaviors and, somehow, transform his observations into a constant flow of retailing ideas. His wife reports that Les will jump out of bed in the morning and say to her gleefully that while he was sleeping, "I just had a great new idea!" He also has the ability to focus on the right ideas, and the skill and experience to execute them. "People are looking for emotional highs," Wexner told me in the course of a philosophical conversation. "Winning companies invent new products that capture the consumer's imagination. We always need emotional products. Otherwise we would all be wearing white wool togas. Human nature causes you to want to be different."

Wexner attributes his success to three factors: hard work, domain expertise, and an ability to see around the corner—to imagine what might be, to connect the economic dots, and to predict where the business landmines might be hidden.

"You have to recognize the importance of observation and to take it very seriously," said Wexner. The world is rich with people, things, and events, and changes constantly. In that richness and change are found the seeds of breakthrough ideas for new business. It's all right there in front of you, if you will just look and try to understand what you're seeing. Whatever you observe that strikes you as interesting, different, unusual, or appealing may contain the germ of a new business idea. Pierre Omidyar was intrigued by how people form communities on the Web. Howard Schultz, founder of Starbucks, was fascinated by the way people drink coffee in Italy. The Albrecht brothers understood that customers take pride in pinching a penny so hard it hurt.

That's why Wexner believes so strongly in the importance of talent. "Thomas Friedman is right. The world is flat," he says. "There's really no such thing as long-term cost advantage on a global basis. Everyone can access the same factories and the same components. The world is commoditizing." So, whether you're playing to the low end or the high end, or trying to hold the middle, you will need the world's best designers, the most talented raw material specialists available, and the manager who can see what has never been created. "This skill set requires experience, intensity, imagination, a furious amount of energy to be ahead of commoditization," Wexner says.

While you're observing, ideas must be allowed to emerge. Let your own ideas come tumbling out and encourage others you work with to contribute theirs. When you see a good idea somewhere else, don't hesitate to grab it and reinterpret it for yourself. Understand consumers, listen to their needs, play back your understanding to them, and respond to and engage with them.

Then comes the hard part—picking up on an idea, interpreting it within the context of your company and competitive situation, and creating the prototype.

Many Ways to Act

As challenging as life in the bifurcating market can be, companies have found ways to act on new ideas and succeed handsomely with them at either end of the market.

In *Trading Up*, we profiled the companies that have done well at the high end, including Panera Bread, BMW, Viking, Kendall-Jackson Wine Estates, and American Girl. In this book, I've shown that there is perhaps even greater opportunity at the low end, and that companies like Best Value Inn, Aldi, Costco, Dollar General, and others are achieving high levels of growth and profits there. There is also a handful of companies that have looked at the market, seen the consumer trade-offs involved, and said, "We can meet the consumer at both the high end and the low end." These few—including Toyota, LG, eBay, Marriott, and Cendant—have indeed found success at both ends.

Then there is the legion of companies that have yet to acknowledge the reality of the bifurcating market and have continued to slog along in the middle, scratching out incremental gains, fighting for share, trying to create the illusion of growth through acquisitions, or the illusion of profits through cost cutting. They often blame their lack of success on exogenous factors—on the rising cost of materials, competition from low-cost countries, currency fluctuations, government regulations, or consumer uncertainty. All those factors may well be in play, but they are rarely, if ever, the fundamental cause of the problem. The reality is that many companies are competing in markets that are shrinking, or operating in categories where the middle is drying up, and they don't realize it or refuse to acknowledge it.

The companies that succeed in this restless consumer market are the ones that face the reality of the bifurcation and look for opportunity within it. They develop a new business model, as LG did. They invent a new way of going to market, as eBay has. They reduce the cost of operations, as Aldi does relentlessly. They eliminate anything unnecessary. They accept the fact that their futures hang on their ability to do one of two things: deliver basic, trading-down goods at unbeatable prices or create trading-up goods with genuine differences that can command a premium.

Most companies simply don't have the patience or stamina required to fully succeed with either strategy. Yes, they usually express interest in learning about how the market is shifting. Yes, they are willing to listen to proposals for various trading-down or trading-up strategies they might pursue. But when it comes to doing the heavy lifting needed to achieve best value or best quality, the struggle is too great for them. It requires too high a level of creativity, too much drive, and too much domain expertise.

Many Traps

As a result, the majority of the companies that attempt to get out of their stuck-in-the-middle position get waylaid in one of a variety of ways.

Companies that pursue a trading-up strategy, for example, will usually make some incremental technical or functional improvements in their offering, and hope that the emotional value will soar. But they don't, or won't, make a full commitment to the strategy. They won't put enough cost into the product. They'll rely too much on advertising to build the brand. They won't listen well enough to consumers about what they like and dislike. They'll copy parts of what other, more successful traders-up do, but miss the central point. Can Maxwell House Master Blend ever capture a coffee lover's heart the way Starbucks does? When it comes to launch, they'll revert to their traditional channels and methods of communication, rather than look for new ways to market. And, instead of seeking out consumers who will really crave what the company has to offer, it will target traditional demographic segments of the population—if that can really be called targeting.

If the company pursues a trading-down strategy, it is just as likely to go astray. The management team will cut costs a little bit and streamline one or two of its processes, but will not have the endurance and fortitude to achieve the benchmark low costs they were striving for. Even if they cut costs a significant amount, they won't cut retail prices as much as they could, because they get enamored of the margins but don't understand that the margins can't last for long.

Many Models of Success

To succeed with either a trading-up or trading-down strategy takes courage. It took a lot of guts for LG Chairman Bon-Moo Koo to get his company to "scale the mountain" and move from a purveyor of dirt-cheap, low-quality home electronics goods to a maker of high-quality home goods that compete at both ends of the market. It was not easy for Neil Fiske to enter Bath & Body Works, with its $2.2 billion annual revenues and nearly 1,600 stores and its traditional mid-price branded offerings and say, "We're going to completely rethink our market, redefine our customer base, and transform ourselves into a partner in 'inner beauty.'"

It took extraordinary perseverance for Fred Carl, an introverted designer and former home builder, to build Viking Range from a one-man operation based in a former cotton warehouse into a world-class manufacturing system. Today, Viking operates three production facilities in Greenwood, Mississippi, all of which are highly automated and equipped with state-of-the-art machine tools. The company employs 1,100 nonunion hourly workers who earn $9 an hour assembling ovens, refrigerators, grills, and other products. All Viking products are made to order and the company stocks only enough parts to satisfy the needs of 1.5 manufacturing days. Everything is shipped from a single distribution center to fourteen Viking distributors who then ship on to retail outlets.

Fred Carl told me that Viking is the low-cost producer in premium appliances. "Toyota has adopted us," Fred says. "Their engineers visit our facilities twice a year to make suggestions. They also take a look at what we're doing and take our experiments back to the Toyota facilities in both Japan and the U.S." One of the most impressive pieces of the Viking operation is the "field repair board." Its function is to gather information from consumers about problems or concerns with Viking products and track them back to the manufacturing line so that any production glitches can be corrected and improvements made.

These models make it clear that—no matter who you are or what your business—the courage can be summoned, the bifurcation strategies can be executed, and companies and categories can be transformed; we've seen it happen in many categories. Over the past five years, we have explored the principles of both trading up and the treasure hunt with clients in many industries and we have watched as many others have adopted and adapted our ideas. In healthcare, for example, consumers are looking for technical and functional benefits they can understand, believe in, and trust. It is around those genuine differences that distinctive programs can be built that will bring in new consumers. In banking, the middle market is rich, needy, and seriously underserved by other financial services providers. Why shouldn't middle-class households have access to some of the same services that wealthier clients enjoy? Why shouldn't their $200,000 investment portfolio be taken seriously? Banks that seek to observe and understand the needs of the middle-class consumer have been able to generate innovations in product, pricing, service delivery, and the operation of the branch networks.

How about that most basic of consumer commodities, toilet paper? Georgia-Pacific (GP), the world's leading maker of toilet paper, has long been in a battle with that other giant of consumer goods, Procter & Gamble. GP decided that toilet tissue need not be a commodity and it need not be stuck in the middle, undifferentiated from its competitors. By segmenting its product line, GP has been able to span the poles, offering a trading-down product that increased sales volume and a trading-up brand that commands high retail prices.

"Paper was a commodity that our competitors thought was like any other consumer category," Mike Burandt, president, North American Consumer Products, told me. "With the Angel Soft and Sparkle brands we created the branded value segment. Angel Soft is the fastest-growing paper brand in the U.S. It provides consumers with a fantastic value. The consumers use this savings in other categories. It may not be sexy to trade down, but if you have a low-cost position, you can do very well. It requires the right foundation and consumer insight."

Market segmentation, which is essentially what we're talking about, has also worked for Wrigley, the world's largest maker of gum, with a 40 percent share of the world's gum market. The company—unlike many other food companies, including Kraft—enjoys strong growth and profits. Bill Wrigley, Jr., chairman, CEO, and president of the company, told me, "Our company was built on consumers receiving value for their money. For years and years, we sold gum in the U.S. at 25 cents for five sticks. During the last five-year period, though, we have seen faster growth. For example, it took ninety-nine years for the Wrigley company to reach its first $1 billion in annual sales, nine years to reach $2 billion, and just four to reach $3 billion. This growth is due, in part, because we segment the market. We now sell five-stick packages at 30 cents, but we also sell Altoids at $1.99 and Eclipse ten-piece packs for 99 cents. We take the trade-up and value price points very seriously."

The 42-year-old CEO is ambitious and expansive in his vision for Wrigley. He has invested heavily in new gum products—for teeth whitening, overall oral care, breath freshening, and revitalization benehts such as "breathe free" in European markets. The acquisition of the Altoids and Lifesavers businesses from Kraft is Wrigley's largest ever, and they may consider others. "You need to take advantage of all your strengths," Wrigley said. "And the time to act is today."

Then there are the small, private companies—whose entire annual sales do not equal a big-company executive's salary—that are building their businesses based on their observations of consumers and their interpretations of the treasure hunt ideas. Baltica, for example, is a maker of architectural and custom hardware such as door entrance sets, thumb latches, door pulls, knockers, backplates, and hinges. Based in Lithuania, the company was founded by Asta Baskauskas. She was born in Lithuania, educated in the United States, and then trained as a dentist, but gave it up to start Baltica with her sister. The company employs fifty craftspeople. "Each of our pieces is a work of art," Asta says proudly. "We use the finest materials and hand cut each piece. We sell primarily by word of mouth." Baltica hardware appeals to the treasure hunter who is looking for a special, unexpected piece that fits her unique value calculus.

Small companies, in fact, have many advantages over their larger competitors when it comes to moving with, or before, the bifurcating market. The primary advantage is to be found in the person of the entrepreneur, founder, or current leader who is motivated as much by dreams and theories as by financial compensation and share price. Smaller companies also tend to be closer to their customers and are better able to observe and understand shifts in consumer needs and pick up on them earlier than large competitors can. And, of course, a small company is generally able to act faster, by converting the idea into a new product or service and getting it into the marketplace before the competitor has called its first steering committee meeting or begun preparing its quarterly "new initiatives" presentation.

Similarly, large companies erect plenty of barriers that prevent them from seeing the market transformation and reacting to it. One is that the leaders focus too much on cost cutting. Rather than find ways to invest in technical, functional, and emotional benefits, companies seek to substitute lower-cost materials and components—as Kraft did with its Macaroni & Cheese—to reduce cost. Too often, the product or service quality gets degraded and the value calculation no longer makes sense for the consumer. Sometimes, the CEO or company leader simply loses his or her sense of imagination and willingness to make a strategic move. The leader may decide to cut back on new-product development, strip funds out of the R&D organization, and end up following a sure path to death in the middle. Large companies often mismanage the value chain. In particular, they outsource one or more of the key customer interface activities (such as surveying, interviewing, profiling, targeting, message development, product field testing, and customer relationship management), with the result that the company stops learning.

Recut the Data

How do you summon the courage necessary to make a move in this market? A good way to start is to take a hard look at the data.

I love data because it is so clear and easy to talk about. When we size the trading-down market, by gathering data on company results and calculating the annual sales in specific categories of goods, we can arrive at a single number—$1.5 trillion—that makes a big impression and reveals a great opportunity. Data can also clearly reveal important trends. When we say, for example, that over the past ten years the middle market for cars has shrunk by 13 percent, for TVs by 51 percent, and for women's apparel by 27 percent, that's stark and compelling proof that the middle is no place to be. Good data provides a rational basis for challenging the prevailing wisdom. When I share data like this with clients, the experience can be highly motivating. People seem to find it easier to summon the courage to make a change when they are confronted with data that shows they really have no choice. They get scared into a state that looks like bravery, even if it is actually not so far from fear.

As much as I love data, I get equally excited about the human issues and emotional factors that are involved in dynamic consumer-goods markets. It is also possible to look at reams of data and still have no sense of what's really going on and what it all means. For example, you could look at data showing the rising percentage of women who are getting four-year college degrees and still not understand the implications for product development and channel management. Data is also backward-looking and favors the average. For example, you might not guess, by looking at the demographic data, that the Nelson family would be in the market for four televisions, one of them a $2,000 wide-screen plasma set. Or that Lauren James, on an $85,000 yearly salary, would be a regular consumer of 7-Eleven soup and free crackers. Or that the single, fashionable Peter Kim would buy all his clothes at season-end sales.

The table below highlights the basic consumer analysis we conduct early in our work. The goal is to be able to explain consumer use, and the products they consider acceptable substitutes, to get underneath usage and understand dissatisfactions, hopes, and dreams. We also try to establish market size, not using the standard industry definition or the definition provided by syndicated data sources.

We know that data is only as good as the analysis of it, and we also know that companies tend to fall into analysis ruts—they keep looking at the same data, in the same way, making the same analysis, and responding to it in the same ways they always have. If the data shows that the company's product is losing share, the leaders often react by spending more money on marketing to the company's traditional consumer base. What the company may not be able to see in the data is the cause of the share loss. It may well be coming from the emergence of several tiny companies that are busily redefining the category, but are not yet on the big company's radar. Or the big company

---

CONSUMER ANALYSIS KEY ISSUES
Identify Causes of Change and Highest-Impact Problems

Consumer usage	Switching analysis
Understand current uses and users.	Identify pattern of switching behavior: purchase pathway.
Attitude/dissatisfactions	Market definition
Assess consumer attitude.	Calculate share in properly defined universe.

THE BOSTON CONSULTING GROUP

---

may be unable to see that some of the discretionary dollars that consumers used to spend in their category have been diverted into a different category altogether. The syndicated providers of data, after all, often don't even report the growth of what they call the "unorganized channels." By the time these small competitors or new channels become visible to the big company, it may be too late to respond. Kraft, for example, as yet has no answer to the rise of artisanal cheeses, fanciful coffee, gourmet lunch meats, or specialty sandwich toppings. Big companies find it hard to compete against entrepreneurs who have vision, category expertise, original ideas, and patented or long-held product formulations and who are highly motivated sellers.

Every data analysis is vulnerable and subject to reanalysis and reinterpretation through different lenses and with different models and as times change. The trick is to know when to recut the data. The trading-up/trading-down phenomenon demands that the data be recut frequently.

How The Home Depot Recut Its Data

Saying that recutting demands to be done is not to say that it's easy to do, because data interpretations get stuck in the collective minds of corporate cultures. The Home Depot, for example, was built on the idea that the customer wanted a large selection of products at low prices with expert service. The store manager was king and his idea of the value calculus ruled. The managers were, for the most part, classic merchandisers who were not coordinated or consistent about either cost or process. They loved goods and stocked what they liked and what they thought they could move. If customers wanted ceiling fans, the managers would find a supplier, negotiate for the lowest price, and then push as many out the door as possible. But, with the rise of Lowe's and other home stores, The Home Depot's dominance in the category was sharply challenged.

When Bob Nardelli became CEO of The Home Depot in 2000, he saw that the company's understanding of the home consumer was dated and superficial. There was very little data to go on, and even less analysis. Nardelli set out to recut the data and redefine the customer's value calculus.

Nardelli knew that consumers at every income level come to The Home Depot not just to buy a single item they need for a home improvement project, but to engage in the process of reimagining their homes. The home is not only the middle-class consumer's most valuable financial asset, it is also the most treasured emotional asset. It is the emotional space that can encompass taking care of me, connecting, and questing. It can be a showplace of trading up, a tour de force of trading down, and a manifestation of the consumer's taste in treasure. So, consumers want to take time to wander the aisles and see what's available, what's new, what might make their homes different or better. The average basket at The Home Depot is about $60 and a significant portion of that amount comes from unplanned or impulse purchases.

Nardelli also saw and valued the essential role of the company's 325,000 associates, and wanted to help them be more effective and focused in serving customers. To do so, he revamped the buying process, which had largely been decentralized and had resulted in many different terms and conditions (sometimes from the same supplier) at different stores. This made it very difficult for The Home Depot to make a national marketing push across the entire chain. If, for example, you wanted to sell a million bags of grass seed at a special weekend price, you could not be sure that the same brand of seed was available in all outlets or at what price it could be offered. By centralizing the buying process, the company could better leverage its enormous buying power and get better pricing and more consistency in the merchandising mix. As Nardelli put it, "Before, we were a thousand businesses united by a brand, but with no common buying process. Today, we are one business with nearly two thousand stores."

Nardelli took a hard look at the data and made important changes to the business based on his analysis of it. The data showed, for example, that a growing percentage of The Home Depot's customers was aging and time-pressed and not particularly interested in the "do-it-yourself" part of home repair or improvement. Based on this data, Nardelli developed an installation services business, a "do-it-for-me" operation that is growing at a rate of double digits. The data also showed that customers wanted greater speed at checkout, so The Home Depot became the first to offer self-checkout. More than one third of all customers now choose that option and waiting time in line has been reduced by as much as 40 percent.

To reinvent The Home Depot required that associates be educated and trained so they could sell in a new way. They had long thought of themselves as people whose main job was to help customers find things in the store and make the best choices about which item to buy and to explain, when asked, how to use it. Home Depot committed some $600 million to a program of recruitment and customer-service training that will eventually touch every associate and outlet.

"Home Depot started in value," Bob Nardelli told me. "In my time, we have tried to do a better job of understanding consumers. We have a formal program for customer engagement in the store. It's about providing the customer gratification, distinctiveness, speed, convenience. Value is assumed," he said. "For many of our consumers it's the thrill of the hunt."

The results of Nardelli's efforts are visible in the numbers. Sales have grown from $45.7 billion in 2000 to $73.1 billion in 2004. Earnings have increased by 64 percent. But even as Nardelli continues to execute against the current recut of the data, he has to be looking for the next one, if The Home Depot is to continue to grow and compete with Lowe's. "In retail, the challenge is always Act II," he says.

What to Look For

What are you looking for when you set about recutting the data?

You want to understand, above all else, the threat you face from competitors at the low end. For example, how many products sell at lower prices than yours? How big a share do those products have of the category? How fast are they growing? It's amazing how quickly value-price companies can grow—as much as 50 percent or more in a period of two or three years. You also need to understand the data on competitors who sell similar products at a premium to yours. Are they attracting your best customers and stealing profit from you?

Recently, we began working with a large and successful company that owns the premium segment in its category. It believed it was gaining share and earning record profits. But its database contained information only about its current retail channels. When we recut the data, by looking at syndicated data on the entire market, we saw a very different truth. Although it was true that the client was indeed gaining share in the premium segment of the category, that segment was in decline. All the growth in the business was in a segment that we identified as "low-value." In the low-value segment, consumers buy products for a purely functional use and don't care about or need the company's technical expertise. They were satisfied to buy a "down-and-dirty" product at a rock-bottom price. The premium product offered by our client, and supported by its considerable expertise, just wasn't relevant any more. The low value is not about showy brands, it is just about functionality. Does it work? Does it fulfill the application? Does it hold up in use? This was tough news for our client—a proud and successful company—to hear. But the recut data was impossible for it to ignore. Now we're working together to see how the company can compete in the low-value segment and also offer products that will encourage the consumer to move "one rung up" on the ladder of benefits. If it can make that work, the strategy will create a new competitive space in the category and help it gain as much as 20 percent of the market. It will require a substantial investment in technology, manufacturing methods, selling capability, merchandising, and targeted advertising. But what choice do they have? To keep looking at the data the old way and continue to pretend their segment isn't drying up?

Many companies, especially those in the middle, look primarily at data on their closest and best-known competitors. This is necessary, of course, but it can become obsessive. Companies worry about minor shifts in the balance of power and make moves designed to attack their biggest adversaries or respond to attacks from them. Meanwhile, the entire category may be undergoing a transformation and the real growth taking place outside the view of the middle competitors. Soon enough, the company may be selling out to the competitor they have nervously watched for so long (as Filene's has done with Macy's—two competitors whose business has been sucked away by premium specialty shops and by the massive value providers like Target and Wal-Mart).

Even so, analysis of competitive data can reveal big opportunities, especially if it shows you where the ostriches are. The ostrich is the business competitor whose stock sells for the average S&P multiple, and that appears to be operating in slow motion. "I'm big. I'm slow. I'm not responsive," says the ostrich. "I inherited my power from earlier generations. I have size and scale, but I don't have speed." When you find an ostrich in your category, you can attack and it can be years before you see a response from it!

You're also looking for data about your own company and its products that reveals your weaknesses. If you were your own competitor, where would you attack? Do you make a product that has too high a cost structure and that makes you vulnerable to a lower-priced option? Is there a region where you have no presence? Is there a channel that you haven't exploited but that competitors have?

Finally, you're looking for the white space. What does the data show you about potential usage, occasions where the consumers are not using your product, times when they are currently using an alternative or substitute?

Think about Lillie and the cockroach, for example. Who knew that the act of killing a cockroach could provide such emotional catharsis? Who knew that a can of bug spray could be used to mount a three-pronged attack, involving not just poisoning, but drowning and decapitation as well? I didn't. The bug spray executive didn't. But, as we learned that day, consumers who live with cockroaches are engaged in a primal battle. They don't actually see many roaches that are bold enough to stride across the carpet, but they live with the unsettling certainty that many more are lurking inside the cabinets and creeping through the walls. Most of all, they live in fear of the scene that we had witnessed in Lillie's living room: a roach parading itself across the carpet in front of visitors. As a result, roach warriors are very willing, even eager, to talk about their various solutions, and are ready to pay handsomely for any weapon that will help them win their never-ending battles. The many insights we gained from our visits to consumers like Lillie had a direct effect on the insect control company's new product strategy, marketing, product positioning, and in-store merchandising. And my client admitted that our adventure had been one of the most eye-opening experiences of his career.

Don't Wait

Above all else, do not wait to take action.

Taking action means innovating, not just doing more of what you're already doing, or considering acquisitions, or increasing your advertising spending in an attempt to attract new consumers. Think about innovation as a series of waves of reinvention and change, each one lasting three to five years, and no longer.

The process of innovation starts with a period of immersion in and exploration of the market. The goal is to develop a deep, almost primal, understanding of consumers, and to search the globe for ideas and inspiration. As part of this process, you need to create a consumer

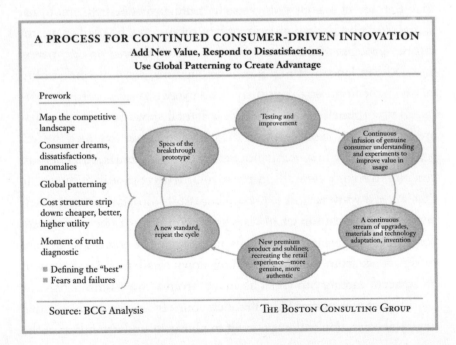

A PROCESS FOR CONTINUED CONSUMER-DRIVEN INNOVATION
Add New Value, Respond to Dissatisfactions,
Use Global Patterning to Create Advantage

Prework

Map the competitive landscape

Consumer dreams, dissatisfactions, anomalies

Global patterning

Cost structure strip down: cheaper, better, higher utility

Moment of truth diagnostic

- Defining the "best"
- Fears and failures

Testing and improvement

Continuous infusion of genuine consumer understanding and experiments to improve value in usage

Specs of the breakthrough prototype

A continuous stream of upgrades, materials and technology adaptation, invention

A new standard, repeat the cycle

New premium product and sublines; recreating the retail experience—more genuine, more authentic

Source: BCG Analysis   THE BOSTON CONSULTING GROUP

purchase tree that maps the various factors that influence the consumer's purchase. You should also create a quantitative diagnosis of your current system, including its most prominent failings and key opportunities.

This painstaking prework will provide you with the facts, understanding, and insights you need to effectively brainstorm ideas and opportunities. It also enables you to create for your R&D team a detailed work plan for delivering technical and functional breakthroughs. Most companies fail to build this platform of knowledge, which is an essential part of a foundation for growth. They are satisfied with a superficial understanding of the market and competition. They prefer anecdotes to data. (Both are necessary.) In making a work plan, they go for simple, incremental improvements. When they launch the "new and improved" version of their product or service, they invest in three months of advertising and hope everything will work out. They have no built-in nurture-and-improve process to ensure that the product is continuously modified, improved, and enhanced. After the initial period of launch and rollout, continued marketing support for the new product is "conditional" on its success. It often fails to materialize at all, because the company has already moved on to the next new product launch, which it will conduct in exactly the same way.

Don't wait to start the process, even if the consumer-goods market doesn't appear to be changing. You must assume that it will change, and sooner than you expect. If you think you are on top of your category at the moment, you can be reasonably sure there is a touch of arrogance that colors your thinking. You'll say to yourself, "No one can challenge us. We're too big, too successful, too smart, too knowledgeable, too rich, too whatever." Every company can be challenged. The truly dangerous challenge is more likely to come from a tiny trading-up startup, or a giant trading-down retailer, or a company in an adjacent category to yours, than it is from a known competitor.

Even as you segment and broaden your offering to serve multiple constituencies, don't allow yourself to blur your understanding of the consumer or to create fuzzy messages. If you can't articulate the benefits of your offering in the length of an elevator ride (of no more than thirty stories), how do you expect the consumer to get the message?

Try to see your category and business as an outsider would. If you were advising others who were facing your business problems, what would you say to them? Would you advise them to do what you're doing?

I carry with me a little checklist for growth, which I refer to whenever I'm on the street or in a mall, looking at new products. The items on the list include:

- Does the product clearly have technical, functional, and emotional benefits?
- Is there a clear consumer target?
- Is the product displayed at retail in such a way that the consumer would describe it as "stunning"?
- Is there a pattern of continuous innovation?
- Is the consumer fundamentally engaged in such a way that she wants to say, "Yes"?

We expect that over the next decade that the bifurcation of the economy will continue. Growth will be at the high and low ends of almost every market segment. Consumer households in the Western world will continue to experience a slow, gradual increase in real incomes. Women will, over the long term, inch toward income parity. Education will drive increasing consumer sophistication in purchasing. There will continue to be a bonanza of growth for discount and splurge retailing. Fragile health, war, terror, and complicated relationships at home and on the job will be the norm. Today's already savvy consumer will only get more skilled.

So, here's my restatement (recut?) of a call to action in a few simple phrases:

- Don't wait for the market to move. Be ahead of the curve.
- Engineer out dissatisfactions in your product.
- Hunt for value in the trade-up and trade-down segments of your market.
- Inspire a continuous search for cheaper, better, more value . . . and better, better, better.
- Attack your category like an outsider who is looking at a blank sheet.
- Pursue the target with energy and relentlessness.

Love Actually

The movie *Love Actually* tells the stories of nine different characters, all in search of love. The stories are told separately at first, but gradually intertwine until the characters all come together in a climactic final scene at London's Heathrow airport. The movie is a bit saccharine and contrived, but what's touching and believable about it is that all the characters are a little confused about their quest for love. Some of them don't even understand that love is what they're looking for. Some worry that they'll never find love. Some fear that they won't be able to embrace love even if they do find it. Some discover that they're already in love with somebody, but didn't realize it.

The simple message of the movie is that love is the driver behind much of what people do and how they behave—and that includes the purchasing of goods and services. The primary consumer in the developed world is female, and a major factor in her value calculus is love. She buys goods that will maximize her chances of finding love for herself, if she has not found it yet. She makes purchases for the loved ones who are already in her life—things that will bring the people in her circle closer together, make them safer and happier, and improve their lives and their futures.

As Sarah Montfort said to us, with tears in her eyes, "I do this because I love my family. I hope that my girls are all college educated, happy, successful, and secure with themselves. I want them to start off with zero debt. I want them to have more than we have. That's why I do it. Every day."

The process of purchasing, therefore, is extremely important to her and she works hard at it. She gathers information about every purchase. She considers each one carefully. She confers with her friends and colleagues about the advantages and disadvantages of various competitive offerings. When she commits to a purchase, she carefully evaluates what she has bought. She discusses its performance and makes her opinions known about it. She keeps an eye on it over time and works to get the most out of it. If she is disappointed with her purchase, she lets that be known as well, and makes careful note of what she has learned from the experience. She won't make the same mistake twice.

Middle-class consumers may not be as colorful as the superrich or the very poor, but they make up the bulk of the market. I appreciate their challenges, solutions, and ideas. I think of middle-class consumers as fundamentally wise. They respect money. They live on salaries that don't change very much from year to year. They have tight budgets that force them to make tough choices and constant trade-offs. Middle-class consumers are also fundamentally smart. They are usually careful, methodical, and analytical in their purchases. They seek knowledge and they apply it to what they buy. They have the talent to find the very best goods and services for themselves. They are not obsessed with goods and don't buy foolishly. They are not fixated on bargains, but they are looking for surprises and want to get value every time. Just because they enjoy the treasure hunt doesn't mean they are irresponsible. On the contrary, most middle-class consumers have learned that they can't have everything, that they have to pick and choose, and they do so with seriousness and resolve.

I think most middle-class consumers are quite happy and fundamentally optimistic. They believe they are leading rich, complete lives.

They don't dwell on what they don't have. They focus, instead, on the potential of the future, the light their children bring to them, and the connected relationships they have with their friends and partners— or would one day like to have. They seek products that appeal to their emotions, imaginations, and dreams. They have fueled a global, consumer-driven economy.

Serving these consumers can be fascinating, exciting, and rewarding. They are looking up, down, and out, in search of ways to provide their families with the things that matter most to them: better education, homes, cars, clothes, trips, and food. They attach a great deal of emotional significance and self-worth to their ability to do so. Helping them make better lives for themselves, and the people they love, is not just about achieving growth and building profit for companies and their leaders.

It can be, at its best, a noble enterprise.

ABOUT OUR SOURCES
AND METHODOLOGY

Research support for *Treasure Hunt* is the work of a team of consultants and researchers at The Boston Consulting Group, most of them located in the Chicago and Munich offices and associated with the Consumer Goods and Retail practice. Many others at BCG participated and contributed in a variety of ways, and nearly all are mentioned with gratitude in the Acknowledgments.

The book is based on several streams of material. The first is the client work that I have done in my twenty-five years as a consultant with BCG, as well as the collected knowledge, experience, and wisdom of my partners and associates at the firm. However, it is important to state that our work with clients is always carried out in confidence and we never disclose who our clients are, the nature of the work we have done for and with them, or their own internal data, without consulting with them and gaining their agreement. The reader should make no assumptions about the relationship of BCG with any of the companies or leaders named in this book.

The second stream of material comes from my engagements and conversations with consumers through a variety of channels and methods, including surveys, polls, visits, observations, interviews, and informal conversations. For this book, the team interviewed some 250 consumers throughout the country. We found most of the people through our professional and personal networks and, although we sought and achieved some diversity in the group we selected for inclusion in the book, we did not attempt to pick a representative sample of the population. Instead we focused on "lifestage" middle-class consumers. Although all of the people we interviewed gave us permission to use their comments and to tell their stories, their names have been changed, as have some of the details that might identify them to others. However, all of the people that we talk about in the book are real, and their comments are extracted from the transcripts of tape-recorded conversations with them. The interviewees provided the information about their assets and expenses, which we did not attempt to verify beyond reviewing with them bank statements, bills, and other materials that they supplied.

A third stream of material is the information gathered from public sources, such as SEC filings, annual reports, and company news releases (which provide data on various measures of performance), as well as the archives of a variety of publications and Web sites.

All of the material was evaluated in the light of the knowledge gained in the course of our original literature review, conducted for *Trading Up*, of more than eight hundred books, articles, and other materials on all manner of subjects related to consumers, consumption, consumer goods, and the consumer goods market. We have continued to gather, digest, and analyze such materials in the three years since the publication of *Trading Up*.

Finally, to create a statistical fact base about consumer spending and attitudes, we have conducted four quantitative surveys of American households in partnership with HarrisInteractive, a leading marketing research firm.

In the first poll, conducted in October 2002, we utilized Harris's extensive panel, composed of 2,333 adults over the age of eighteen with annual household income over $50,000. Using a twenty-five–

minute Internet survey, we asked questions regarding luxury purchases and attitudes about luxury shopping and spending in general, as well as specific questions about the luxury categories most important to those adults. All data was weighted using Harris's proprietary propensity-weighting technique to be representative of the general population of adults with household income over $50,000. The data was analyzed using a variety of statistical techniques. The groupings of emotional drivers were derived through factor analysis, a multivariate statistical method that aligns attribute statements onto common factors or vectors on the basis of their intercorrelation.

We conducted another HarrisInteractive survey in October 2003, polling 2,105 consumers with household income of $50,000 or more. The results were consistent with those of the first survey and confirmed that the emotional drivers had not changed and that the most important trading-up categories were also the same.

Our third BCG–HarrisInteractive survey was fielded in late October 2004 and included over 2,100 adults in the United States with household income of at least $50,000 per year. This survey included questions pertaining to trading down, as well as trading up, in over fifty product and services categories. It also examined attitudes toward spending and life in general. Some of the specific quantitative findings are included in the text. The qualitative findings helped shape our thinking throughout this book.

We conducted a fourth survey in November 2005. This survey suggests the trading-down movement is becoming even more pronounced. Consumers are holding their wallets close in and believing they can find more value at discounters and private labels.

ACKNOWLEDGMENTS

Treasure Hunt is the work of a small core team of people at The Boston Consulting Group, many partners and associates throughout the BCG organization, and several important partners and collaborators outside the firm.

John Butman and I here collaborate on our second book. It is an interesting partnership. John is a fantastic writing partner—curious, intelligent, a keen observer of people and consumption. He stands for what he believes in and has an engaging and keen wit. He has made the writing of *Treasure Hunt* a delight.

Members of the core team for the project include Julie Gish, Amanda Brimmer, Dave Kluz, Lucy Brady, Barbara Hulit, Angela Guido, Lucy Marinangeli, John Budd, Catherine Roche, Isabelle Boergel, Jill Corcoran, Sanna Mari Virtanen, and Amadou Sanankoua. Julie was the master of much of the consumer research, literally living with many of the individuals profiled in the book. Amanda was a research machine, unearthing details about the categories and companies profiled in the book and creatively feeding implications and ideas. Lucy and Barbara were key thought partners in the development of the theory of trading down. Angela joined the team to make sure all the facts were in order and tirelessly kept our final drafts from going off track. Catherine managed our European research effort. Dave helped to lead the research effort on several critical categories and companies. Isabelle helped us deeply understand the European pursuit of value.

We received very valuable support and guidance from our senior management at BCG. Hans Paul Buerkner, BCG's CEO, told me, "Take your dream and write this book." Hugh Simons, BCG's CFO, found the money for the research and project team and provided encouragement and support. In addition, my successor as global practice leader for our consumer practice, Patrick Ducasse, provided advice to globalize the message and bring Europe and Asia into our view. Patrick and the consumer practice manager, Emmanuel Huet, provided detailed input on sequential drafts.

I must also thank BCG's co-chairmen, John Clarkeson and Carl Stern, for years of mentorship, for encouragement in developing our consumer understanding discipline, and for support in making this book happen.

Once again, Bill Matassoni stands out as a key contributor to our work. Bill is the steward of the BCG brand and a well-known figure in the world of consultancy marketing. Early on, he recognized the potential for *Treasure Hunt* and has provided advice, needed criticism, editorial guidance, and more. The key publishing partners who helped create *Trading Up* were also instrumental in the development and publication of *Treasure Hunt*, including our agent, Todd Shuster, of Zachary Shuster Harmsworth, and our editor, Adrian Zackheim, the founding editor of Portfolio. At Portfolio, Will Weiser has provided enthusiastic support and ideas.

Special thanks go to BCG colleagues Miki Tsusaka, Mike Deimler, Tom Lutz, Jeff Gell, Kermit King, Marin Gjaja, Hubert Hsu, Sally Seymour, Antonella Mei Pochtler, Sebastian DiGrande, Angus Thompson, Angela Zaeh, Nicola Pianon, Gerry Hansell, DG Macpherson, Doug Hohner, Federico Lalatta, Elizabeth Rizza,

Lindsey Argalas, Raymond Nomizu, Merel Vehneman, Hal Sirkin, John Wallace, Mark Kistulinec, Rich Hutchinson, Sharon Marcil, Christine Barton, John Bogert, Colm Foley, Kate Sayre, Mary Egan, Cliff Grevler, David Pecaut, Joe Manget, Ian Frost, John Garabedian, Hiroaki Sugita, Matt Krentz, Steve Gunby, Bjorn Matre, Christian Veith, John Wong, Wahid Hamid, Marcus Bokkerink, Sabra Krock, Joon Ma, Taka Mizukoshi, Tom Wurster, Willie Burnside, Dan Jansen, Nicholas Keuper, Takashi Mitachi, Rene Abate, Frans Blom, Rainer Minz, Daniel Stelter, Ron Nicol, Carsten Kratz, Peter Goldsbrough, Jacques Chapuis, Joerg Matthiessen, Rich Lesser, Walter Sinn, Philippe Guy, Alan Jackson, Debbie Lovich, Dieter Heuskelm, and others. Jeannine Everett has had a serious role in teaching me the discipline of consumer market research. George Stalk has been an inspiration and encourager throughout the process.

An important and enlightening part of our research was the interviews we conducted with the leaders of our featured treasure hunt and trading-up companies. They are noted throughout the book and thanked for their contributions and insights. We also want to thank the dozens of consumers we interviewed, both formally and informally, as part of our research. Many of them appear in the book and, although we gave them fictitious names, we did not significantly alter their stories or the critical details of their lives. We also thank the more than ten thousand consumers who participated in the Harris-Interactive poll and the dozens of those who agreed to further interviews with our team.

The core *Treasure Hunt* team has had the benefit of an expert and hardworking support team. In Chicago, my executive assistants, Kristin Claire and Amanda Vrany, have always cheerfully and fully supported every request for materials for this book. Kristin just had her tenth anniversary with me and has played a major role in many of our efforts.

We also received valuable support from a number of outside contributors. At Sommerfield Communications in New York, Frank

Sommerfield, Penny Peters, and Elizabeth Koons expertly helped us bring our ideas to the press and the outside world.

Throughout the course of our work on the book, we have turned to our colleagues at BCG for their ideas, insights, and counsel. We are fortunate to have a worldwide network of people with extraordinary expertise and experience in a wide range of practices, disciplines, and industries. Vera Ward, Pat Heidkamp, Bill Hagedorn, Jill Jackson, Wanda Perkins, and Rudy Barajas provided extensive and knowledgeable research support. Our thanks for publication support also go to Chris George, Eric Gregoire, KC Munuz, and Christine Vollrath.

Thanks to Nina Abdelmessih, Niki Aryana, Tommaso Barracco, Ivan Bascle, Jorge Becerra, Jean-Marc Bellaiche, Lamberto Biscarini, Rolf Bixner, Marge Branecki, Patrick Campbell, Phil Catchings, Thierry Chassaing, Carlos Costa, Nils Daecke, Francois Dalens, Steve David, Rob Davies, Joe Davis, Christine DeLeon, Stephan Dertnig, Jeanie Duck, Eva Estermann, Reggie Gilyard, Karen Gordon, Emile Gostelie, Oliver Graham, Marcus Grundke, Mark Hoffman, Rune Jacobsen, Barry Jones, Martin Koehler, Jeff Kotzen, Edwin Lai, Marjorie Lee, Tom Lewis, Ross Love, Robert Maciejko, Kate Manfred, Steve Matthesen, Heino Meerkatt, David Michael, Arnaud Miconnet, Anna Minto, Yves Morieux, Atsushi Morisawa, Nicola Pianon, Anthony Pralle, Stefan Rasch, Byung Nam Rhee, Martina Rissman, Just Schurmann, Marty Smits, Karen Sterling, Garrick Tiplady, Jari Tuomala, Tom von Oertzen, Adrian Walti, Elmar Widerin, Alan Wise, Marie-Therese Zambon, Carole Whittemore, Jim Andrew, Jim Borsum, Paul Gordon, Eric Olsen, Paige Price, Dave Rickard, Carl Rutstein, Rohan Sajdeh, and Simon Stephenson. Special thanks to Bob Contino, David Cahill, and Christina Coffey on the Chicago production staff and to Jon Desrats and David Douglas on the New York production staff. Thanks also go to Jonathan Cowan, David Webb, Vikas Parekh, Peter Dawe, Marc Fredman, Leslie Spengler, and Amy Davy. Expert advice was provided by Christine Beauchamp, Jim Jewell, and Jeff Mory.

INDEX